GORILLA CONVICT

THE PRISON WRITINGS OF
SETH FERRANTI

EDITED BY RON CHEPESIUK

13-digit ISBN 978-1-4675-2662-3
10-digit ISBM 1-4675-2662-2

TABLE OF CONTENTS

FOREWORD

Every now and again serendipity will bless a man in pursuit of his own destiny. And that's how I found Seth. Seth Ferranti, artist, playwright, journalist, scriptwriter, publisher and all around good guy. There are many words that can be used to describe this man. But the one I use most often is "friend". I met Seth by way of solicitation. I was an aspiring novelist and Seth was an established publisher with two titles to his credit at the time, those being: Prison Stories and Street Legends Volume 1. I really enjoyed Street Legends—mostly because I'm a convicted felon and felt that his interpretation of prison life and its hardships was accurate. Some of the things he exposed were subjects that resonated in my mind, but I wouldn't dare discuss. Not to mention that the proverbial yeast he sprinkled in made it one hell of a read.

Soon after that I was hooked. I also began to notice the name Seth Ferranti popping up in numerous periodicals I was reading. The Don Diva's, F.E.D.S.', Smooth's, Source's, Hip-Hop Weekly's- he was everywhere. That's when I knew he was on to something. The thing that surprised me most, though, was his race! His flow is very soulful, something an avid (black) reader can sense most times, but every so often a man will surprise you and reintroduce you to your own ignorance.

There are three kinds of Street Nigga. 1) The real. 2) The fake) 3) The bitch nigga. It is extremely difficult to gain the approval of the real; yet through Seth's accurate and objective reporting he gets to the heart of matter he's reporting on because his personal experiences allow him to weed out false players looking to inflate their own credibility and egos.

And because of his sordid past, he is able to see through the (often times) vicious propaganda that mainstream media uses to secure convictions against society's "undesirables", often resulting in railroad style convictions. He showed this skill in Street Legend Volume 2, when he dug into my own case and exposed gentrification as the source of our indictments.

His fiction writing is good, but his strong suits are journalism and screenwriting. The screenplay for "The Supreme Team" may be the greatest piece of street reporting since "New Jack City." Still, with all his work in magazines, books, and web-media, Seth and his wonderful wife, Diane, find the time to tend to the needs of their friends. Seth is always willing to lend a hand-up, not a hand-out, and for a real man or woman fighting the good fight that is the best you can hope for. And yet, he and Diane will exceed even that. Seth Ferranti is not only a great writer and a true voice of his generation, but he is one of the highest caliber of human beings and will continue to enjoy success in whatever it is he chooses to do.

—Lamont "Big Fridge" Needum, USP Lee 2011

INTRODUCTION

Seth "Soul Man" Ferranti has been a prisoner of America's failed War on Drugs since 1993 when, after spending two years as a top-15 fugitive on the U.S. Marshal's Most Wanted List, he was captured and sentenced to 304 months under the federal sentencing guidelines for an LSD kingpin conviction. Seth's current release date is November 2015.

Many prisoners facing such a long period of incarceration would have given up on their future, but not Seth Ferranti. During his incarceration he has worked hard to better himself and to prepare for his eventual release back into society. He earned an A.A. degree from Penn State, a B.A. degree from the University of Iowa and an M.A. from California State University, Dominguez Hills, and he plans to earn a doctorate degree.

Along the way, Seth has become a publishing phenomenon. Indeed, his writing has led to the recognition, behind bars and in the street, that he is a true crime writer of note and a chronicler of gangster stories that might not otherwise be told. Since the late 1990s, Ferranti has published six books and several articles in such magazines as Don Diva, F.E.D.S. and Street Elements. His book, "Prison Stories," is a series of short story vignettes that captures the gritty essence of prison life. In a review, Don Diva Magazine commented that "an episode of Oz couldn't capture prison the way Seth "Soul Man" Ferranti does in "Prison Stories.""

Other books profile some of the legendary as well as lesser known African American gangsters, including Kenneth "Supreme" McGriff, Frank Matthews, Wayne Perry and the Boobie Boys. Curtis Scoon, producer of Black Entertainment Television's popular "American Gangster" series, said that Ferranti "provides a unique perspective of the gangster's creed from the belly of the beast. Few writers can claim such first hand access to men as feared and dangerous as those found in Street Legends."

Seth was a prolific writer but by 2005 only so much of his writing was getting published. He needed another outlet to have his voice heard. So he started his popular Gorilla Convict blog. "I was reading about blogs, which were becoming popular back then, and I decided, publishing-wise, that was the way to go," Seth recalls.

The blog took off. Today, Seth's blog gets 15,000 to 20,000 unique visitors and over 250,000 hits a month. The blog has allowed him to develop a huge following. "The blog lets me communicate with the public so I can create a dialogue with them," Seth explains.

Still, it hasn't been easy. You see, the prison industrial complex doesn't want its inmates to express themselves, and it certainly doesn't want to let the public know about the living conditions they endure in its gulag. As a prisoner, Seth has almost no rights. For instance, the authorities, at any time, can go online and view everything Seth has written on his blog. As Seth explains, "I've received a real negative, almost censorship type reaction from staff in the different prisons I've been in, they try to intimidate me. They take away my privileges to get me to stop writing."

But Seth has refused to be crushed by the American prison system. "Their attitude has just made me want to write more," Seth says defiantly. "I have battled them the whole way and will never give in no matter how hard they retaliate against me or harass me."

This collection of essays gleaned and edited from the Gorilla Convict blog is a tribute to Seth's spirit, talent, writing and perseverance.

They reflect his thoughts, observations, investigation, interactions and dialogue with other inmates, past and present, from America's prison industrial complex. As these essays show, Seth Ferranti is a keen observer of prison life, the urban scene and American society. We hope you enjoy them. We know you will be enlightened and informed.

—Ron Chepesiuk, Editor

I

THE STATE
OF THE PEN

ONE

The State of the Feds

W HEN I FIRST entered the netherworld of prison in 1993, the last vestiges of the convict were dying out. The convict is the ultimate prison ideal that has existed in prisons throughout the ages and has been portrayed and glorified in countless Hollywood movies. It is possible that convicts still exist in the state systems and the higher maximum level type federal prisons, but I am here to tell you that in the medium and lower security levels of the Bureau of Prisons convicts are a dying breed, if not already dead and stinking.

Convicts lived by a set of codes, had certain tenets inherit to their incarceration, and carried an "us against them" mentality, no matter the odds. Convicts brought about Attica. They stood for something- honor, respect, and loyalty. But those ideals, whether wrong or right, are dead in the federal system. They exist in rhetoric and legend but not in word and deed. Very few in the federal system live by these codes. They are definitely and clearly the minority in prisons today whereas only 10 years ago they constituted the majority.

Today the feds are dominated by prisoners and inmates. I would break it down like this- 10% convicts, 30% prisoners, and 60% inmates. Prisoners are the logical descendants of convicts and still hold much of their values. But prisoners usually aren't willing to take the stand that a convict would. Convicts stood at Attica, not prisoners. I doubt that a prisoner would make a stand even if he wanted to. At least a prisoner has the potential to be a convict. Inmates have no potential at all. Inmates are scared-ass motherfuckers. Straight Joe Citizens. Running to the man and shit. They don't ask any questions, challenge any rules, and follow orders to the timid side of the letter. They don't want to make waves. They don't stand for anything. They have no ideals, only those that the institution forces upon them. They just want to do their time and cooperate with the police. Anything to make their time go by easier. They see nothing wrong with dry snitching, helping the man out in anyway, or even snitching outright. Inmates are why the federal system is so fucked up today.

The emergence of inmates and the snitch culture they perpetrate can be explained by two reasons. The first is the fed's directive of locking up so many illegal immigrants. Nearly 30% of the federal prison population is made up of INS detainees. And for the most part these people aren't even criminals. They are just illegal, deportable aliens who have no papers. They aren't criminals, thieves, rapists, drug dealers, murderers, stick up kids, or white collar criminals. They are just hardworking foreigners trying to make a buck. The U.S. dollar, you know.

But our government has locked them up, gave them a sentence, and thrust them into federal prison creating a new sub-culture of inmates and over-populating the system at the same time. Convicts would never put up with triple-bunking but inmates will. Like I said, these INS detainees for the most part aren't even criminals and probably never broke the law. But their papers weren't in order, so they get locked up and they make up the fastest growing segment of the federal prison population.

The second reason for the emergence of the inmates and the snitch culture that they thrive in is that the BOP has taken away the power of the convict. The convict's greatest weapon was the threat of violence. The threat of violence allowed the convicts to intimidate and control the prisons and their populations and enforce their code on all persons living on the compound or within the prison system. But the BOP and the feds started casing dudes up in the 90's for any violent infraction committed in prison.

It used to be a convict could kill a fellow prisoner and only receive a shot and hole time. Some prison killings might make it to court but most didn't. Back then there were hardly any witnesses willing to testify, but today it is a different story. The BOP even has an incident report category for killing another inmate and appropriate sanctions. It is a 100 series shot—one of the most severe. It used to be all this stuff was handled in house. Assaults on staff, on other prisoners, killings, stabbings, extortions, drugs, and rapes were mostly handled in house.

But as the federal prison population expanded, the U.S. Attorneys started trolling the prisons for cases. Convicts started catching street charges for infractions that happened in prison and additional time was added to their sentences. This effort systematically stripped the convicts of their greatest weapon—the weapon that let them enforce the codes that they lived by—the threat of violence.

It used to be that known snitches were checked in and not allowed to stay in the yard. There might have been some instances where a known snitch was a bad-ass dude or straight killer and walked the yard freely, but it was very rare. Convicts took it as an insult if one of their homeboys, who was a snitch, walked the pound freely. And in the convict world an insult could lead to death. Now, though, the snitches thrive. The Bureau of Prisons is a straight snitch culture. They used to have to hide in protective custody but now walk around in the open. And it's not like they are killers or hard men either. They are just conniving and calculating little cowards.

They openly work for SIS, the prison investigative services, and get convict types locked up in a minute under a lengthy investigation. In prison, the convicts are still feared, but the administration has enabled and even encouraged the activity of snitches so that they can operate within the prison walls with impunity. So the prisons have seen a role reversal. It used to be the snitches were locked up for their own protection because convicts were the majority. But now convicts are locked up in the hole because snitches are in the majority. It is all part of the vicious cycle of the inmate-snitch culture that dominates the prison system today.

Also, the rapid rise of the federal prison population has played a part in the proliferation of the inmate class. When I first entered prison in 1993, the BOP's population was about 50,000. Now in the present that population is fourfold standing at almost 200,000. So in approximately 10 years a definite shift has occurred in the demographics and character of the prison landscape.

I came in as a young kid, a fish really, with no prior prison experiences and no inkling on how to act or behave. I had seen the movies, so I just thought I had to act tough. But an old head convict took me under his wing. He checked my paperwork to make sure I wasn't a snitch, vouched for me, and showed me how to act. At this time, though, there were probably five old head convict types for every new fish coming in. So if the fish thought he was a bad man or tough or anything like that, he had five convicts to show him the error of his ways.

But now it is different. For every old head prisoner that was schooled in the convict ways and has been doing his time like that, there are twenty new young kids coming in who want to act tough and show that they are hard. Five to one odds are good in the convict's favor. But one to twenty? You get the picture. A lot of old head prisoners don't even bother with all the young ones coming in, so they don't get schooled in convict etiquette and nobody shows them how to act.

So this circumstance combined with the illegal alien aspect has created a whole new prison sub-class and majority that now dominates the prison hierarchy and perpetrates the current inmate-snitch culture. Convicts talk about getting your respect, but nowadays that is a losing proposition.

If a prisoner tried to live by convict ideals in the current snitch culture, he would be drawing a line in the sand all day and spend all his time in confrontations. This has led to the prisoner minority mindset where the convict ideals are recognized and valued but not necessarily put into practice at all times. At least the prisoner acknowledges the convict code. The inmate doesn't even recognize it.

By casing dudes up for prison violations that used to merit only hole time, the feds have stripped the convicts of their power. Back in 1994 I saw a dude get busted with three grams of heroin, do six months in the hole, and then come back out on the pound. Today that same dude might be looking at 18 months in the hole and an outside case that could give him an additional sentence of three years. The feds have seriously upped the ante. Any assault might bring three to five more years of incarceration, and a murder could get somebody life without parole.

By stripping convicts of the threat of violence, the feds have drastically altered the prison hierarchy. An old junkie told me in the early 90s that prison was the perfect place to enjoy his habit. Even if he got busted he wasn't losing nothing, he said. Because being in the hole was still being in prison. The time is still ticking but on the street, he told me, going to jail is a big loss of liberty. I wonder what that old convict would say today, knowing that a dirty urine or possession of heroin charge would get him 18 more months of prison time.

I don't claim to be a convict but never would I be an inmate. I am a prisoner, nothing more, nothing less. The War on Drugs has killed the convict and the current inmate-snitch culture may be a safer environment, but it is definitely much more treacherous. Respect, unity, and loyalty used to be cherished prison maxims upheld by men of honor—convicts to the world. Hollywood has immortalized them and glamorized them. But just as the dinosaurs disappeared so too have the convicts being replaced by snitches, inmate police, and double crossers who will stab you in the back figuratively but not literally because they don't have the heart to face you like a man.

TWO

Trials of a Hustler

I N PRISON, THERE are many obstacles to a prisoner's freedom. The razor wire topped perimeter fences, the walls and gun towers all ensure that the number one obstacle—escape—doesn't occur. There are also other obstacles in prison for those prisoners who wish to legitimately better their situation. When a prisoner takes it upon himself to do something positive during his incarceration, often times, the staff and administration at the facility deliberately try to make it hard on him. Anyone would think it would be the other way around—that prison staff would encourage prisoners to pursue positive objectives. That, however, isn't necessarily the case.

Case in point: Wahida Clark, inmate. Wahida Clark became an Essence bestselling author and was profiled in King magazine and numerous other publications while she was and still is serving time in a federal prison. Wahida recently became the subject of an intense bidding war between several major publishers. As Wahida, the author of several lit classics, "Thugs And The Women Who Love Them," "Every Thug Needs A Lady" and "Payback Is A Mutha," gets ready to hit the streets in the summer of 2007 after serving a 125-month fed sentence for money laundering, mail and wire fraud, she'll tell anyone that is willing to listen that it hasn't been easy.

Wahida has endured her trials and tribulations to be sure. Even though the First Amendment applies to all Americans, even those in prison, Wahida's keeper, the Bureau of Prisons, has continually tried to make her feel as if she were doing something wrong simply because she started writing, got several books published and decided to carve out a future for herself. She was singled out and punished for trying to make something of herself. So much for rehabilitation.

Wahida's personal story demonstrates all that is wrong with our criminal justice system...where close-minded, robot-like administrators who can't think for themselves are permitted to make arbitrary decisions that drastically affect the lives of inmates. Even though the prison authorities tried to intimidate Wahida into not writing any more books with their rules and regulations, they were unsuccessful. They couldn't shake her. The girl is gangsta. Trips to the hole and constant harassment by the feds couldn't break Wahida. Just as she faced down the 10-year sentence without flinching or breaking weak, way before the current "stop snitching movement", Wahida faced down her captors, stared them straight in the eye, defied them and kept on writing. But let her tell it...

"I was at the federal prison in Lexington, Kentucky," she says. "At the time, my first book was floating around at both the women's prison and next door at the men's FCI. One morning around 5 a.m., I was awakened and ordered to get dressed and report to the Lieutenant's office where the SIS Lieutenant was waiting to speak with me."

As anyone in prison knows, the SIS Lieutenant is like the FBI. They investigate prison disturbances, riots, escape attempts, stabbings, murders and drugs. Only the most serious offenses, however, are brought to their attention. So as expected, Wahida was seriously surprised to be called in to see the SIS Lieutenant. Wahida had never received a shot (an Incident Report) in all her years of incarceration. The SIS Lieutenant was hot on her trail, though, and wanted to know how she had managed to write a book in prison.

"I explained to him that a former inmate, who used to be a literary agent, had been incarcerated at the Lexington prison. I also explained that the camp administrator had approved her to give a creative writing class where the curriculum consisted of a crash course on writing and getting published. Upon graduating we received a certificate." Wahida pointed out.

This piqued the SIS Lieutenant's attention even more, but with a prison administrator's close-mindedness, he probably thought something nefarious had resulted. A prisoner writing a book...definitely illegal, the SIS Lieutenant most likely thought.

"He asked me if I had a copy of my book," Wahida states. "I told him 'yes', and he sent me to get it. When I returned and handed it to him, he asked me whether the staff knew I had written a book. I told him of course and showed him where I had thanked the staff in the Acknowledgements Section of the book. Since the inmate copier had been broken at the time I was trying to send my manuscripts to publishers, several staff members were kind enough to make copies of the unpublished book for me."

No big crime, right? Attempting to do something positive. Unfortunately the end result was big trouble for Wahida.

"We are going to have to conduct an investigation," the SIS Lieutenant informed Wahida. "We are going to have to put you in "lock up" in the county jail for your own protection while the investigation takes place." Wahida couldn't believe it, but what could she do?

"I was at the mercy of my keepers," she says in reflection. "Here I was doing something positive, something legitimate for my future and the prison authorities acted like I was smuggling drugs into the prison or something worse. I was pissed off." And she had a perfect right to be.

"It was New Year's Eve in 2002 and we had our seats ready to watch BET's top 100 videos of the year and here I was on my way to some freakin' county jail. I was furious. The damn phone calls at the county were $22 for 20 minutes. We were locked down 23 hours a day. The food and commissary sucked. No microwaves. No radio. No music. We couldn't have books or magazines. I was livid."

To add insult to injury, about a month later, Wahida was served two shots. "One for running a business and the other one for introducing contraband into the prison," she says. The contraband was her book that several of the other prisoners had legitimately ordered from the publisher. There was a big furor "since the staff was supposed to be mad at me for thanking them in my book, but in reality most of them had talked to me to make sure I had the correct spellings of their names and asked me to make sure I put them in there." So it was a situation of damned if you do and damned if you don't. That's just how it goes in prison when you do things out of the ordinary, even if it's something positive.

The end result of the interrogation was that Wahida was informed the charges would be expunged. Wahida thought they had been. "Until recently," she says. "I was told that the charge of conducting a business still remained. I was also not allowed to return to the Lexington prison again. Bureau of Prisons Lexington wanted nothing to do with me." The official verdict Wahida received went like this. "The DHO (Discipline Hearing Officer) stated that it was a gray area and that I could write but not get published. She informed me that it was best not to. She stated that even though they applauded my efforts, thought it impressive that I was doing something positive with my time, the idea of prisoners writing books was still a gray area." That's how the BOP applauds prisoners who are trying to do extraordinary things behind bars. They throw them in the hole and try to intimidate them into not pursuing their goals. But Wahida made the best of a bad situation.

"My husband kept reminding me of how he wrote 'Uncle Yah Yah' parts 1 and 2 when he was in the hole." Wahida says. "So not only did I begin penning 'Payback' (her current bestseller), I also started my marketing campaign. I had already hooked up my flyers and noticed that everybody was writing somebody. I started collecting addresses and began sending out my promo kit. I became a mailing machine. I even had the girls in the pod stuffing and addressing envelopes for me. I had so many names I couldn't even write them all. I think that's what really made my name and books ring bells." Talk about underground marketing.

On September 3, 2003, Wahida was transferred to the women's prison in Alderson, West Virginia. "Before I was released from intake, SIS looked in on me." Wahida says. "I was like, oh, brother here we go again. The officer asked me what had happened. I gave him the short version. He basically told me to stay out of trouble. I explained to him that the shot I had received was my first shot ever and that I didn't get into any trouble." And for real, who in their right mind would call writing a book getting in trouble? Only a mindless BOP bureaucrat.

"As I started learning the ropes around Alderson, the staff began to constantly scrutinize my mail and sent a lot of it back." Wahida says. "I received a stack of flyers and was called down to the Lieutenant's office. They informed me I couldn't have them. I said cool. The next week, I received five books which my family wanted me to autograph and send back. I was once again called to the Lieutenant's office. They indicated that I couldn't sign the books, I said cool. The next week I got a stack of letters. Again the staff wanted to know what they were. I told them it was fan mail. They sent them back."

It seems kind of ironic that when someone takes the initiative to rehabilitate themselves, the people in charge of their rehabilitation fight them the whole way. But in prison, that's how it is. It's a Catch-22 situation. Wahida Clark, however, has stood strong. As her release date approaches, she is more than ready to hit the streets and enjoy the fruits of her labor.

"They harassed me consistently until Martha got here," Wahida says referring to Martha Stewart who also served time at Alderson. "I guess they figured if they were gonna give Martha special privileges then they would have to extend the same courtesy to me as well. Now that Martha's gone, it's back to he same old thing...harassment everyday." Wahida is dealing with it though. She knows that this too will pass. Things are looking very good for Wahida's future with a release date in the summer of 2007. Wahida is ready to make her mark in the publishing industry with her own Imprint, Wahida Clark Presents. Vickie Stringer, Teri Woods and Nikki Turner watch out. Wahida will soon be on the loose.

THREE

The Lorton Experience

I N 1910 THE U.S. Government acquired land along the Occoquan River in Southeastern Fairfax County, Virginia. This site became the Occoquan workhouse, designed first as a workhouse and later as a reformatory for the District of Columbia. Inmates worked on a 1,200 acre farm raising hogs, cattle and chickens and built many of the buildings in the complex, including the dorms, dining hall, laundry, bake shop, ice plant and hospital. Two sections were added later: the Lorton Reformatory in 1913 and finally the penitentiary in the 1930's historical documents relate.

For the last 75 years, the Lorton prison housed prisoners from Washington DC. The often poor inner-city blacks were bussed south from the crime ridden neighborhoods and the DC jail into rural Virginia where the prison resided. The complex consisted of several compounds: from Big Lorton, which was considered the hill where the modular intake unit was to the Wall, the maximum security compound to Occoquan the medium prison to the minimum down the road to Youth Center 1 and Youth Center 2 where youthful offenders were housed.

The vast complex was home to over 7,000 prisoners in the mid 90s, 44 percent over its capacity. Tales of corruption, vice and violence concerning life at Lorton abounded. It was known as the worst of the worst. The toughest prison in America, where allegedly drug lords like

Keith "Fly" Gaffney, who was featured in Don Diva magazine, held sway, controlling both prisoners and guards alike. The prison was so corrupt that prisoners had access to guns, knives and an assortment of weapons from which to battle each other and the guards. Drugs and prostitution were rampant. It was even said that the female guards used to sell their bodies to prisoners. And escapes were the norm rather then the rarity. To separate fact from fiction and rumor from actuality, to get the real take on Lorton, we contacted some real O.G.'s in the know, convicts who served time at the notorious prison.

"Lorton was a place for the fittest and only strong men survive," says Oscar a penitentiary veteran who did time there back in the 90s. His homeboy Tank concurs. "In DC every man is for himself," he says. "So it's either you or him. Due to such dangerous people, it makes one's heart hard and cold so you don't have a problem with putting the knife in people." This was the mindset of the prisoners at Lorton and ex-cons in the city, and the administration wasn't much better.

"Corruption first started at the head. The mayor of Washington DC was corrupt so his institutions were as well," Tank says of noted crack head mayor Marion Barry. "Lorton was a corrupt criminal reformatory. Being in Lorton was like being on the streets." But the corruption at Lorton eventually led to its closure.

Before closing in 2002, Lorton grew to an extensive 3,200 acre complex, historical documents relate. The District of Columbia Department of Corrections did not have the funds needed to construct housing for the exploding population or to maintain the facilities and adequate staffing levels. So the federal government agreed to take over expenses for DC prisoners in 1997 as part of a bailout of the financially strapped district. The agreement meant the Lorton complex would close and thousands of DC inmates would be absorbed into the federal system.

"In May 1996, the first shipment of prisoners went to a CCA in Youngstown, Ohio," Oscar says. The prison run by Corrections

Corporation of America experienced problems from the jump. Two inmates were stabbed to death, 40 assaults were reported, six prisoners escaped in a 1998 breakout and inmates won a $1.65 million class action lawsuit that accused guards of excessive force. These were hardened convicts from Lorton. They knew the score and the routine. The CCA prison was closed as DC prisoners were shipped into the federal system.

In the federal system rumors of the incoming DC prisoners were rampant. "They're gonna take over the compound," prisoners said. "Don't let them out of the hole," they told the warden. "They're gonna fuck things up," they said. The Lorton prison had such a fearsome reputation that the federal prisoners didn't want to be on the same compound with the DC convicts. But the DC dudes had different ideas.

"I thought it was going to be a good thing to get away from Lorton," Dingus another penitentiary veteran says. "But the rumors about the feds have not panned out, especially dealing with the parole." Tank has a different take. "Well, when they started shipping us, I was thinking the jail conditions was going to be a lot better, but no, the feds are some shit." Only Oscar had serious regrets on leaving Lorton, "I was thinking, oh, shit, there goes the neighborhood." But what was the real reason Lorton closed? Was it the corruption? The financial difficulties of DC? Here's a different angle.

In July 2002, Fairfax County received title to 2,440 acres of the Lorton complex and was tasked with the challenging decisions of how to use the property to its fullest potential as a world-class asset for Fairfax County residents. "Lorton sits on some valuable ground on top of hills and the locals wanted their land so they could build shopping malls and other ventures," Oscar says hitting it on the head. A mix of retail, residential and educational uses were planned and have come together with a school being built and a tract of million dollar houses being built on the former prison land. And what has been the result of the city inmates being transferred to far-flung prisons away from their families in the Bureau of Prisons?

"It is very stressful and burdensome on me and my family. And very expensive," Dingus says. "The telephone is about 100 times the price than it was at Lorton." Oscar echoes this sentiment. "I thought it was downright unfair. I just didn't complain because I knew there were others in the boat with me. All of us DC dudes want to be closer to home. It's aggravating that we have to plan a visit a couple of months before the actual visits occur as opposed to getting visits four days a week down Lorton." Dingus goes even further saying he and his homies feel "helpless, voiceless, and disenfranchised" being flung all across the nation and far from home.

Another aspect of the prison closing was the loss of jobs for the already low income DC community. Dingus says a lot of the guards were "devastated because they felt like they weren't qualified to do anything else." Oscar elaborates, "A corporal down Lorton made over $80,000 a year. Wardens in the feds are around that much." So the closing hurt the financially strapped residents of the District. "The staff at Lorton was some mixture of DC, Maryland, and Virginia C/O's but mostly DC officers." Tank says and it wasn't uncommon for staff to have relatives incarcerated at the prison they worked at.

"Convicts had family members as guards doing time with them." Tank says "But things like that had to be kept quiet," Oscar relates. "I had a cousin who worked in my dorm where I slept." And this led to corruption inside the prison. "With family, friends and loved ones working as guards, there was nothing one couldn't get. The convicts ran the joint." Tank says. And given the choice, most of the DC prisoners would rather be back at Lorton.

"I would prefer Lorton so that I could see my family more often," Dingus said. And Oscar says, "If I could choose to do two years here or eight years in Lorton, I would prefer Lorton. Everything was convenient and simple. I would've been home five years ago if I were down at Lorton. The reason is the feds are hitting me with their guidelines." But Dingus admits that, "Some like it because you do not have the violence, but some hate it." It's like Oscar says, "We all know that the feds is the home of the snitches. So we are certain to watch and move accordingly."

And in looking back the DC convicts reminisce. "The joint was sweet." Tank says. "You could sneak or get a gun in a food package. There was a lot of murder, robbery and drugs." Oscar concurs, "Convicts aren't going to stop making because they come to jail, especially a DC convict. It's in our nature as Washingtonians to simply go hard as a man." But Dingus keeps it real, "People just so happen to fall victim to the hands of the violent elements and un-calculated extortion and it changes you, makes you harder, not better or worse, just harder." And that about sums up the Lorton experience.

FOUR

Supermax

T
HE ABU GRAIB photos exposed torture, humiliation, degradation, sexual assaults, assaults with weapons and dogs, extortion and blood sports. The world, the media and the public were appalled and outraged at the images captured- prisoners with nylon bags over their heads, naked prisoners spread-eagled on wet floors in isolation, handcuffed to the wall, deprived of sleep and being kicked in the stomach repeatedly by guards. Prisoners were shocked and stunned that, with no regard for human decency, they were burnt or branded and their family members threatened. These images that emerged from Abu Graib made the headlines but in reality all they did was expose the brutal underbelly of the beast and the procedures practiced regularly by guards in U.S. jails. All of the above are the modus operandi of the lawful, state-of-the-art prison. Nowhere is this more clear than in the growth over the past 25 years of what's known as super maximum imprisonment.

On the cutting edge of technology, Supermaxes are known for their strict lockdown policies, lack of amenities and prisoner isolation techniques. Originally set-up in 1972 at USP Marion to house the most violent, hardened and escape-prone criminals, they are now used for leaders of criminal organizations and gangs, serial killers, persistent rule breakers and political prisoners like spies and terrorists. With limited access to visits and phone calls, Supermax prisoners are confined alone in tiny cells up to 23 hours a day. They are isolated yet under intense surveillance. Their keepers want to know when they sleep, when they eat and when they shit. Every aspect of their lives is under official control. They're offered one hour of recreation in a small cage that's often referred to as a dog kennel. They have no communal eating areas, no opportunities to work or to attend educational programs. There are no windows, only solid doors with slots for passing food trays and cells with the lights kept on 24 hours a day. The cells are designed to keep the sound out, so prisoners rarely hear another human voice. The isolation is total, and these underground control units often referred to as ADMAX, SHU, ADSEG or IMU are constructed with fortified tunnels, double doors, remote control locking mechanisms and furnished in concrete and steel, equipped with around the clock audio and video surveillance The most infamous of the Supermaxes is ADX Florence, the Federal Bureau of Prisons maximum security prison.

USP Marion replaced the notorious Alcatraz and ADX Florence replaced USP Marion, which was put on indefinite lockdown from 1983 to 1994, demonstrating the need for a permanent lockdown prison. Hence the construction of ADX Florence, which has been called the Alcatraz of the Rockies. "We just needed a more secure facility," said Tracy Billingsley, a BOP spokeswoman. "We needed to bring together the most dangerous who required the most intense supervision to one location." And many states followed the feds' lead. California copied the concept with Pelican Bay and now there are over 57 other Supermaxes with over 13,500 beds in the U.S. Bob Snelson, a union leader at ADX said, "Most of our inmates are very violent. They have short fuses. We are dealing with people who can go from reading the bible to trying to kill you."

People like Luis Felipe aka King Blood, leader of New York's Latin Kings, Larry Hoover the leader of Chicago's Gangster Disciples, Mexican Mafia leader Ruben "Nite Owl" Castro and Aryan Brotherhood commission members Barry "The Baron" Mills and TD "The Hulk"

Bingham, who were all charged with running their gangs from their ADX cells after receiving natural life sentences for their prior offenses. But the list goes on—notorious DC hit man Wayne Perry, Lorton prison kingpin Keith "Fly" Gaffney, B-More drug lord Anthony Jones, NY City street legend Peter "The Pistol" Rollock and mob turncoats Anthony "Gaspipe" Casso and Sammy "The Bull" Gravano. There's also a literal bombers row at ADX, with Richard Reid, the shoe bomber; Ted Kaczynski, the Unabomber; Eric Rudolph, the Olympic Park bomber; Ramzi Ahmed Yousef who planned the 1993 WTC attack; Timothy McVeigh's partner Terry Nichols and 9/11 terrorist Zacarias Moussaoui. The father of actor Woody Harrelson, Charles Harrelson, who killed a federal judge, is there, as well as white supremacist Mathew Hale who tried to kill a federal judge, Robert Hannen, the FBI agent who spied for Russia and Yu Kikumura, the Japanese Red Army member who plotted to bomb the NY Navy Rec Center. Krista Rear an ADX spokesperson said, "Sometimes we receive inmates here at ADX as a direct court commitment. The rest of our inmates are here from other penitentiaries where they were unable to be safely and securely housed in a more open population setting." And with only 490 beds only the worst of the worst make it to ADX.

Terrorists, big-profile mobsters, gang leaders and white supremacists are imprisoned there along with political prisoners, prisoner organizers, prisoners who file lawsuits and voice other complaints about the system. And there have been many complaints from critics and former ADX prisoners that the Supermax is inhumane and cause its occupants to go crazy. The attorney for Luis Felipe aka King Blood said that his client broke down from the stress of isolation and requires medication. Christopher Boyce a convicted spy who was at ADX said, "You're slowly hung. You're ground down. You can barely keep your sanity." And Eric Rudolph, the Olympic Park bomber wrote the following words to a newspaper, "Supermax is designed to inflict as much misery and pain as is constitutionally permissible. It's a closed off world designed to isolate inmates from social and environmental stimuli. It's a political prison. The government not only uses it to house problem inmates, it also uses it to add an extra measure of punishment for those inmates who have been convicted of politically motivated offenses."

To get the real deal about ADX we reached out to penitentiary veteran and DC Blacks gang member Little Caesar who's been doing time in the federal system since the 70s, with stints at both USP Marion during the 80s and ADX Florence in the late 90s. Of his time in the Supermaxes, Little Caesar says, "It's like being in a tunnel for years where your radio and communication frequency has gone out, where you can't reach out to anyone and it seems no one can reach you. But you've got to navigate through the darkness with hopes that there is really a light at the end of the tunnel."

Little Caesar was first sent to lockdown at USP Marion after an attempted murder charge "on a rat that was trying to make bones to join the AB's by cutting a borderline retarded brother's throat," he relates. "I pled out on the case and got a fresh 37-month sentence." And a one way ticket to the toughest penitentiary in America at the time. "Marion was the toughest in regard to psychological effects. The early 80s was an era of aggression, an ear of murder as well as malicious wounding," he says. "It was different then. Back then a motherfucker had to have good game on how to get out on the pound, be prone to violence or under somebody's wing in some kinda way. I was fortunate enough to be around a lot of men.... convicts." And as part of the feared DC Blacks gang Little Caesar made his way.

Little Caesar the convict who eventually ended up in ADX Florence in the late 90s, has been locked up with a who's who of American gangsters. "Nicky Scarfo, John Gotti, Jeff Fort of El Rukns, Big Naughty, Rayful Edmonds before he turned rat, Kenneth "Supreme" McGriff and many other kingpins and gang leaders," he says. He reveals that the worst part of ADX Florence was the mental abuse. "The psychological abuse administered by staff was a key mind controlling factor." Little Caesar asserts. "There were subtle as well as overt battles of the mind, and with the state of chaos being what it was, you always needed a source to stabilize your thinking to keep you from crossing the line of psychological to physical warfare because the circumstances were so unusual. The underlying conflict between races and the different gangs and territorial factions was constant and kept both inmates and officers alike off balance. They constantly had to worry that the next incident might surely erupt in violence."

Little Caesar eventually completed the three-year step program that keeps inmates in their cells 23 hours a day for the first year and then gradually socializes them. In the last year, prisoners can come out of their 7-foot by 12-foot cells into a pod like area with other prisoners to see how they act. "It was a matter of coming to grips with the fact that people were just people," Little Caesar says. "That shit will make or break you. It's incumbent upon each individual to either build themselves up or allow themselves to fall deeper into the folds of the system. The longer you're in a situation like that, the more you become a part of the environment, and the more you become a part of the environment, the harder it is to sustain one's sense of purpose and sanity relative to societal norms." And we know that the feds bury undesirables at ADX with no chance of ever coming out or completing the step program.

Undesirables, political prisoners and those convicted of continuing criminal activity from prison that the feds want to hold limbo incommunicado just like the war detainees at Abu Graib and Guantanamo Bay are housed at ADX—that is, whoever the government wants to keep on ice and away from the public eye. In ADX rehabilitation is not an issue. Punishment, control and cutting the individual off from the rest of the world is the MO. Every occupant is kept in near total solitary confinement. Beds, desks and stools are all made of poured concrete. Toilets have a valve that shuts off the water in case flooding occurs (prisoners are notorious for flooding their cells with water) and the sinks have no taps just buttons. A 42-inch window four inches wide looks out on a one man rec yard, and a 12-inch black and white TV shows closed circuit classes in psychology, education, anger management, parenting and literacy. The extreme isolation is the way the BOP achieves extreme control over the individuals incarcerated there. But recently there have been numerous problems at ADX.

Opened in 1994 to replace USP Marion, where 20 prisoners and two guards were killed by the likes of AB member Thomas "Terrible Tom" Silverstein the preceding decade, ADX Florence was hailed in corrections as the safe new model for high-security prisons. But after 11 years with no murders, there have been two since February 2005. Clearly things at ADX are heating up, and critics are attacking the Supermax structure from all angles. With budget cuts forcing 3,147 critical shifts left unfilled in the last couple of years, a CNN report called it Superlax. A report by the inspector general found that the BOP is unable to effectively monitor the mail of terrorists and other high risk inmates in order to detect and prevent terrorism and criminal activities. Inmate cells are no longer being searched on a regular basis, and the fact that the Aryan Brotherhood and Mexican Mafia gang leaders ran their criminal empires from isolation make it worse.

"Every thing is changing—the laws, the penalties, the technologies and the old methods for controlling communication are passé, caput," says Little Caesar. And he's right. When gang leaders in the most secure facility in the U.S. can smuggle out instructions and direct their organizations from their prison cell, something is definitely wrong. "They have cut the staffing budget so short that it's just a matter of time before we have a riot," Union rep Mike Schnobrich said. And ADX union leader Bob Snelson reiterated this, "When they are supposed to get an hour of recreation a day and they get none for weeks, or they can't make a phone call for weeks, they go into a killing fury." And with threats of violence or murder against guards doubled from

55 in 2004 to 110 in 2005, there is room for concern. Officers are regularly pelted with urine and feces, and one counselor was attacked by a prisoner with a papier-mâché spear and nearly had his eye cut out. But the pendulum can swing both ways, and it does. Prisoners have been gassed, beaten, pepper sprayed, 4 pointed to the bed, strip searched constantly and extracted from their cells forcefully. Mind control, medications and chemical weapons are used to incapacitate prisoners. A guard at ADX said, "It's chilling to walk down the cellblocks and glance through the Plexiglas sally port chambers into the cells and see the faces inside. It's a bunch of terrorists and psychopaths. Inmates run showers all day and night and scream for hours when the water is cut off. Other prisoners yell that CIA agents are monitoring their thoughts. It's sad. Many have lost all hope." With the routine excessive force, tasers, chemical sprays, shotguns, sensory deprivations and overload, pacification with drugs and violent cell extractions, Supermax looks more and more like the feds are waging war, a security war.

Over the past 10 years, prisoners' political and civil rights have been severely disabled. The language of security has authorized Supermax imprisonment by treating it not as punishment but as a set of administrative procedures for managing high-security populations. The procedures now legally sanctioned were once considered violations of the U.S. Constitution's Eighth Amendment, which prohibits cruel and unusual punishment. "These are the most dangerous of people," Attorney General Roberto Gonzales said. But does that justify the way they are treated? The militaristic aspects of policing have intensified the use of lethal force inside the Supermaxes. The sophisticated weaponry and surveillance equipment- metal detectors, x-ray machines, leg irons, waist chains, black boxes, holding cages and all the rest have dehumanized the prisoners. So how should we expect them to act?

"I have seen them rot," prison expert James Aiken said. "They rot." And maybe that is what our government wants. Or maybe it's like the former warden of ADX, Robert Hood who was remembered as especially restrictive and sadistic by former prisoners, said, "No one's getting out of Supermax, period, end of story."

If that's the truth then our society has truly degenerated. If a man doesn't deserve to live in society, then why not put him out of his misery? Why this sadistic nature for the ultimate retribution? Is that what all the tough on crime rhetoric is about?

FIVE

On the Inside: Rats and Snitches

W HEN THE FEDS prosecute a case, they are vicious, brutal even. There aren't any pleasantries. They are out to draw blood, inflict harm and all that. It's like all those defense lawyers are saying, "When the indictment is coming down, it's like a buffet. First come, first serve. So you better be first in line." And they are talking about first in line to snitch.

But you know those are just some sucker ass lawyers talking. And they are some bloodsuckers too. Working in cahoots with the government. All they want you to do is snitch, to make their job easy. The majority of lawyers, paid or appointed, will sell you out in a minute because this is the feds. This is the war on motherfucking drugs.

So you know you got all these cats snitching on their cases, trying to get that 5K1 or rule 35. It is wrong we know. It is the coward's way out we know. But some dudes ain't trying to do no time. They never heard of "if you gonna do the crime, you gotta be willing to do the time." They would rather live with the knowledge of what they did to somebody's mother, brother, sister then face up like a true soldier. Death b4 dishonor, you heard. That's on them though. They are the sucker. They gotta look at themselves in the mirror everyday. Maybe everybody doesn't know about them, but they know about themselves. When they wake up every morning they know they are rat-snitch motherfuckers.

But you know what I really don't understand. I don't understand these motherfuckers that rat and snitch in prison. What the fuck is wrong with them? They aren't getting any time cuts in here. Maybe they're trying for extra good time. But they must be stupid because in the feds you're only getting 54 days a year.

But still you got cats in the feds, be it a low, medium, or USP, snitching on motherfuckers left and right. And they snitch on some petty-ass, trivial shit too. I want to know what the fuck they are snitching for. What do they get out of it?

Let me try to lay it out for you. This kid has been around. Nine years in the feds and five institutions- Petersburg, Manchester, Beckley, Fort Dix, and Fairton. The kid has seen a lot of bullshit. So let me kick it to you.

You got some chump-ass motherfuckers in here working for SIS. They got the LT's # on their phone list. Calling them from the unit all stealth-like. Letting the man know what is going down in the unit. Who got the dope and shit like that. These cats are vicious. At some joints they are right out in the open. It's like snitches-are-us, like it's a franchise or something. I'm telling you the feds are bad. It's treacherous.

They are snitching to eat first in chow or to get an extra piece of chicken. Cats are snitching to get close to some government bitch. They're giving motherfuckers up for a 305 contraband shot. They sell out their homeboys to avoid 30 days hole time or to keep that measly 54 days a year. Shit is getting stupid in here.

I've seen crews of dudes, supposedly homeboys, doing their thing you know, making moves or whatever. One of the crew gets a dirty or something. He doesn't tell his homeboys. The fucker ain't trying to go to the hole. He's scared to death of the hole. So he rats out all his homeboys to SIS and they all get pissed. The dirties come back and they go to the hole. But the one cat never goes. He snitched his way out of it.

You got dudes in here who are always in trouble, always getting busted for fighting, for wine, for drugs. But they never do no hole time. They never lose their commissary, visits, or phone. They are always making some excuse about how they beat this shot or that one. But they don't ever show no paperwork. And in the feds nowadays ain't nobody calling them on it. They just let it slide. The times are crazy. What happened to honor? Respect? Integrity?

The convicts in here are very few. There are a little more of what you could call prisoners. But the majority of people in the feds today are inmates, straight-ass sucker motherfuckers too scared to make a move or to defy the man. They will drop a note on you in a minute. And they ain't just dropping notes on serious shit either. Motherfuckers will drop a note on you for a fucking onion, son.

Cats are dirty in here. Let me tell you how they do it. You might have that Grade 1 in facilities or Unicor, but the grade 2 dude is looking to make a move up. The motherfucker will drop a note on your ass saying how you are about to fuck-up so and so and boom—you are in the hole under SIS investigation for possibly months.

And these snitch ass rat bastards aren't just snitching for those government jobs. They will tell to get your cell or your bottom bunk or even your pillow, dog. It is sick. They will tell because they are jealous of your girl they saw in the visiting room or heard about. They tell because they hate on you because you get mad letters at mail call. They will tell to fuck up your hustle from the kitchen or laundry. They will tell for anything. It doesn't matter.

And don't let these police try to take something from one of them snitches, like their good time, their visits, their payphones, or their commissary. If these police threaten them with that, those cats will tell in a minute. They will tell anything. They will make it up. Anything to keep their little privileges, to keep their little luxuries.

And you better watch out if you are watching TV, too. Because these cats go hard on the TV and a lot of them won't check you to your face. If they think you are cutting into into their TV time or moving in on their government TV, watch the fuck out. It's on. And I ain't talking about no fighting either. Most of these cats are cowards. They'll tell on you straight up.

Motherfuckers are scared to death to go to the hole. If you really think about it sending a prisoner to the hole is the worst thing these BOP people can do. They are not gonna beat you up. They are not gonna put a gun to your head. All they're gonna do is say, "You need to cooperate or go to the hole."

Big fucking deal. Go to the hole. Don't give them the power. Be a convict. Take the power back. Something for you players on the street. Go to trial. If everybody stood firm, there wouldn't be all these bullshit cases. Death before dishonor, you heard. True soldiers only die once.

II

PRISON LIFE

SIX

Prison Gangs and the Analogy of Hate

P RISON IS A cauldron of hate, a mixing pot of volatile tempers and personalities that can incite violence in a nanosecond. The territorial, drug and monetary beefs from the streets bleed over into the prison yards as racism intensifies and the hate it spews forth explodes in the form of prison gang warfare.

In prison a convict's skin color defines him. It is his flag or calling card, an affiliation to belong or to be part of a group. And with our nation's prisons bursting at the seams with a 30 percent over capacity rating, violence has surged. Earlier this year, Harley Lappin, the director of the Bureau of Prisons, told a congressional subcommittee, "We are managing more dangerous and aggressive offenders, including more gang-affiliated inmates, and we are encountering increases in inmate assaults on other inmates and on staff."

In prison, different races of gangs clash to control their immediate surroundings. Be it drugs coming into the prison, gambling, or extortion rackets, violence is the common denominator. And it's not just white or Spanish against black. It gets a little more complex in the belly of the beast. Welcome to the world of prison gangs.

White Gangs

"Hate is always a common analogy," says a tattooed skinhead and Texas Mafia member who did time in the vicious Texas State system in the 80's. He explains how "there's very few similarities between the states and the feds." Claiming that there's way more gangs in the state. He continues, "In Texas in the 80's there was over 300 body bags a year. Hate wasn't even really acknowledged. It was more about the color you wore, the ink on your body, or your patch."

He names the white gangs that operate behind bars, "The Aryan Brotherhood or the Brand as they're called in the feds. The Dirty White Boys or DWB's for short. The Aryan Circle (AC's), White Knights, and Texas Mafia (TM's)" He explains how there's "a bleed over of all those gangs in the feds now," but that the "originals are dinosaurs" and most likely locked down 23 hours a day at ADX Florence, the BOP's Supermax penitentiary that houses the likes of the Unabomber.

But even with the restricted mail and phone monitoring these dinosaurs are still calling the shots from their prison cells as a case out of USP Leavenworth involving the AB's in the mid 90's illustrates. Back then, the feds started a program where they had some of the AB's on ice. They were on 24 hour lockdown and the only way they were let out of the program was if they debriefed with the feds and told the BOP of their gang affiliations.

As dudes filtered back into the system, the AB's started putting hits out on their own members. Anybody who debriefed was marked. "Weeding out their own trash," says the Texas Mafia member. "Cleansing our ranks."

And in prison race on race killings are common. The Texas Department of Corrections has a video tape of a murder that happened in 1984 that they still use to this day for guard training purposes. AB Virgil Barfield killed Calvin Massey an affiliated TM. A straight white on white killing. The AB butchered the affiliated TM stabbing him 78 times, then cut his head off, stood up and smiled at the camera that was recording the murder. "Shit like that goes on all the time," says the Texas Mafia member. "It has nothing to do with color, but with affiliation."

Most of the white gangs are racist skinheads who favor Nazi imagery and their affiliations vary. The Hammerskins are an offshoot of the AB's but they are more extreme in their political and social beliefs. They consider Hitler a hero to the white race and say things like "all niggers should die." They refer to blacks as sub-humans. The Brand, another AB shoot off, is a more federal prison thing. They are represented by a clover leaf tattoo. The DWB's are ranked by state and sport a tattoo of their home state. They also have a splinter group, Bruden Waffen "88" that wears a fist double lightning bolt tattoo. They are the DWB's elite hit squad.

All of these groups are highly into the Nazi swastika and the lightning bolt thing with the spider webs and white pride tattooed on the backs of their arms. They look upon Hitler as a demigod. Like, "Yeah, he was doing the right thing." They are equal opportunity haters, lumping "Jews, niggers, spics, and race-mixers" in the same category. If it's not white, it's not right with them.

Mostly though, they just exploit their own people; that is, other whites. And a lot of them are dope fiends. But they will kill in a minute, if provoked. "Most of these dudes got so much fucking time, they got 175 years. There is no deterrent when somebody has over a century worth of time." says the TM member. And he concludes with: "These are racist gangs, but they hate their own race just as much, just another culture of it."

Black Gangs

A lot of black gangs are embedded into American popular culture. The two most famous, the Crips and the Bloods, were immortalized in the Sean Penn film, "Colors", and have been name dropped by rappers like Snoop Dog and Tupac. These gangs have moved past the race barrier, for you can now find Crips and Bloods of any color, race or creed. And these gangs are represented in prison also, but it's more broken into geographical regions. Like the Texas blacks hate the New Orleans blacks or the DC dudes hate the Virginia ones. Any group can find a reason to be prejudice. Be it color, ethnicity, or where you're from.

The major black gangs in prisons today are a spillover from the ones on the streets. There's the aforementioned Crips and Bloods, the Gangster Disciples- who are led by Chicago native Larry Hoover, who calls the shots from the ADX Supermax in Florence, the Vicelords- another Chicago spawned gang—and the Black Gorilla Family. As seen in movies like "Blood in and Blood out," gang life starts on the streets and permeates the prisons, where incarcerated leaders call the shots from their prison cells determining who lives and who dies.

In the late 60's and early 70's in the California State system, a race war waged. The Black Panther affiliated George Jackson and his cohorts would attack random whites on the tiers and in the yards just because of their white skin and blue eyes. It was in retaliation for white oppression of blacks. Edward Bunker, a white convict and author wrote of the whites hate of George Jackson and his ilk in his memoir, "Education of a Felon," just as George Jackson wrote about his crusade against the establishment in "Soledad Brother."

Many black dominated religious groups like the Five Percenters, the Nation of Islam, and Muslims also promote black solidarity with themes like "the blue-eyed, white devils" or by referring to all establishment or government-related persons "as those crackers." The Five Percenters even claim that white people are a genetic experiment gone wrong by ancient African scientists.

But the white-black hate that surfaces in prison has a long and disturbing history in our country. Beaconing back to the days of the KKK, the ultimate hate group, and the endless atrocities and lynching of slavery. With black males dominating the prison population it could be said that prison is just another form of slavery for the black man in this country.

Spanish Gangs

In total, there's seven different Mexican or Chicano gangs, and just like the movie "American Me" that told the story of the Mexican Mafia, they started from the inside out. But there's a big California/Texas thing going on with the vatos. It's like one of the California vatos says, "It could kick off whenever. But the Cali/TX thing doesn't mean you hate them. It's just an area thing."

The Mexican gangs can be broken down like this. There's the Cali Mexican Mafia and the Texas Mexican Mafia. They don't mess with each other. Then there's the Surenos (meaning southern) and Nortenos (meaning northern), as in southern and northern California gangs, that unite in federal prison but in the state might be at war with each other. Then there's the Texas Syndicate, which is a prison based gang that stretches back to the 70's in the Texas State System and the Texas Aztecas. And finally there's the Pizas and the Neros who are Mexican Nationals and not Chicanos like the above groups. The Pizas is just a loose collection of all Mexicans from Mexico and the Neros are Mexico City-based Mexicans.

The vato from California says of the Texas/Cali split, "It could be war or it could not be war. It's an on and off going thing." But basically he explains, "There's three groups in the feds: Cali, Texas, and the Pizas." He says how the number 13, which is tattooed onto a lot of the vatos' necks, is a California thing. "The homies got their own thing." Also prevalent are a lot of teardrops which represent murders or hits.

And in addition to the Chicano gangs, other Spanish nationalities are represented in prison too. The biggest among them being the Latin Kings, who are mostly New York and Chicago based and are comprised mainly of Puerto Ricans. Their leader, Luis Felipe aka King Blood, is locked down for life at ADX Florence.

Asian Gangs

The most prominent Asian gangs are mostly Chinese and basically New York based. Some of the more high profile ones are the Flying Dragons, the White Tigers, and the Green Dragons whose whole crew is in prison. Another notorious Asian gang is the Vietnamese BTK, as in Born to Kill. A lot of their members are in prison too.

All these Asian gangs prey on their own communities in the real world, fighting over territorial or monetary beefs. In prison, however, all the Asian guys usually come together despite their differences. Its like one Green Dragon member says, "Each prison has no more than ten Asian guys. So whatever beef existed in the streets is squashed." He continues, "Our culture is different. If there's a beef we solve it. And unless a guy is an asshole or a rat then everybody is a friend."

He explains how the Asian gangs like to "keep it close" and how "most gangs have politics. Still the bosses do business within the Asian community." He mentions some other Asian gangs also, 24k is a Korean gang, Fu Ching- a Fukinese Chinese gang, Go Shadows- a Chinese group, KP (Korean Power) and Goblins- both Korean gangs. "All of these gangs are New York based," he says. "And they all have members in prison. But the numbers are small so we all come together in prison."

As the different races of gangs vary so does the hate that they promote. From the KKK to the Mafia to the biker gangs like the Hells Angels and Pagans, American society is flush with gangs that hate another group for one reason or another, be it for monetary, territorial, ethnic, color or religious reasons, or for a long standing blood feud like the Hatfields and McCoys. Hate promotes more hate and violence inspires more violence. From slavery to Hitler to the Columbine killings, it's all the same.

Maybe it's like Nobel Peace prize winner and Crip founder Tookie Wilson surmised in the recent made for the TV movie "Redemption." He said that when you got hate in your heart it's easy to hate someone similar to yourself, one who walks like you, talks like you and looks like you. Maybe it's the self-hate coming out.

But on the other side of the coin, maybe it's the differences between the races. The differences between the haves and have nots. The differences between the prisoners and their keepers. The differences between the establishment and the minorities that incubates hate and makes it fester. In prison it might be all of the above. And in prison hate can equal death. Death to one and death to all.

SEVEN

The World of Prison Tattoos

IN THE BELLY of the beast a convict's tattoos can define him. Being sleeved out or tatted up is a sign of respect or a mark of belonging. In the pen dudes wear their territorial and gang affiliations on their sleeves. Their street names are proudly emblazoned across their stomach or backs, as are their girl's names, the joints they've done time at and the number of years they've spent inside. Like a mural depicting history a convict's life can be dissected by checking out the ink on his body. In the nether world of corruption and violence convicts take their tats seriously.

Homies mark themselves accordingly, and they're not looking for no jive ass sucker to put some inferior work on their skin because tattoos are permanent. There's no laser removal in the joint. And you better be sure you belong to whoever's sign you're wearing. Don't be putting no clover leaf tattoo if you're not a real AB, because you will get fucked up. And dudes have been bodied for less than some bad ink. It's like penitentiary veteran and jail house tattooist Chuck says, "In this environment, if your work isn't stellar or near perfect, a dissatisfied customer is apt to stab you in the fucking neck rather than withhold payment, or report you to the better business bureau."

And Chuck should know. He's done 16 plus years in prison. From, "T.D.C. (Texas Department of Corrections), where I split my time between the Beto #1 unit and the Darrington Unit," where only the worst of the worst are housed, to "USP Allenwood, FCI Beckley, FCI Beaumont and FCI Gilmer in the feds." He says.

Being an inkslinger in the pen isn't a cakewalk. It's not like the guards set up shop for tattooists. Everything is done on the downlow, for getting a tattoo or inking one is grounds for a shot and trip to the hole, if you are caught, that is. "Some guards love to catch someone blasting a piece or getting inked," Chuck says. "But I've had a number watch me work and supply me with latex gloves and alcohol pads. I've even had a few who would give me the greenlight to work if I gave them a machine to turn in, as if they found it."

And the cons in here don't have a fancy tattoo gun. They make use with what they can find and put together on the compound. "In T.D.C.," Chuck says. "Spinner motors were unobtainable in the early 80's, so I would appropriate electronic relays and remove the 110 volt coils, which I combined with a plastic frame, band steel off vegetable crates, and Bic pens cut down for barrels." Engineering skills come in handy it seems. And in prison a tattooist has to keep the gun hidden too, because guards will confiscate them as contraband in shakedowns. "Every machine is designed for easy quick assembly and disassembly to be hidden in as many places as possible." Chuck says. "One piece is easier to replace than the whole thing."

Chuck describes tattooing in prison as, "Challenging, sometimes rewarding, but mostly a pain in the ass for many reasons," the quality and lack of ink foremost. "People make ink by burning articles of plastic, and collecting the soot as a base." Chuck says. "I've made it a habit of never using made ink. It doesn't flow worth a shit, and I won't compromise quality art or my time with inferior ink." But that doesn't stop a whole a lot of other dudes who perpetrate the myth of jailhouse tattoos with subpar work. Chuck says he uses India inks such as Speedball, Black Cat or Higgins, which he can acquire from facilities, or through the art program.

And for the needles Chuck says, "The only material I've ever used for needle stock is stainless steel guitar strings (the core)." With music programs at most prisons it's not that hard to get a pack of strings. And considering that most musicians are frequent customers it makes it real easy. An inkslinger like Chuck doesn't work cheap though. Like he says, "Good tattoos aren't cheap and cheap tattoos aren't good."

He'll charge "in the neighborhood of $35 to $100 for a small piece." And in prison where most dudes are making $25 a month that's a lot of money. "In the past I've priced arm sleeves at $250 per arm, and back pieces at $500 up to $2,000." Chuck says, "I've been paid in everything from commissary items, such as food, cigs, shoes, sweats, radios, stamps to contraband items (i.e. drugs) to money sent from the street to my inmate account."

As to the pieces he does Chuck says, "They have to have a pretty specific idea of what they want before they even come to talk with me if they want me to design it from mind to paper to flesh." Chuck specializes in surreal imagery involving guns, demons, inner hells and the cesspits of prison. Alluding to all the cover ups he's done over the years, he adds adamantly, "I will not put wives, or girlfriends names in ink though."

And Chuck doesn't discriminate either. "It doesn't matter to me who they are, or who they know and run with gang wise." And he's tattooed mad gang members with their telltale gang emblems, from Aryan Brotherhood members to Mexican Mafia vatos to Black Gorilla Family members, and even a bunch of wiseguys. But Chuck is very aware of health hazards. "Health hazards have become a major fucking concern in the past fifteen years or so." He says. "Since I can't screen nor trust, or believe what anyone says in here, I treat everyone the same concerning Hep C and AIDS. Everyone gets their own needles and barrels, any ink that hits the cap and isn't used is thrown away with the cap and latex gloves are always used." You can never be too careful when you're dealing with a bunch of junkies, crackheads and low lives.

Of the drawbacks to slinging ink Chuck says, "Dealing with a bunch of motherfuckers you don't like nor respect isn't always kosher. I've told some flat out I wouldn't work on them. And a lot of these dudes don't have the heart or balls to attempt to jump me but they'll rat a motherfucker out in a heartbeat and bring down the heat, so that I'll have to close shop for a minute." So being selective does have its price, but like any discerning businessman, Chuck is trying to make some money.

"I've had good runs where I pulled in over five grand in a three month period." Chuck says. Even though most dudes in prison don't have anything, a few big Willies can keep Chuck busy and in the money. But dudes are always hustling in here anyways, trying to come up by smuggling drugs, running a parlay ticket, stealing food from the kitchen, manufacturing shanks, or even doing tattoos. But everything has its risks and Chuck has spent plenty of time in the hole, "suffering for my art," as he puts it.

And after 16 plus years as a prisoner and inkslinger, Chuck looks back. "I've always possessed an artistic talent for drawing and painting. That aspect came naturally. Some early tattooing experimentation came at my own expense, but I started tattooing regularly and making a name for myself in the T.D.C. in the early 80's." And Chuck found that, "Besides the money it generated, it helped to pass the time." And inside that is what it's all about: making the days go by.

And to his counterparts on the streets, Chuck says, "If they had to do arm sleeves or back pieces with single needle alone, let alone a portrait, they would pull their fucking hair out in frustration." But still Chuck sites inkslingers like Paul Booth as his role models. "Under the umbrella of creativity, passion of trade and business savvy- definitely Paul Booth," he said.

EIGHT

Homo Thugs

YOU SEE THEM in every prison. Homo-thugs creeping on the low, acting like they're gangstas, going hard and then breaking weak, swearing they ain't faggots. But let me tell you. If you let a man suck your dick or you hit one of them gumps, you are a straight queer. Ain't no ands, ifs, or buts about it. Well maybe there are some butts about it, but you know what I mean. These dudes up in here are crazy. Closet homos, for real.

I've seen it all over the feds. And it ain't like some macho movie shit in here, like fuck or get fucked. These dudes are just straight homos. But they're swearing they're not. I've seen them all up with the gump on the pound, and then they're fronting in the visiting room kissing up on their babymama and their kids. These dudes are sick, for real.

If you can't get no pussy what would make you wanna let a man suck your dick? I mean if you're straight, that is. If you're a gump, then that's what you are. Don't fight it. Don't deny it. Be who you are. But in here you got a whole bunch of dudes faking it. Like they're tough. Like they're gangstas. Like they're hard. Yeah, they're hard alright. Hard for another man to suck their dick.

And these homo-thugs blend in too. All up in the click with their homeboys, but hanging with the gumps on the downlow. They're watching the videos on BET, fronting and rapping like they're gangsta, keeping it real and shit, talking about that Lexus they used to have. I keep waiting for the day when another brother will call one of these homo-thugs out. "You ain't no gangsta nigga, you a homo-thug." But it doesn't happen that often. Dudes are letting shit ride. They don't want no drama, I guess.

These dudes are all up on the court balling and everything. Sweating up on a motherfucker. Who knows what they got? A lot of these gumps got the package, but that doesn't stop none of these dudes getting theirs. They're digging that gump's back out. Tearing that ass up in the name of what? Getting theirs? That shit's crazy.

And some of these homo-thugs are getting mad love from bitches. Their babymamas are taking care of them, and they're all up in the feds hitting faggots. And they're thinking these faggots are bitches too. Prison bitches they call them. Yo, that's my bitch, you hear them say, referring to the gump. That ain't no bitch motherfucker, that's a motherfucking man, just like you.

And some of these gumps have tits too. The homo-thugs love that shit when a faggot with tits hits the pound. All types of drama will jump off as all the homo-thugs fight over the gump, stabbing each other up and shit like they're fighting over a fine ass broad.

I can see why some of these dudes with life do it. I mean fuck it. They got life. They're trying to get something. But they got homo-thugs in here that are short and they go hard on that gump shit. All up in recreation or education sweating the gump to meet them in the bathroom or even moving up in the gumps cell for some all night action. I'm like damn, these dudes are short. What are they thinking?

I've heard of dudes that got dilemmas when they hit the street. They got their babymama and their prison gump on the street waiting for them, and they're not sure which one they want to go home to when they get out. They're talking about the gump got a good job and their babymama is on welfare. Damn, and these dudes swear they're not gay.

I say fuck it, come out the closet. Move to San Francisco. I ain't gonna knock a person for being gay, but don't be no hypocrite. Like, yeah, I ain't gay, but I'm fucking with gumps in prison. C'mon man, that shit is retarded. Either you are or you aren't. There's plenty of dudes that have been in 20 or 30 years that never went that route.

There's a saying in here that after 10 years it's all legal. Meaning that after 10 years in prison it's all good. You can fuck with a faggot and not be queer. But c'mon, that's some bullshit. And some dudes jump right off the boat and into the water. They're like, damn, I'm getting me some, like there ain't no difference between ass and pussy. These dudes are going hard like they're in ancient Greece or something. They think they're Trojan warriors. They go raw dog too. No wonder so many homo-thugs got AIDS, trying to say they were shooting up and shit. All up in the joint going hard on heroin. But motherfucker, you ain't shot no heroin. You're a straight gump.

Going back out to the street and giving their babymamas the package, that shit is foul. These dudes are outta control. And it doesn't matter where they're from either. In the prisons a lot of dudes label DC guys as homo-thugs. And to a point it's true. But not all of them are like that. And I even believe the word, gump, came from the DC prisons like Lorton and the like, but for real I've seen homo-thugs from all different places- Carolina, New York, Philly, Jersey, Virginia. It doesn't matter. Some of these dudes get in here and they think they're home free. Like its ok, I was in prison. It doesn't count. Stop fooling yourself man. That is some bullshit.

I've even seen some Muslim dudes who are supposed to be all righteous and shit on that gump shit. Like they say, it takes all types. But these homo-thugs are a breed of their own. And they stick together too. You see them on the yard all late when it's dark. Walking around the track with their gumps or they're playing ball and their gump is up in the stands cheering. And these same dudes, these homo-thugs will swear they're not gay. They'll go home to their woman swearing they never did no shit like that. But in here dudes know. And once you're labeled a homo-thug the label sticks, you can't shake it. Change your ways when you hit the streets. Once a faggot always a faggot.

Hip-Hop Does Not Mean Gang Related

Hip-hop doesn't mean gang related, but some in the media would have you believe it does. To the delight of hip-hop's opponents and the consternation of its defenders, rap music has a long history with the penal system. And with the recent gang legislation bills passed in Congress rappers better watch out.

"The same techniques that were used to investigate the Mafia and drug gangs are being used on rappers today," says Lisa Evers, host of New York's Hot 97's "Street Soldiers" program. The feds targeted Death Row CEO Suge Knight in the 90s, and Y2K5 saw them indict Murder Inc. With Irv Gotti's arrest and the continuing probe investigating Ja Rule and other Murder Inc. artists and employees, the feds are portraying the record label as a violent, criminal street gang allegedly led by Supreme Team founder and ex-con Kenneth "Supreme" McGriff, a former 80's drug baron, who after spending a decade locked down emerged to make strides of his own in the rap world as a film producer. The straight-to-DVD flick, "Crime Partners," which featured Snoop Dog and Ja Rule, was among his credits. But with Gotti acquitted the feds case against Supreme seems weak. The trial starts in March.

In the mind of legendary Geto Boys alumni Scarface, there is no doubt that hip-hop is being targeted by law enforcement officials. "They are about to make the rap game illegal," he says. "It's going to be like the dope game. It seems like it, because they're trying to kill this shit. They want this shit dead. They don't want any nigga in power, period. They don't want niggas making money off this shit."

With the ever popular cell block video setting and affixed gang colors, hip-hop has been tattooed with the markings of gang and prison culture. But it's just entertainment, right? Maybe not. "They don't call it gangster rap for nothing," says FBI agent Fred Snelling, a primary on the Murder Inc. case.

And incarcerated O.G. Tank, who's doing life in the feds, says, "Rappers have taken on the persona of the hood stars who are now in prison or dead. They think it's slick to be linked to the streets with their gangsta image and street credibility to boost record sales, but with that gangsta image comes some very real gangsta problems." As Irv Gotti has found out, even 50 Cent says as much. "I think it's sad, Irv Gotti's situation. He tried to become something he never had the heart to be. That's where Gotti came from. He was DJ Irv ahead of that."

And in reality Murder Inc. is no more a violent street gang than the U.S. government is. And the alleged leader, Kenneth "Supreme" McGriff, is just an ex-con who was trying to go legit. But with the feds' war on rap it's open season on every money getting dude in the hip-hop industry, especially if they got a criminal past. "They doing some foul shit to Preme," says Choke, a B-More native who did time with Supreme. "The feds won't be happy 'til they bury Murder Inc." But the Death Row case showed that reality isn't always stranger than fiction and sometimes entertainment is just that, entertainment. No matter the connotations the media, critics and the government would have you believe.

NINE

Aryan Circle

IN PRISON BATTLE lines are drawn along racial, territorial and geographical distinctions. And in this country, the US of A, it's been reported that about one fourth of all male prisoners are gang members. And on some compounds a convict has no choice but to join a gang. Either that or he gets extorted, checked in, beat down or turned out. That's just the nature of the beast in the netherworld of corruption and violence.

The feds have reported that prison disturbances have soared by 400 percent as a direct result of gang activity in Y2K. Inmate gangs operate ruthlessly with mafia-style codes and constitutions and fight with the raw brutality of pit bulls. A gang provides not only protection from other gangs, who are more than willing to fight gangs of their same race, but also a sense of family, an identity that transcends the individual. In the belly of the beast, gangs offer a respite from the feelings of isolation and powerlessness. They empower prisoners and give status in a world where a man isn't considered a human being, only a number to be corralled, fed and counted like human cattle.

Though the prison subculture exists in relative obscurity, hidden behind concrete walls and razor wire, a prison gang out of Texas, the Aryan Circle, has sent tremors through the vast corridors of the prison industrial complex. The newer white supremacist gang in the Texas prison system, they are making a name for themselves and growing quite violently with deadly attacks against the Texas Aryan Brotherhood, TDC corrections officers, and other prison gangs.

The Aryan Circle originated in 1985 "because we got tired of the AB's turning out their own kind," says Johnny Bravo, a 37-year-old TDC gang war veteran now in the feds. "It started at Beto #1. Now we are the largest white organization in the TDC (Texas Department of Corrections)." Robert Walker of gangsorus.com, a prison gang identification website, verifies this. "The AC was founded in 1985 by Mark Gaspard and was formed due to the fact that some whites had become too radical in their beliefs." Not to say that the AC needs his verification. But it's nice to be recognized by the so-called experts.

"The president of the AC is a legendary dude in the TDC," Johnny Bravo says. "He was an ex AB member. The Texas AB's are different than the Cali faction, and the AC is not like the AB's." And Johnny should know. He's been locked up for a minute. "When I get released next year it will be 21 years. I've been locked up since 1985." He names the prisons he's been locked up at, "Beto #1, French Robinson- the worst prison in Texas, Sugarland, the Wallace Unit, Clemons, Coffield Unit, Allred- I've stayed years in every one of them."

And Johnny says the Aryan Circle is "based on white separatism." Beliefs include separation of the white race from all others for the betterment and preservation of the race. Johnny breaks it down, "Our own schools. Stick with your own kind. Have babies with your own kind. 1488." They consider their enemies to be all who are against them and those who attempt to oppress them, Johnny explains, "We wanted a brotherhood. To stick together and watch each others back. Your own kind you can trust." And in the brutal world of the TDC prison system this bonding was necessary, and at times vital.

There are over 25,000 known gang members in the TDC, and their influence, and control within the prison system has grown exponentially in the past five years. "Its easy for a gang to prosper in that environment," says Sammy Buentello, chief of the TDC Security Treat Group division, where all confirmed and suspected gang members are documented. In 1999 federal Judge William Wayne Justice cited the race-based gangs, and their system of thug rule in a still ongoing case, known as the Ruiz case that deplored TDC prison conditions. Justice found slave like conditions in "a prison underworld in which rapes, beatings and servitude are the currency of power. Inmates who refuse to join race-based gangs may be physically or sexually assaulted. Vulnerable inmates are subject to being bought and sold among groups of prison predators."

Johnny Bravo breaks it down like this, "As soon as a white dude walks in the door everyone is lacing up. Right off the rip you're fitting to fight, fuck or bust a 60. A 60 is commissary, so you gotta spend. That's your limit. It's really rough and segregated there." And whites, who are the minority in Texas prisons, gravitate toward the likes of gangs like the Aryan Circle. The gangs often recruit like fraternities, and specifically, target prisoners who are serving short sentences. New inmates who can't fight or afford protection find themselves paying an even higher price as a sex slave. "I think it's a very destructive system," says Dr Dennis Jurczak, an expert witness and psychiatrist. "And I've been in many systems. I've never seen one as repressive as I have seen in Texas." But the system is also one of the most racial.

"Back in the day we were proud. We were representing our race to the fullest. Loyalty, dedication, solidarity, kinship." Johnny Bravo says in describing what the AC means to him. About his comrades he says, "Most of them are max security. We stayed locked down the better part of the year for racial riots." Concerning the conflicts with blacks, he breaks it down.

"Bighead is a legendary dude." Johnny says. "I've seen him walk up into crowds of toads, and spit in their faces. He got a riot started in commissary by farting, and a toad said he'd stick a dick up his ass. The riot started in Beto #1. We got locked down for nine months. Bighead is still in the TDC. Been in there since he was 17. He's probably 36 now."

According to Johnny, "Everyman in the TDC—white, black, brown—will get tried. If it's one on one he's a man, but if two blacks whip a white, and the other whites don't do nothing they're hit. We're gonna get them." At one point in the TDC, the feds came in, and said they needed to integrate. They handcuffed the prisoners and tried to force integration, but Johnny lays it all out, "We don't house with them period. TDC had interviews, and they classified you: RR-racially restricted whites only, RE-racially eligible or RB-racially black. That's just how it was. If you got caught talking to a black other whites will stay away from you. The toads hate you, they don't like you homie. When they look at you, they look at your ass or your money. Texas' prisons is the most racial place." And the biggest problem is that the prisoners who spend part of their lives in this violent, degrading environment do get out.

Case in point- the senseless June 1998 James Bryd murder in Jasper, Texas. Two men, having paid their debt to society inside the brutal world of TDC and swearing allegiance to the sacred principle of Aryan Racial supremacy, were released. They plucked up a drunken black man off the street, chained his ankles to the back of a pick up truck, and dragged him to his death. "Texas prisons breed that," Johnny Bravo says of the horrific event.

Johnny goes on to say how the AC started in prison and made it to the world. "They got different chapters like motorcycle clubs." The gangsorus website says the AC is believed to consist of three branches—incarcerated men, incarcerated woman and an external branch, which consists of non-criminal white men in the free world. Their hierarchy consists of a president, vice president, majors, captains and several other titles.

"We got patch numbers," Johnny says. "If dude claims to be AC, I'll ask him where'd you get prospected at? I could write back to Texas and find out. Everybody has a patch number. If I walked up to a dude today, and I said, where'd you get picked up at? And he said, I just heard about it. Nah, you can't do that."

About potential members Johnny offers, "We would lace them up. Tell them a toad will come to them and pull their cord. We would tell them what to do, and if they fell short of that he was hit. You had to be a man. If you're a man we got your back. Why would we help you if you wouldn't help yourself." And the AC was no strangers to conflicts.

"We had a lot of confirmed wars down there." Johnny says. "The original thing with the AB's was a bloodbath. There were no in-betweens. You're either with them or not. We've been at war with them, The Black Gorilla Family, the White Knights, and the Texas Emes (Mexican Mafia). And if you go down to Texas and you're a Latin King, you are dead,"

About the conflicts Johnny says, "We gave them a chance to cover up or disband, but we didn't give the Emes that chance. The reason the war started with the Emes was behind a handball game. They were playing handball, there was a bad call, and the Eme hit the AC guy. When dude woke up, he wanted to know who did it. He got a shank, and killed the Mexican he was playing handball with, but it was the wrong one. Four years and 13 deaths later we signed a peace treaty. That happened in 1996. The faxes were going around the TDC like crazy. They put all the ACs in one unit. They cleared out units for us. The shit was kicking off everywhere. In transit. If we saw the Emes in the chow hall we'd stab them. A four-year riot behind a handball game. We had a green light on them on sight. Wherever you went, whatever compound, a green light. If we found out about an AC not jumping an Eme on sight we'd run court on him. Took it up in front of the district captain. Shot word to the president." And disciplinary measures such as cover him up, smash and beat him down, PC him, give him an extra duty type deal, or loss of rank would come back down. "There's a chain of command," Johnny says. "Everything comes down from the top. We got hundreds of lifers. Most of the brothers got big time. A lotta lifers. Texas gives out life like crazy. I've seen people come in with five and get a life."

And looking back now Johnny Bravo, who gets out soon, says, "I'm through. It's known all over the system that I'm through. I'm nothing but a heat stick. I can't do nothing. Lots of reasons too. It's bad inside. All the young kids think with their fists. It's violent. Back in the day we had a reason. Now the reason is violence." And in the TDC, where they isolate gang members, and place them in lockdown status to discourage membership, maybe it's not even worth it anymore. But there's an uneasy balance between necessity, and what's right or wrong. To Johnny Bravo being in a prison gang like the AC was a badge of honor, but now with huge organizations operating in prisons across the nation, it's like he said. It's just a heat stick for everyone involved.

TEN

Mob Parties in Prison

T HERE'S A SCENE in "Goodfellas" where Ray Liotta, who plays Henry Hill, and some other mafioso are in the joint. They're in a backroom or a mop closet at the prison, but due to their Cosa Nostra status, they are living large, drinking, and eating Italian delicacies, having a blast like they're at a social club or something, joking and laughing like they're not even doing time, living it up in the feds.

Well, some people might think that's just some Hollywood fantasy. I mean, it's a movie, right? But I am here to tell you that scene is not some made up act for a movie. That type of get together or party happens all the time in the feds. It ain't no country club and maybe prisoners aren't eating as well as they were in the movie, but they're still eating good or as well as they can. Whatever they can buy from the commissary or get out of the kitchen. Prisoners in the Bureau of Prisons are trying to live as nice as they can even on the inside and a lot of the mob guys are living pretty well, throwing parties for all different occasions. Like when a prisoner is getting released and going home or on holidays like Christmas or on someone's birthday or for the time honored American tradition, the Super Bowl party. Those are the most popular and it's not just the Mafia guys throwing them. The Spanish, Black, and Muslim communities get in on the act also. But in prison nobody can throw a party like the wiseguys and most dudes on the block are trying to get down.

When I was at FCI Fort Dix, a low security prison in central New Jersey, a couple of years ago, I saw and attended a lot of prison mob parties. Let me first state that I am in no way connected or affiliated or otherwise a member of any organized crime family. Yes, I have an Italian last name, but my father and grandfather were career military men, and I grew up in the suburbs of California, not exactly a Mafia hotbed. But anyway, during my 11 calendars in the feds I have met and associated with many East Coast Mafia types. Some of them were the real genuine thing, while many other were fake, wanna-be, hang-on-the-coattails type. It seems that all these East Coast dudes in federal prisons of the Caucasian persuasion want to be connected or down with the mob. I don't know why, but hey, forget about it. I guess they've seen too many movies.

In Fort Dix, though, they had lots of Mafia dudes, real and imagined. There were the New York guys, the Philly guys, and the Jersey guys. Most of them stayed with their own cliques or crews but when some Big Willie Joe Mafia guy threw a social they all came out of the wood-work and made an appearance. In building 5702 on the eastside of the compound, many parties were thrown. This was due to the presence of "Little Nick" Corozzo, a reputed Gambino capo and personal friend of John Gotti who was supposedly in line to take over the Gambino family. He was doing a short bid and considered himself lucky. And at Fort Dix he was the center of Mafia attention on the compound.

For the parties he threw for whatever reason, usually when one of his guys was going home, he would get his crew of Boston roughnecks to hold down a multi-purpose room on the second floor. Effectively the room was off limits unless you were invited to the party. These events would usually be held in the afternoons on the weekend or after the count on weekdays and would usually last several hours as the waves of mafiaso, connected guys, wanna-be's, hangers on, and respected prisoners showed up, paid their respects, ate or drank a little, then left to make room for the next wave. Because for real, it wasn't no banquet hall "Little Nick" was renting. It was a tiny little multi-purpose room adjacent to the row of dorm rooms where prisoners slept. Usually it was used as a card room or game room to play dominoes and the like, but when "Little Nick" wanted, it was turned into a sort of Mafia social club.

There would be a couple of tables pushed together with a white sheet laid overtop like a tablecloth. A bunch or catered like appetizers and snacks would be spread out over the table on cardboard trays. Crackers with tuna salad, deviled eggs, pepperoni slices with olives and cheese, little burritos, chocolate chip cookies, various types of chips—basically anything that could be bought from the commissary or stolen from the kitchen. Usually a Mexican or Colombian prisoner would be hired to prepare all the snacks and appetizers and have them ready at the appointed time and place. It wasn't fancy by real world standards, but in the joint it was nice. It was almost like a catered banquet.

Also there would be a trash can filled with ice and sodas—Pepsi, Coke, Mountain Dew, Minute Maid Orange, Sprite, etc. The Mexican or Colombian, who was overseeing the festivities on "Little Nick's" behalf, would run back and forth to the microwave and hot water dispenser, preparing cappuccinos, coffee, or tea for prisoners as they arrive. Paper plates, napkins, and paper cups would complete the set up so prisoners could pass by the buffet table, fill up their plate, grab a soda or coffee, then sit against the wall in a folding metal chair congratulating the guy who was going home, joking, laughing, making future plans, and remininiscing.

These events were usually pretty crowded and people would be spilling out into the hallway making room for the new guys showing up. The whole Mafia cheek kissing, handshakes, and slaps on the back would go around as every new prisoner showed up making their way to greet the host, "Little Nick" and whoever the honored guest and party was being thrown for.

A lot of other prisoners who weren't Italian or weren't invited would walk by the multipurpose room looking on with envy. If "Little Nick" saw them he would tell one of his crew to give them a soda or something and send them on their way. Generosity was one thing but having undesirables hanging out at a mob party.... no way. "Little Nick" would rather swim with the fishes.

Most times a prisoner who had a good rapport with the cop working the unit would go to him in advance and explain what was going on so the cop wouldn't get all excited and alarmed and hit the deuces when he saw a big group of guidos loitering around his building. Most cops didn't have a problem with it and sometimes when the lieutenant made his rounds he would even drop by the mixer and pay his respects. But I've seen lieutenants bust up the little parties, too, to everyone's dismay. And if anyone complained they'd go straight to the hole. Imagine that—going to 24 hour lockdown because you were having a birthday party. Forget about it.

The mob guys are funny too. They may have all these regional and inter-family beefs and talk mad shit behind each other's backs, but when there's some pasta or free food to be had they put on their best face and all come together like the best of friends. Nothing like a bowl of prison microwave prepared spaghetti to mend differences. And I've seen mob dudes get all offended if they're not invited to a certain party or don't get their bowl of pasta. They might be ready to whack somebody. Good thing they don't have any guns in federal prison. Because, for real, a lot of these mob guys aren't trying to fight. They're straight killers and like the old saying goes: boys fight, men kill. So ain't no Mob guy fist fighting. He'll whack someone, if only he had a gun. Imagine being whacked because you didn't offer the Gambino capo a bowl of pasta.

I also spent some time at FCI Fairton, which is a medium to high security joint in southern New Jersey, about 45 minutes away from Atlantic City. At Fairton I just happened to be in the unit, B-Left, with Michael Perna, the consigliere from the New Jersey branch of the Lucchese crime family. Now Michael Perna was a class guy. He held pasta dinners every Sunday for all the Italians on the block. He was literally feeding 15 or 16 guys every weekend. He was generous to say the least. And he went all out for holidays and special occasions. His Christmas parties were legendary.

The prisoners who cooked for him, usually it was some Italian guy from Boston or Philly, spent all day cooking the sauce or gravy as Mikey called it. Heavy on the garlic and pepperoni, but very smooth and zesty, the red sauce always turned out nice. Three or four card tables were put together in the common area to form a banquet table, and white sheets were laid overtop like tablecloths as all the seats were arranged. Made guys at one end with Mikey and the other Italians and hangers on at the opposite end away from the really good conversations.

Appetizers consisting of salami and pepperoni slices, mozzarella and Velveeta cheese, olives, and Townhouse Crackers were prepared and ready to serve on a cardboard tray. A mop bucket filled with ice and sodas sat at the foot of the table. As all 15 or 20 guys sat down at the table after the 4:00 p.m. stand up count, paper plates were handed out as the appetizers were passed around with Mikey always offering more and making sure everybody was served. Then the main course of ziti with red sauce was served with a dash of parmesan on top in plastic microwave bowls. As everyone ate with their plastic utensils and drank sodas dudes talked, joked and wished each other Merry Christmas. Then for desert chocolate donuts were set out along with Italian sweetbread and chocolate-mint cookies. For real, the spread wasn't bad. Mikey always threw a nice dinner party. But it was more an in house thing because, previously, Mikey had problems with the SIS Lieutenant who is in charge of investigating occurrences at the prison. Sort of like the FBI on the inside.

Well, one of Mikey's guys had went home some time before, and Mikey had thrown him a party with guys from all the other units stopping by B-Left and joining in the festivities. The unit cop had ok'd it, so Mikey thought he was in the clear. But some inmate police or jailhouse snitch had dropped a note to SIS informing on the party, and about a week after Mikey's guy was released Mikey was called down to see the SIS Lieutenant.

The SIS Lieutenant told Mikey that he knew about the party and that he had it all on tape and was going through the tape to identify all the all the prisoners who had visited B-left on the day of the party. The SIS cop seemed to think something nefarious was going on. Mikey tried to explain that it wasn't a big deal, just a going away party for one of his guys. But the SIS Lieutenant seemed to take the matter very seriously and told Mikey that if he didn't cease and desist with his party throwing activities, then he would be thrown in the hole. He also told Mikey that he would be informing the probation officer of the prisoner who went home that Mikey had thrown him a going away party before he left the institution. It was like this some kind of violation of his probation.

But Mikey just kindly told the SIS Lieutenant that he wouldn't throw anymore parties and blew the guy off. Fucking jerk off, he probably thought. But that's how it is in here. Imagine the audacity of the SIS Lieutenant to actually think that he could get the released prisoners probation revoked because Mikey threw him a going away party. Forget about it. And by the way, Mikey doesn't throw mob parties anymore. He began having dinners.

III

STREET
LEGENDS

ELEVEN

Rick Ross

FREEWAY RICKY IS a big name in the drug world. The dude is straight gangsta. He's been profiled on BET's "American Gangster" series, was the subject of numerous street DVD's and has appeared on several magazine covers, such as ASIS and All Hoods. The dude is a bonifide ghetto superstar who's ready to hit the streets and get into the entertainment world. Freeway Ricky is also trying his hand at the book game. Dope game, been there. Street legend, done that. Prison celebrity, check. Urban lit author—add that to the list.

Freeway Ricky's resume is on blast. The dude is multitasking and he's becoming a multimedia icon. Check out his new novel, "Black Scarface," that he wrote with acclaimed street lit author and Philly rapper Jimmy Da Saint. Also check out Freeway Ricky's social networking website, freewayenterprise.com. Here is what's going on with Freeway Ricky Ross right now. And we aren't talking about that fake ass officer, Ricky, the studio gangsta. We are talking about the street legend and certified LA gangsta. Straight out of federal prison Gorilla Convict brings you the exclusive.

How did Black Scarface come about?

Jimmy had just got out of the hole, had a note from a guy that owed me some money. Jimmy is a very smart dude, who's always looking for angles, but at that time he wanted to help me. He asked me why didn't

I have a novel out. I told him I really wasn't interested in doing novels. He had like 30 written, so he offered me one. I told him that I just didn't want to put my name on anything and that's when he came up with the idea of us writing together.

How instrumental were you in the writing and publishing of it?

I help create scenes. The story is based on both of our lives and things that we've experienced and seen in our lives. We'll be publishing it through Jim's company but I'll be there right with him every step of the way.

What is it about?

It's about a mother's love for her son, who's determined to see him be successful. And a young man that refuses to lose.

Can we say it's the Rick Ross story fictionalized? Why?

No, I won't say that it's the Rick Ross story fictionalized. Even though it does relate. Jim and I fought on a lot of issues, even though he's my man, we clashed on a lot of issues. And since there is no question that Jim is a better writer than me, I used to let him win.

What other plans do you have as an author?

At the present time I'm finishing up my autobiography. Jimmy is also helping me with that. I put together what I feel is a dream team, along with Kwame the author of Dutch, Monique Hall, and Barbara, the editor of Dutch 1, 2 and 3. I plan on taking readers through a step by step journey of how a tennis player who was anti-drug one day became a drug dealer the next.

What else is going on?

I have a deal set up where I can do multiple movies as well as starting my record label, video games and books. My website, **www.freewayenterprise.com**, is starting to take on a life of its own. We've already started filming a reality show. Man, it's off the charts. I feel like the luckiest man in the world.

Anything else?

Yeah, man, I just want to tell everybody out there what's up. All you have to do is put your mind to it and you can do it. It's wide open. Make sure you all check out the website. I'll be doing major moves off of it. So become a member of this new movement. Also check out Young Bucks new CD with Bigger Ranking. It's off the charts. Also I'm still looking for artists to kick the label off. So if there's anybody out there that wants to be down they can e-mail me at freewayrickyross49@ yahoo.com.

TWELVE

Pappy Mason, Street Legend

HOWARD "PAPPY" MASON was a soldier. In one of the most violent eras in New York City history, Pappy Mason rose above the rest to cement his reputation as one of the most feared men in the five boroughs. When the South Jamaica crack wars were in full swing and bodies were dropping by the day, Pappy held court in the street and reigned as king. He was the one that nobody wanted to fuck with. He was the baddest man on the block. To put it quite simply, Pappy Mason was a legend in his own time.

In the mid 80s the crack vial spawned violence and bloodshed, paper chasers and four corner hustlers, drug empires and kingpin galore. And in the annals of mythical drug lore, Pappy Mason has stood tall over time as the man, the myth and the folk hero that inspired Jay Z, Nas and 50 Cent to lionize him and his exploits in verse. "They was legends, myths like urban-legends myths," Irv Gotti said of the Southeast Queens hustlers. And for real, can't nobody front on that. But let's go way back before Pappy was the certified street legend that he is. Let's look at how he got to be who he was.

"There's not a lot of history on this dude," says BC, a Queens's hustler from the era. "They say this nigga was from the Brook, from Brooklyn somewhere." And Bing from the Supreme Team confirms, "Pappy Mason was from Brooklyn, Crown Heights, not Queens." But that didn't stop Pappy from becoming a Queens's legend. It's said he was born in Alabama and moved to Crown Heights at a young age. At the time Brooklyn had that thug shit on lock. Of the five boroughs Brooklyn was known for producing the thoroughest, grimmest dudes. Pappy, who was a natural born fighter, came up in this thug culture and learned how to be a man on Brooklyn's tough streets, first as a member of the gang, the Jolly Stompers, and later as a stick up kid. Back in the day, Pappy was not known as a drug player, but he was known as a hothead who took no shorts and who hated the police. At a young age he was telling the police in his neighborhood to "suck my dick." He held a big middle finger up to authority. It was just how he was cut. Pappy had a problem with authority from the jump, and his preferred way of handling that problem was with his fists.

His violent ways and fights with police landed him in juvenile detention facilities like Warwick and Spofford. He did a five-year sentence for attempted murder as a teenager and couldn't stay out of trouble. During one of his many stays at Spofford Youth House, Pappy met another young kid who was good with his fists and hailed from the Seven Crowns gang. His name—Lorenzo "Fat Cat" Nichols.

The two young toughs hit it off and bonded over their ability to knock motherfuckers out. They both had the I-am-my-brother's-keeper mentality and saw the ideals they valued in themselves in each other. Spofford was an institution for bad and troubled teens. Only the worst of the worst were sent there. Kids came in bad, but after years in that madhouse authorities called juvenile detention, they came out worse. Pappy turned his hatred for police into a hatred for C/O's and clashed with the staff repeatedly. "Pappy's the only person I know back then who had seven years and did everyday of it," Fat Cat said. "He left not owing a day." And when Pappy left in 1983, he had already spent a quarter of his 23 years in prison.

"In every hood people make a name for themselves." Bing says and Pappy was no different. By the time he hit the bricks in '83 his man Fat

Cat was well established as a drug dealer on 150th Street in Southeast Queens. Pappy went to the block looking for Cat and Cat hired him on the spot for $1,000 a week as security. "Pap's got a good heart," Fat Cat said. "If he's your friend, he's your friend. But if he's your enemy that's something altogether different." Pappy was the dude crazy dudes would think twice about trying. With his no-nonsense attitude, he was vicious. And don't get if fucked up. Pappy was fiercely loyal to Cat.

"When you hear Cat, you hear Pap," says BC of the pairing. Pappy emerged as Cat's man on the streets. Cat wanted Pap on his team because he knew Pap had that mad heart. And Pappy did his job with a vengeance. He pistol whipped a prostitute who stole from Cat in broad daylight on the block. He shot a rival dealer who tried to encroach on Cat's territory, and he shot a customer dead outside a church because the customer had the nerve to complain about the purity of Cat's product. Pappy's viciousness and image enhanced his already fearsome reputation. He had a strong mystique around him. With his Rastafarian dreadlocks and adopted Jamaican patios, dudes thought he was from Jamaica. "That dude with the dreadlocks. That's Pappy." One informer told the police. "He's Fat Cat's enforcer now. He the craziest guy out here." And street tales tell of Pappy sticking hot curling irons up dudes' asses to torture them or get them to talk. The dude was vicious. He definitely did not play. And Pappy's work was rewarded by Fat Cat. He handed Pappy a lucrative drug spot in Forty Projects to ply his trade and get money. Pappy took the spot and ran with it.

The enforcer for Cat's crew formed his own crew. Pappy's suborganization was called the Bebos. The Bebos grew dreads too and sold cocaine and heroin. "The Bebos were underneath Pap. He was the head nigga in charge," BC says. "He was amongst them Bebo niggas from Forty Projects." And along with the dreadlocks Pappy's crew emulated him in all matters, from his violent ways to his speech patterns. "They used to try and be like Pap talking Jamaican and the like. A lot of dudes were under Pap. He had a strong influence in our hood." And the Bebos adopted Rastafarian culture as their own. "They got a thing where they call one love and when Pappy say you do, you do." Scott Cobb, a Bebo said. "One love means do or die. We all tight, we family. When Pappy gives you an order you do." Pappy was down on 150th Street but his crew held it down in Forty. "Those Bebo niggas they were out there," BC says. "They had leather jackets with Bebo on it." And Phillip "Marshall" Copeland, another Bebo said, "There was no boss with us, every man was for himself. Bebo is a way of life to Rasta man and Jah for real." But still, even with his own crew and spot, Pappy was in charge of Cat's security.

"When you think of Pap, you think of an enforcer for Cat," BC says. And Prince from the Supreme Team said, "The first person I met from Cat's crew when I came home from state prison on July 1, 1984, was Pap." Pappy was a wild dude in the streets too. He didn't give a fuck. He was blatant when it came to violence. "He had his own identity as far as getting busy," BC says. "He was a loyal, faithful soldier. In my hood it was all Cat and Pap." Even the infamous Supreme weighed in on Pappy, "He was a real thorough dude."

And when crack hit it changed Queens dramatically and when the violence erupted, Pappy was at the center of it. "He was a wild nigga," BC says. And Pappy Mason didn't play. When Fat Cat was arrested in 1985, Pappy crept on the arresting officer as he escorted Fat Cat to a police car. Pappy slipped behind the cop and was prepared to shoot the cop to free Cat so they could make a get away, but Cat shook his head no. So Pappy crept back into the cut, gun still in hand. Pap used to visit Cat in jail at the Queens House of Detention and even threatened Fat Cat's girl after his arrest. "I don't know what you know," Pap told her, "But Cat says you better forget it." And when Cat's parole officer was killed for violating Cat's state parole, Pappy was the main suspect.

On February 28, 1985, Queens's detectives arrested Pappy for the murder on the strength of Cat crew member Perry Bellamy's statement. Bellamy told the cops that he lured the PO to the ambush spot where Pappy gunned him down. When the cops arrested Pappy, he had a loaded .22 caliber Derringer in his boot that he was trying to get at before the officers arrested him, adding to his charges. Asked to cooperate into the affair and implicate Fat Cat for the murder of the PO, Pappy told police, "I ain't no Perry Bellamy." That was in reference to the snitch in Fat Cat's camp. Because of his refusal to break the street code, Pappy joined his boss in the Queens House of Detention. And during Pappy's incarceration his legend grew.

"He was a big presence in Queens," BC says. It's said that while he was incarcerated, Pappy, in a visit at Rikers to take care of future Bebo ventures, gave Phillip "Marshall" Copeland a gold and diamond ring that was shaped like Africa and worth $40,000, which he took off his finger. Pappy would call from Rikers to his crew in the streets and go on tirades about the cops and the word on the streets concerning the PO killing was that "the Bebos did it." But Pappy maintained that, "I didn't kill no PO." And before trial started in January 1986 one Queens native said, "There's not a single soul who is gonna come in and testify against that boy." In the borough that was the prevailing sentiment. Pappy had that much juice on the street and his cold blooded antics put fear into people's hearts. "He was a motherfucking killer," BC says. "His influence was so strong. He had a big influence." The prosecutor and judge in the case were living under constant anonymous death threats during the weeks prior to the trial, and right before the case started, the star witness, Perry Bellamy, refused to testify. Pappy had got his man. Only Bellamy's taped confession was played for the jury.

"They was all there when the PO got killed," Perry Bellamy voice said on the tape player. "Pappy, he just opened fire. Pappy got him. That shit was swift." But without a live witness willing to testify, the jury hung. As Pappy made bail in February 1988 after the hung jury, he formed an imaginary gun with his thumb and index finger, turned to the prosecutor and pulled the trigger. Pappy Mason was free again. But this time he would only be on the street for 10 days. But during that 10 days he set in course the motions that would shock the nation. Pappy was on bail and drinking a beer on a South Jamaica street corner when a beat cop accosted him. "Do me a favor," a cop called the Iceman told Pappy. "Don't drink beer in front of me." Pappy was stunned. No cop ever told him what to do. "Do you know who I am?" He demanded of the cop. "Yeah, the guy who is going to put his beer in a paper bag." The cop replied. "Fuck you," Pappy screamed and a shoving match ensued. After a couple of seconds Pap walked off, his beer on the ground spilling on the pavement. Pappy was in a rage. "That cop has to die," Pap said. "He dissed me." Death threats against the cop followed, and he was pulled from the streets for his protection. Pappy's gun case, for the Derringer he was arrested with, was remanded a week later and Pappy was back at Rikers. He had only lasted 10 days on the street since the Rooney murder. "He was out before they remanded him," one local said. "He was organizing at that time. It was already planned." Pappy Mason was about to set in motion a jarring set of events that would have repercussions for the decades to come.

"We lose one, they lose one," Pappy allegedly told Marshall. Pappy wanted the Bebo's to send the police a message. He wanted to send a message out. The message was that even though he was behind bars he still gave orders. The message was devastating. Pappy wanted a cop hit. He was eventually convicted on the gun charge, but that was the least of his worries.

"When Pap went to jail after Cat, most of Cat's strength in the streets was gone," Prince said and Pappy knew this. He needed to do something drastic to keep his power and hood in check, something unheard of. His message was carefully constructed to have a maximum effect. Early in the morning of February 28, 1988 NYPD Officer Edward Byrne, a 22-year-old rookie was shot five times in the head while sitting in his patrol car in Queens 103rd precinct protecting a witness whose house had been firebombed after he testified against some local drug dealers. The rookie's murder was front page news all over the nation, and it kicked the War on Drugs into high gear and led to the creation of New York's Tactical Narcotics Taskforce (TNT). Informants said some Jamaicans from Brooklyn killed the cop. Pappy went to prison the day before the officer was killed.

Four suspects, all Bebos, were immediately arrested—Todd Scott, Scott Cobb, David McClary and Phillip Copeland. Off the jump, three of the four suspects made video taped statements implicating themselves, Fat Cat and Pappy. The only one who didn't talk was Phillip Copeland. The police played it up to implicate the drug lord Fat Cat in the media. "This was an order, not for the murder of a particular officer, but any officer for the purpose of delivering a message of death to anyone who opposed Fat Cat," Lieutenant Phillip Panzarella of the Queens Homicide squad said. But behind the scenes a different tale was emerging.

"Cat was mad about what that stupid motherfucker Pappy did," Viola Nichols, Cat's sister said. "What Bebo did was fucked up," Cat raged. "Now nobody will make no money." In a call to Viola, Pappy explained his reasons, "The man dissed me." It was because the police officer ordered Pappy to put a can of beer in a brown paper bag. But as Cat found out Pappy had the wrong cop killed. The execution style murder was said to have been ordered by Pappy from prison for revenge against the police. And to make matters worse, on August 12, 1988, the feds indicted Fat Cat and his whole crew on racketeering charges. The New York Daily News headline read—"Fat Cat's Empire Crumbles; Feds Bust Drug Clan, $20 million in Dope Seized, 30 Suspects Nabbed in Massive Raid." The suspects included Pap and Cat's mothers. While all this was going down, Pappy was sentenced for the gun and received a three-and-half to seven-year sentence. At sentencing he told the judge, "You gotta do what you gotta do. I look crazy, so people are going to judge me on that. This is two cops I supposedly allegedly killed. Cops come to me at precinct and say I'm the leader of a drug ring. I've never been arrested for drugs in my life. I don't know what they're talking about." The federal racketeering and conspiracy case included charges that Pappy and Fat Cat orchestrated and gave the order to kill the cop. The four suspects in the state case, the triggerman and his three cohorts, had already been convicted and sentenced to 25 to life. Now the feds were going after the ring leaders.

"Todd Scott and them niggas are from the projects... Forty Projects." BC says. And Todd Scott is the one who said that Pappy ordered the hit. But he wasn't the only one who betrayed his man. It's alleged that on September 29, 1989, in a secret court session, Fat Cat agreed to testify against Pappy Mason. "The feds offered me and Pap 40 years under the old law to cop out to 848 for our mothers freedom," Cat explained. "Pap said he wasn't going to plead guilty. I took the plea." There was a lot of outrage in the streets at the time concerning Fat Cat's alleged duplicity. And there was outrage at the prosecutor's office, too, where one prosecutor said, "Using Fat Cat to get Pappy is like using syphilis to get gonorrhea." But to this day Pappy maintains that, "Cat never testified against me. His name is not in any of my paperwork."

Pappy Mason went to trial alone in the federal racketeering case. "I'm not letting these crackers roll me," he said. About his mother facing the indictment, he explained, "My mother knows about white people. She said, God will make a way." Harry Butchelder, Pappy's lawyer, tried to enter an insanity defense at the November 1989 trial, but it didn't play. Pappy was violent in court and the judge isolated him. So in effect he boycotted his own trial, preferring to follow the proceedings on a specially installed speaker system in his cell. "They did me wrong," Pappy said. "Jah is good, it was no trial. It was a KKK meeting for real. That was not an indictment. That was the government." Scott Cobb was a witness, saying he knew in advance of Mason's plan to kill a cop.

The order was given to Marshall, who was instructed to pay $8,000 a head. Mike Bones, from Cat's crew also testified and Viola Nichols, Cat's sister, spent three days on the stand. Fat Cat was never called.

"They say that me and Pappy planned this," Phillip "Marshall" Copeland said. "But me and him never talked and I didn't go see him, so I can say that he didn't play no part in it." David McClary, the accused shooter denied Pappy ever gave him an order. And even Pappy claimed innocence, "No, hell no, why would I kill a cop?" Still Pappy was convicted and sentenced to life imprisonment after the jury deliberated three days before finding him guilty. "I look at it like this—they used me and my boy to make points during that election year," Marshall said, summing it all up from his point of view. But whatever the truth is, the legend lives on.

"I am a man amongst men. I am God's son," Pappy Mason said. "I am strong I will never give up on Bebo. I'm the hip-hop kid from Southside Queens." And a lot of the kids who grew up on hip-hop and later became rap stars looked up to Pappy. He's had a strong presence indirectly in their lives, and this has translated to their songs. Nas on God's Son's Get Down spit, "New York streets where killers'll walk like Pistol Pete and Pappy Mason, gave the young boys admiration." Nas also namedropped Pap in The World is Yours. "Facin' time like Pappy Mason," he rapped. And Southside Queens most controversial rapper, 50 Cent, used Pap's name in verse, too, in the Ghetto Qu'ran where he alluded to Fat Cat snitching on Pappy. "I used to idolize Cat/Hurt me in my heart to hear that/He snitched on Pap/How he go out like that?" And 50 also big upped the Bebo's in his song, "Go against crews like Bebo and killers like Pap Mason." Other rappers like Ja Rule, Fat Joe and Ghostface have also saluted Pappy in verse.

"He defied the police in the street. He defied them in jail. How real is that?" BC says. "Some niggas don't bend, they don't move, they fight. It's in the nature of a nigga like Pap. He was a cool ass nigga but he could get violent in a minute. Bug out and all that shit. But still the nigga was cool." And for a guy with such an outlandish legend, he wasn't a real big dude, only standing maybe 5-foot-8 or so but what made him who he was, was that pit bull heart and attitude. That take all comers mentality. Like they said, "Pappy didn't take no shorts." But looking back another hustler from the era said, "I think these guys were living a movie. They used to watch "Scarface" and "The Godfather" and they wanted to be like that." Maybe so, but whatever the reason, Pappy has gone down in infamy as one of the most notorious killers to ever walk the streets of New York. And even to this day the fearless soldier Pappy Mason, who some say is as strong as an ox, is ready to go to war.

Tales from the pen have circulated of Pappy battling the goon squads and cell extraction teams. They say he wraps his head with towels to soften the blows from guards' batons and saturates his body with baby oil to wrestle with the guards so they can't grab a hold of him when they storm his cell, six deep, to try and subdue one man. They say he wages a constant battle against the guards by throwing shit and piss at them through the little door trap where they put the food tray through. Because you know Pappy Mason is in 24-hour lockdown. He long ago forfeited his right to be on a regular compound. "Pappy Mason's burnt out. I was with him at MCC in '92. He had dreads down to the floor, slept underneath the bed, smoked a carton of cigs a day," said one federal prisoner.

"They said in Attica he was bugged out." BC says. "He was crazy but that don't take nothing away from him. Street niggas love this dude because they know he gets busy." Pappy's life now consists of threatening officers, cell extractions and cutting up snitches that he hates with a passion. After 18 years at USP Marion, Pappy was transferred to ADX Florence in Colorado, the Bureau of Prisons Supermax and home to the most notorious criminals in the U.S. It's said that the feds shoot him up with large doses of Thorazine to keep him docile. Pappy even admitted this. "The government shot me up with Thorazine, but Jah makes a way, so God brings me back to Bebo. I am not crazy, I am in prison for something I did not do." Pappy is still at this time fighting to overturn his conviction and life sentence in the feds, waging a constant battle on multiple fronts.

"The nigga took that time. He ain't crying, he took it, he doing it." BC says. "You got to salute a nigga like that. I just know this nigga is burned out but Pap a stand up nigga, they love that nigga son. They love that nigga because he stood up. He's in the joint and he still don't give a fuck. His influence is so strong a heritage that's not even his salutes this dude. The Jamaicans claim Pap like he's one of their own. He's not. He's American." And on the whole Fat Cat snitch fiasco Pappy stands firm.

"They lie on Fat Cat and me, word to mother." Pappy said. Pappy calls Cat his brother. But street legend discredits Pappy due to him being shot up with Thorazine. Some dudes say he doesn't know what he's saying, but whatever the truth; it's caused a lot of controversy. Not enough to diminish Pappy's infamy though. Even though he's been locked away from the world for the last twenty years, his legend lives on, as does his link with Fat Cat. "They will forever be linked together." BC says, but unlike Cat, Pappy will forever be recognized as a stand up dude. Fat Cat's credentials, right or wrong, are in question. A chilling fact rises to the surface though, in this story—that is, no matter who ordered it, the bullets that killed Edward Byrne were meant for the other cop, the one called Iceman.

THIRTEEN

Hip-Hop, Guns, Gangstas, and The Feds

G ORILLA CONVICT WRITER Seth Ferranti, Soul Man federal prison register #18205-083, is in the 12th year of a 25-year mandatory minimum sentence for dealing LSD. In 2004 he got to know alleged New York drug kingpin Kenneth "Supreme" McGriff at FCI Gilmer, a medium-to-high security federal prison in the foothills of West Virginia.

"To finally meet the man 50 Cent rapped about and who was considered a street legend was inspiring." Recalls Soul Man. "We talked a lot about book, movie, and writing projects and the entertainment world in general — all legal ventures. I was always telling him that he needed to tell his story, because for real, Supreme is one of the classiest dudes I have ever met. But with all the allegations surrounding himself and Murder Inc., he wasn't willing to do an interview, despite getting letters every week from newspapers, magazines and book publishers that were interested in his story. When the Murder Inc. indictments came out, and before they took him back to court, he came and told me that I could do a story on him, but he didn't want it to be in his words. He wanted it to be in the words of his peers. He wanted his fellow convicts to tell his story, so that is how I came up with this piece.

What the feds are doing to Supreme is nothing new. They do it to people from the hood all the time. The prisons are filled with Black men, young and old, and they are all serving decades of their lives. More times than not, the punishment doesn't fit the crime. To an insider like me, it seems that the feds, in the name of justice, manufacture these big conspiracies and turn things into what they are not. But it's not justice; it's a travesty. And what they are trying to do to Supreme is a mockery of justice. For real, the man is like a gangsta philosopher. He is eloquent, deep thinking, and kind, not full of himself like most people who have a measure of fame or notoriety. Just check out how those who actually know him describe him. "

Rap and crack were both born 20 years ago, and more than a few rappers boast on their records about starting their labels with drug money, and with lyrics reeling out like taped testimony, it's no wonder the feds have taken notice. Hip-hop performers have long argued that they've been unfairly targeted by police, and now it seems rappers are viewed as the new Mafia by the feds. Death Row was the first label targeted in the mid 90s and then Y2K saw the feds investigating claims that Kenneth "Supreme" McGriff bankrolled Murder Inc. In his day Supreme was a king of the streets who held court in Queens. He's spent the years since the 80's split between doing various bids and returning to his hometown streets in South Jamaica, Queens.

The New York City street legend has been at the epicenter of the swirling allegations surrounding Murder Inc. since their 1997 debut, and in January 2005, Supreme, rap mogul Irv Gotti and seven others were federally indicted on charges ranging from money laundering to racketeering to murder. If convicted Supreme faces the death penalty. But charges of Murder Inc. being a criminal organization seem more gangsta-rap fantasy than reality. To comprehend the totality of this case, it's important to understand the life of Supreme, who is now 44-years-old and being held at MDC Brooklyn.

"The brother Supreme grew up in the '60s and '70s, when guys in the life had a semblance of principles," says Terry Trice, a close friend of Supreme's and a D.C. convict who has done 30 years. "He stays true to his word as a man." Supreme grew up in Southeastern Queens, and Terry says, "His whole family is square. All his brothers and sisters are professional people in their own lives."

"He lived right across the street from the Baisley Projects." says Tuck, a former Supreme Team member who has been incarcerated since 1990. "His pops was ex-military, a marine or something, a strict disciplinarian. Preme grew up on Foch Blvd. and the Guy Brewer intersection in South Jamaica, Queens," an area that spawned some of the biggest names in the city's drug lore.

"What probably influenced him getting into the life was becoming a Five Percenter." Terry says. "With a lot of them coming out of prison, it had to influence his decisions." And his whole crew was also Five Percenters. "Supreme is his given name. He's been in that since he was eight or ten," Terry says. Tuck adds, "He doesn't drink, smoke, or eat red meat, in accordance to his beliefs."

In Queens, the conflicting streets of private homes and grim city housing projects gave birth to another factor that proved pivotal in the young Supreme's life—the Seven Crowns. According to legend, Seven Crowns was an early 70s street gang that started out selling marijuana and then graduated to heroin and cocaine. In 1979, the gang split up, dividing up their turf into several territories and launching the careers of some of New York's largest urban drug dealers—including Lorenzo "Fat Cat" Nichols, Howard "Pappy" Mason, Tommy "Tony Montana" Mickens, the Corley brothers, and Supreme. Supreme's notorious beginnings have hung over his head, both enhancing his infamy and leading to his current predicament. Tuck, who also grew up in Queens, breaks it down. "Pappy Mason was with Fat Cat. Pappy's crew was the Bebos. Cat had 150th Street. Wall Corley had Forty Projects and Supreme had Baisley Projects."

The 1988 cop killing of rookie officer Edward Byrne brought the Seven Crowns alumni unwanted attention. Pappy Mason and four others were quickly convicted and sentenced to life for the murder, but in the eyes of law enforcement, Supreme and the other Queens drug dealers have always been associated with this tragic event. Besides, Supreme's had his own tangles with the law.

"In 1985, Preme had a state case." says Tuck. "He got arrested in a house with drugs. He was sentenced to nine years to life, but he only served 22 months because an appeals court threw out the conviction. But then the feds got him in '87. He copped out to 12 years. No co-defendants. The feds just wanted him."

Supreme had been charged with running a Continual Criminal Enterprise, and as he sat in federal prison, his crew ran wild under his nephew, Gerald "Prince" Miller, who is now doing seven life sentences in federal prison. "Supreme was the originator of the team." Tuck says. "Who doesn't know that? But I was down with Prince and we were getting money."

"When you look at "New Jack City," you know who that movie was about," Tuck says confidently. Even though Supreme had begun serving his time and more or less left the game, the CCE charge and kingpin status conferred by the feds immortalized him in the eyes of Queens' urban youth.

In early 1993, while Supreme was paroled, his crew was going on trial. Tuck remembers the trial, in which he was a defendant, "Preme was released from his federal sentence around February '93, so he was home when our trial began. Our trial lasted exactly two months. During the testimony of one of the defense witnesses, Preme was sitting in the audience with a dude I grew up with. While the prosecutor was cross-examining the witness, she shocked the whole courtroom by turning around and pointing to Preme and saying, 'Isn't he the founder and leader of Supreme Team?' Of course, the witness denied knowing anything about him being the leader of anything."

Robert Simels, Supreme's former lawyer, has said that regardless of what his client may have started, he saw the light after spending time in jail. Terry concurs, saying, "When he saw so many thousands of young guys who grew up similar to him and who were never getting out, he decided to do legitimate stuff." But it wasn't all smooth sailing. "He was going back and forth on violations," Tuck says. "Out in '93, back in '95. Got out and was back in '97."

"He did his time for the CCE," says DJ, a B-More native who spent a year as Supreme's cellie. "He came home and his whole crew was dead or doing big numbers, but the feds still wanted him off the street, as if he was a threat to society." To the feds, Supreme was public enemy #1, but to hip-hop artists, the name mattered.

"A lot of dudes getting legitimate money want to touch gangsterism, but when it comes time to help somebody realize their dreams, they back off," Terry says. "Irv Gotti didn't. He tried to help somebody who was through with the life. Supreme said Irv was basically a very good friend. A dude that was willing to give him a chance."

With Gotti's backing, Supreme formed Picture Perfect Films and put out "Crime Partners," a DVD adaptation of the Donald Goines novel that starred Snoop Dogg, Ja Rule, and Ice-T. He also acquired the film rights to four other Goines' novels, including "Black Girl Lost." "He knew, for the most part that it ain't a black or white thing," Terry says. "It's a rich or poor thing."

"The first thing the feds said is that its drug money," adds DJ. "Everything that he did when he came back to the streets was legal, but still the feds say it's drug money."

"Success would have been assured without interference from the feds," Terry says. Regardless, Supreme's story took another turn. As the fed's latest investigation took off, a Queens kid — Curtis Jackson, who you may know as 50 Cent — put out Ghetto Qu'ran where he spit, "When you hear the talk of the Southside, you hear talk of Team/ See niggas feared Prince and they respected Preme/For all you slow motherfuckers I'ma break it down iller/See Preme was the business man and Prince was the killer."

"Preme is a legend." Tuck confirms. "He's proven and he's not a rat. That fact alone, in this day and time, says a lot. Stand-up men are no longer the rule. They are the exception to the rule."

The rappers 50 and Ja Rule's status was less clear, as they continued beefing about a world that Supreme had known far better than either of them. "The Ja Rule-50 Cent beef was partly because Supreme spoke up for Ja Rule and 50 Cent took this as a rejection of him." Terry says. "Supreme thinks 50 Cent is an angry young man who's been venting, and his venting could be construed as un-gangsta, because real men don't put stuff out to the public that could bring about an investigation." Adds Terry, "Supreme looks at 50 like he's confused. If half the things that are said about 50 are true, then he needs to send half his loot to Supreme."

With the ongoing investigation, 50 Cent's lyrics obviously added fuel to the fire. "That chump 50 Cent wouldn't even be a factor in the rap game if his lyrics weren't snitch-oriented." Terry says. "He owes all his success to the media and his beef with Murder Inc."

In January of 2002, FBI agent Gregory Takacs started investigating Supreme's ties to Murder Inc. Two affidavits heightened the investigation and led to the January 2003 raid of Murder Inc. The first, prepared by IRS Special Agent Francis Mace, said, "Gotti is the public face of the label and that McGriff was the true owner of the company." The affidavit alleged that Supreme used the label to launder drug money and linked him to a narcotic-related double homicide that occurred in Maryland in 2001. The IRS sought forfeitures from Supreme's Picture Perfect Film Company. The second — prepared by Detective William Courtney, who was with the NYPD's High Intensity Drug Trafficking Taskforce, linked Supreme to the 2001 Queens Village revenge slaying of Eric "E-Money Bags" Smith.

Supreme was also facing a couple of gun charges, one stemming from a July 2001 traffic stop in Harlem, and another for attending a 2001 firearms training course. He was arrested in a Miami Beach

Hotel in November 2002 and pled guilty in April 2003 for taking target practice at a Glen Burnie, Maryland firing range —a charge unheard of until this case. On November 4, 2004, he was sentenced for the New York City gun charge and received a five-year concurrent sentence that would have put him out in the summer of 2005.

For more than two years, law enforcement officers and agents from the NYPD, IRS, FBI, and ATF investigated Supreme. They allege that upon his mid 90s release from prison he rebuilt his violent drug organization with several new members, since the Supreme Team were all in jail. The feds actively built a case that Supreme never left the drug game, despite evidence to the contrary. His former attorney Simels maintained that his client is the victim of wild innuendo, and that his name comes up with every unsolved crime. "In Supreme's situation, he is a perfect target because of his past, and because the hip-hop generation accepted him and put him on a pedestal as an example of what a gangsta should be," Terry says of his man.

"It's like a vendetta against Preme, what they're doing right now." Tuck says of the indictments. "Dudes change over the years, but with the feds, it's like once a drug dealer always a drug dealer. These days, being a drug dealer is worse than being a rapist." The investigation, overseen by U.S. Attorney Roslynn R. Mauskopt, saw the feds work two angles to the case. First, in November 2003, they indicted Ja Rule's manager and a Murder Inc. accountant with laundering more than one million in cash. Then, in a separate indictment, a Queens couple was charged with the E-Money Bags slaying.

"It's like Supreme said, 'They could have easily not been on the indictment by saying what the cops wanted them to say.'" Terry says. Supreme's former lawyer accused the government of pushing cooperating witnesses to falsely implicate the ultimate targets of the probe, and their case hinges on the testimony of Jon "Love" Ragin, the leader of a large-scale credit card fraud ring who worked on the Crime Partners DVD with Supreme, and when he got busted in August 2003, he turned government stooge rather than face a 15-19 year sentence. About Ragin, Terry says, "This creep, nothing he says has any validity. He started a lot of this when he went on the run and got caught in the forgery ring. The feds seized the film company due to this dude's lies."

When the indictment came out the government quietly backed off its claims that the seed money for Murder Inc. came from Supreme. In fact, this is the reason the investigation was initially started and this allegation appears nowhere in the 37-page indictment. Concerning the murders in the indictment, Terry says, "Supreme's never been in that part of the game. It's clear he's a negotiator. To kill someone is to create a problem and a negotiator would never do this." Terry goes on, "The governments gonna paint you however they wanna see you. If you're not gonna lie on somebody or try to put somebody in jail or comply with the government, then they're going after you." And this is the position that Supreme finds himself in, but like the street legend he is, he's ready to battle for his life in court.

"From my point of view," says Choke, another Supreme confidant, "they're trying to judge him from his past. All these articles talking about the Supreme Team... that shit was 20 years ago." And Terry sums it all up, saying, "The whole investigation started trying to link Murder Inc.'s start-up to drug money from Supreme. Now, it's turned into a gangsta-rap fantasy." And that gangsta-rap fantasy could end up costing a man his life.

FOURTEEN

Alpo and Fray

A LOT OF factors figured in the death of the Washington DC street legend, Fray, but the main reason was Alberto "Alpo" Martinez. When the soon to become infamous rat Alpo hit DC in the late 1980s, Fray was a well established and respected hustler at the top of DC's street hierarchy. Fray didn't take kindly to New York dudes coming from up top to set up shop in the city. He despised dudes coming down to Chocolate City and hustling on the home turf. But it was more than that. The slick New York dudes would come down with kilos and game, flossing and shining, fucking all the DC girls, turning the community out, and getting DC dudes to betray and murder other DC dudes. Just fucking shit up in general and then leaving the mess for Fray to clean up. Fray didn't like to feel he got played on any level, and dudes like Alpo were snakes, fucking it up for the home team.

Fray's attitude toward outsiders, especially the dudes from New York, was to lean on them. He put his muscle game down and dared the New Yorkers to make a move. Fray felt secure in his city and he put his mentality in effect. When Alpo came into town, flossing and fronting that gangster shit, Fray called his bluff, got shit off him and didn't even pay him. He treated Alpo like a sucker. He was leaning on the New Yorker and saw him as a coward even before he started snitching. Fray had the 411 on Alpo from the jump. Before he knew him he saw the snake for what he was. In retrospect, Fray played Alpo for the buster he was.

"I saw Fray take 10 keys from Alpo one time," one hustler says. That was how Fray treated the kid. Fray got in touch with some of his people from New York and they warned him that Alpo wasn't right. They told Fray that Alpo had set some people up in New York, good dudes, on some flip shit long before he began to tell. He was a shiesty dude and Fray was forewarned. Fray knew Alpo wasn't a true gangster. He knew Alpo was fronting because zebras can't change their stripes, once a sucker always a sucker. But even suckers can bust their gun and Fray didn't foresee the coward's treachery. He was too secure in his status in the city.

Fray was in the life though and death was an occupational hazard. It happened to lesser men everyday. Fray just never envisioned himself falling prey to the game. He never thought he would be a victim. The Washington Post headline read, "Alleged Drug Figure Slain on DC Street." The man known as Fray, government name Michael Salters, had met his demise. He was described by law enforcement officials as one of the city's largest drug dealers, but it was noted that his real power lay in his ability to referee turf disputes among rival drug dealers. So, in other words, Fray made big power moves, and due to this, he was a man among men, respected, feared and loved. That didn't stop him from being gunned down on the streets he came up on. On July 16, 1991, in an ambush at First and Bryant Streets Northwest, an unidentified gunman opened fire on Salters' car, Washington DC police reported. The death of a street legend was the result. The city was rocked by his murder.

Afraid that Fray was going to have him killed, Alpo paid a DC dude to kill a DC legend. Fray's body, still inside his bullet-ridden car, was left outside the entrance to the Washington Hospital Center shortly after 10:30 p.m. Fifth District Captain James Coffey said. Fray was pronounced dead at about 1 a.m. that morning. The police department said Fray had been shot at least six times. A relative of Fray's was driving a van behind Fray's car east on Bryant when he was cut off by another car near First Street, police said. An occupant of the vehicle that cut off the van opened fire on Fray. An uninjured passenger in Fray's car then drove him to the hospital.

"I was in prison when Fray got killed." His relative says. "I'll never forget when dude came to my cell and told me that your cousin got killed last night. I got on the phone and called home and couldn't believe it. I wondered who would jump out there like that. Fray had that much pull in DC. It hurts to even talk about this shit because nothing was really done to answer that shit. How can a nigga like Fray get killed and niggas don't tear the city up and go to war. The only person I can say really did something was his nephew Poochie." Darrell Salters aka Poochie, Fray's nephew, was a stick-up kid who robbed and kidnapped drug dealers. He did a lot of shit behind Fray's murder but was eventually gunned down himself. It was said that Poochie killed a few big names in the game behind Fray's murder, but no one knew if he got the right people.

"I heard that this guy Brooks and Alpo were scared of Fray. That's what I heard," Fatts says of what the streets were saying about Fray being taken out. About the murder, the rat Alpo said in F.E.D.S. magazine, "Fray was about to get back in position in DC. He had a list of names or people he needed to eliminate and I was at the top of his list. I found out because I was feeding someone in his camp he wasn't taking care of. That same person ended up killing him for me." At the time though, no one knew who killed Fray. It was a complete and utter shock that a man of his stature could be taken out like that. His friends, family, allies, associates and enemies were all dumbfounded. If the Ambassador of Chocolate City could be touched, then anyone could be touched. It was a sobering reality.

On March 5, 1993, a 27 count indictment, stemming from the Alpo case, alleged that his crew was responsible for nine homicides from 1989 to 1991. According to the indictment, when Alpo learned of Fray's plans to kill him, he and Wayne Perry paid Michael Jackson nine grand in cash, a half-kilogram of cocaine and a 9 mm handgun to kill Fray. The allegations were never presented in court, but Alpo admitted to them in the magazine interview. So did Wayne Perry, who said of the matter in Don Diva magazine, "As far as the Fray thing, I'm gonna tell you about it. I wouldn't if it could get someone in trouble, but the rat already told it. But dig, that was a cruddy snake move. And his trusted friends got him, not me. They put it out there that I did it. Yes, I was after Fray because he put a hit on me. He said he had to get me out of the way so he could extort Alpo. Alpo was scared of Fray but I wasn't. And Alpo felt okay as long as he had me. So I end up finding out about the hit on me and I got at those in Fray's crew who took the hit and let Fray know that he was next.

"But I couldn't track him down. So those snakes, who used to be down at that shop on Georgia Avenue and were close to Fray but were scared of him, played both sides. So Alpo and them set it up for Fray's close buddy to hit him and then tell all Fray's people that I did it 'cause he was close to me too. But he is a snake and has no loyalty." The snake Wayne was talking about is Michael Jackson. "He even told the feds that he heard that he and Marky and Mario got Fray. The dude is a snake. All the time he was the one that did it and the dudes at the shop was all in on it. Now dig, one of my kids' mother heard the whole lie about me killing Fray at Fray's funeral where all the dudes and the dude that got Fray were saying I did it. At the time I don't know all of this and the dude who did it was my man at the time. I still didn't know he did it until we got locked up. The dude knew my daughter's mother heard him at Fray's funeral, so he hurried up and came to me to tell me she was at the funeral telling people I killed Fray. The dude knew I would believe him and ask no questions, just do what I did best, which I did. And that's my only regret. May she rest in peace. Michael Jackson is a snake."

Before his untimely end, Fray was the subject of a five-year investigation by the Washington Metropolitan Police and the FBI. Fray had been implicated in drug deals of more than 200 pounds, but he had proved to be too well insulated from direct involvement to be charged. Agents at times put Salters under intense surveillance and interviewed drug dealers who said they had worked with and for him. His name also came up in wiretapped conversations. A dude from the R Street case was heard on a wire saying Fray had paid the District Attorney five grand for information. That's how far his reach and influence carried. But the feds never got him. Fray met his maker in the streets, in a burst of gunfire like a true outlaw. Some rappers rap about it but Fray lived it. He was the epitome of the original gangster. For a man like that, all that can be done is to honor his gangster, his name and his legend.

FIFTEEN

The Real Rick Ross

I S THE RAP game the new drug game? With all these rappers fronting, styling and profiling you would think so. From its origins in New York to LA gangsta rap to the bling-bling of the 90s to the South's ascension, hip-hop has always took its cue from the streets. And Y2K7 finds cocaine rap en vogue with artists like TI, Jeezy, the Clipse, Lil Wayne and Miami's own Rick Ross doing their thing telling tales of street life and the drug game. And with BET's "American Gangster" series detailing the criminal exploits of real life gangstas, such as Fat Cat, the Chambers Brothers and Freeway Rick Ross, a correlation can be made and a question posed—where does reality stop and entertainment begin?

Hip-hop artists have long borrowed monikers from street legends just as they've told the drug lord stories in the rhymes. From 50 Cent, who took a Brooklyn stick-up kid's name to Scarface to Biggie referring to himself as the black Frank White, juxtaposing the gangster creed of death before dishonor and portraying the criminal lifestyle in videos has been a recipe for success. By promoting the thug life image of a hustler from the streets who lives by the code of omerta many rappers have made a career. Call it fake, call it fronting or what you will, the formula has worked and a multitude of cardboard gangstas are flashing gang signs and making their would-be criminal associations known in their videos on MTV, VH1 and BET. But as Irv Gotti found out, it can go too far, as in all the way to a court of law. And the way some of these entertainers portray themselves they shouldn't be surprised to find themselves in court. I mean get real. Case in point is the rapper Rick Ross.

William Roberts aka Rick Ross who released "The Port of Miami" last August promotes himself as the most respected hustler in hip-hop. And to be fair he's had a lot of success. But to hear this dude talk you'd think he was the second coming of Tony Montana or is in the penitentiary. But he's not and never was although the dude who he took his name from is Freeway Rick Ross, an alleged Hoover Crip from Los Angeles, California, who was one of the biggest drug dealers from the 80s, and is seen by some as being responsible for the nationwide crack epidemic that plagued inner city areas in the crack era. BET's "American Gangster" told his story, but we'll retell it quickly here.

Freeway Rick went from a low-budget car thief who stripped stolen vehicles near Harbor Freeway to selling cocaine by the ounce. The he met Danilo Blandon and Norwin Meneses, two wealthy Nicaraguan cocaine brokers determined to finance the ousting of the Sandinista and reestablish the Somoza government in their country. Through them Freeway Rick started getting kilos, and with Blandon's cocaine he was the first to mass-market crack. Ross flooded cities across the nation with the inexpensive ghetto-designed drug, and by 1984 it's alleged he was getting 100 kilos a week. By 1985, it's also said he had earned two hundred million dollars and from 1982 to 1989, it's said he moved three tons of cocaine.

The thing was that Freeway Rick was unwittingly supplying the money used to buy weapons for the Contras, a CIA backed anti-Sandinista squad of guerrillas trying to overthrow the government in Nicaragua. It all came out later that Freeway Rick was an unknowing pawn in Oliver North, Ronald Reagan's and the CIA's game of running guns to the Contras and returning with plane loads of cocaine that hit South Centrals streets as crack. The story was big news in the 90s. Very well publicized and California Representative Maxine Walters upped the ante by putting pressure on Attorney General Janet Reno to reveal the corruptness of Reagan's administration after the story broke. Gary Webb, a reporter from the San Jose Mercury News, investigated and broke the story. His investigation culminated in a book and later his death under mysterious circumstances. All that is said to make a point and now back to the rapper Rick Ross aka William Roberts.

"I just put a couple of names in the air and that Rick Ross shit just ringed to me. I didn't know anything about the dude personally, but the name sounded right to me. To be honest I didn't know shit about him," the rapper said recently in F.E.D.S. magazine, but this is after a previous article where he admitted to being a drug lord historian. He commented on how that was his thing, tracking the careers of the notorious underworld gangsters. "I started hearing more about the dude from the West Coast. I actually spoke to him over the phone. We got to chop it up. I always acknowledged him, but I don't want to make it like it is." Obviously, he took the name to emulate the infamous kingpin.

About the whole deal, the real Rick Ross, in a recent AS IS interview from prison, said, "You know in the hood anytime someone takes your name they are supposed to show some respect and I feel he should show me some." So I guess all that chopping it up shit from the rapper is some fantasy. It doesn't sound like Freeway Rick talked to his namesake. So Rick Ross the convict was the real drug dealer. That is an undeniable fact.

But Rick Ross the rapper, what are his credentials? "I was a fan of the game. I sat on the porch and listened to the Cadillacs go by." Ross said. "I was booming weed at 15 and had a bird at 17. I bought my first crib when I was 21. You know I'm the boss. I come from the cocaine capital. I was in the midst of the murder game on some real shit." Yet he isn't in prison and hasn't been. What is he, untouchable? He hasn't heard of conspiracy charges. Even the real Rick Ross, who unwittingly sold drugs for the CIA, wasn't untouchable. The rapper has even said how the money he makes from rapping can't even support his lifestyle, implying that he's still in the streets and in the drug game. I guess he's not worried about an indictment, because his raps are filled with allusions to the life and his part in it. But is it his life he's rapping about? "All those things he saying is true but true for my brother." David Ross said in the same AS IS interview about the rapper, but Rick Ross the rapper keeps the illusion going 24/7. "You know Noriega was down there in FDC forever man, with all my dogs. I used to send messages to him. So that's why I put his name in there." He said in F.E.D.S. "I've been involved in that kind of shit where robberies took place. I wasn't even there. My homies pulled it off and came off so lovely. Go buy two homes, here's your cut, a gift, it's easy." But it you were really involved in that type of shit would you advertise it? I don't think so.

"He found an opportunity and he exploited it." The real Rick Ross said on the rapper: "I don't know if there's anything I really want to say to him." And remember this is the dude the rapper said he chopped it up with. So maybe Rick Ross the rapper lives in a fantasy world, a carefully constructed facade and image built on lies. Because if he was the real don that he claims to be in his rhymes, he would be counting millions instead of rapping about them.

"In the late 80s, Rick was counting a million dollars a day." His brother David said. "The million dollars couldn't be carried alone, no one person with a duffel bag. You couldn't even pick it up. Two counters and you could count a million dollars in about ten hours." Now what does the rapper know about that? Nothing. "I feel that god had put me down to be the cocaine man." Freeway Rick said, "I owned lots of property, I owned one motel. I had one of the first custom tire wheel shops in LA, beauty salons, shoe stores, junk yards, auto body shops and numerous apartment and housing buildings." That's the real life of a hood legend and ghetto baller. A real big time drug dealer is looking for ways to legitimize his shit. The rapper Rick Ross is only selling illusions, albeit, successfully.

But fuck it, its only entertainment, right? Drug game, rap game—the lines are blurred. "I just took the same formula of ripping that dope up, taking it to the streets and making a nigga buy that shit." The rapper said on his M.O. And if anyone believes that they'll believe anything. Not to say you can't respect the hustle, because dudes music is tight. But if you're an entertainer, be an entertainer. Don't try to be something you're not. Could you imagine the real Rick Ross trying to get in the rap game?

But the subject of Freeway Rick singing has come up—singing to the feds that is. Allegedly he cooperated with the feds when the whole Contra affair came to light and subsequently received a reduction on his current sentence for that cooperation. Even on BET's "American Gangster" it said he cooperated, so how gangster is that? "I don't think it was snitching." Rick Ross said in AS IS magazine and AS IS co-signed dude saying, "AS IS has love for Rick, we gonna ride with extenuating circumstances for Rick." What do you think? Dude snitched on the government, if you want to call it that. It is what it is. But what about AS IS?

AS IS is the brainchild of Shabazz who used to write for Don Diva, the original street bible. With AS IS in circulation it now makes three street themed magazines- Don Diva, F.E.D.S. and AS IS, with Felon a fourth that probably isn't operating anymore. There's been a couple of others like Troy Reed's Faces, but it didn't last either. Clearly Don Diva is #1 on the food chain, and, with the success of BET's "American Gangster," the numerous books coming out and mainstream hip-hop mags like King, XXL and The Source featuring gangsta content, it's no wonder the rappers are following the trend. This gangsta shit is bubbling and pretty soon, slowly but surely, the tales of America's black underworld gangsters will go mainstream in the entertainment world just like the Mafia. Vicious gangstas from the crack era are finally getting their shine on. Fake ass rappers or not.

SIXTEEN

The New World
of Islam

I N THE 1960S and 1970s a quasi-militant Muslim sect, the New
World of Islam (NWOI), emerged as a force to be reckoned with. Its
main base on South Orange Avenue in Newark, New Jersey, was known
as Temple 25. The religious group was suspected of having staged more
than 100 area armed robberies to raise money to further the cause of
the New World and to finance a black separatist community. During
the course of this robbery spree, six murders, including that of the head
of the NOI Temple, James Shabazz, were laid at the door of this group,
along with those of two police officers who intervened in robberies
staged by members.

Federal authorities described the NWOI as a Black Muslim splinter
group that was one of the most violent criminal organizations in New
Jersey. The quasi-military group advocated black superiority, a separatist movement and armed robbery to raise money. They were getting
theirs and didn't have any qualms about what they did to get it. While
pursuing their militant brand of Islam, members of the group were
tied to a number of bank robberies and several murders including two
beheadings and the slayings of two police officers. The New World was
not playing. Authorities even said that they plotted to have the judges
on their cases kidnapped. These brothers were thorough, straight up

Muslim gangsters. Death before dishonor and all that. But they were also righteous soldiers in their faith. Willing to get down for a cause and fight for their people.

"We didn't set out to hurt anyone but we needed money." Hijr Najee says. "Brothers were committed to a movement and we needed funds. The most perfect robbery was one where a shot wasn't fired." But shots were fired and people were killed. There were high speed chases and shootouts with police. These brothers were not joking. They were righteous but deadly. They were serious about theirs and had little tolerance for those who didn't follow the rules. "The brothers were totally against drugs," Hijr Najee says. "We had numerous opportunities to get into drugs. Big dealers wanted us to invest. But the brothers didn't want to be associated with that. Weed was legal in the nation but drinking, heroin, cocaine, cigarettes; they didn't want us to mess with that."

The New World got theirs like Bonnie and Clyde, the ski mask way. They were on that "Set it Off" tip. They weren't drug pushers or dope dealers. They knew what was killing their community. They were trying to rectify that situation and get out from under the white man's rule by establishing their own society and way of life. Loyal soldiers like Hijr Najee worked their way up in rank, proving their resolve and heart by their deeds, not their words. In the New World it was all about action, talk was cheap. "You had to work your way up in rank," Hijr Najee says. "I started elevating in rank when other brothers had to leave. I was minister of the city. That fell into my lap. At one time they were keeping me away from the underground stuff." But like all things the underground didn't stay underground. People talked and it got exposed.

Throughout its existence, the group robbed banks to sustain its members, according to testimony in the federal racketeering trial. Men wearing ski masks, storming into banks, waging high speed chases and having shootouts with police while fleeing with money was their M.O. Members would select and case the banks and other businesses and thereafter plan in detail the execution of the robbery of those targeted institutions. Police identified Al "The General" Dickens as the head of the group and criminal mastermind behind the armed robberies. "All the money went to finance the New World." Hijr Najee says. "We were trying to build communities in Calhoun Falls, South Carolina, and Salem, New Jersey. We wanted to get the property. We wanted to build the houses, a separate community. That's what we intended but it got crazy. We started robbing the same banks twice."

Despite the noble intentions, the robbing hustle didn't last. Brothers started going to jail, but for the most part they kept their mouths shut. That was the code installed by the General. "We wanted that loyalty." Hijr Najee says. "Brothers used to put other brothers in jeopardy and brothers wouldn't tell. That's what happened to James Scott. We always had a link up with the prisons. I was going to visit the brothers in liaisons. I became James 'Superman' Scott's liaison." The arrests brought attention to the group. With law enforcement closing in on the sect due to the murders, the New World was attracting way too much attention—attention that had the feds lurking around the corner.

Several New World members were convicted of the September 1973 slaying of James Shabazz, the local NOI leader, even though Al Dickens was found not guilty of planning the homicide. The murder of Montclair Police Sgt. Alfred Sellick on January 17, 1976, also attracted a lot of unwanted attention as a close connection was found between the accused gunmen and Dickens. One of the defendants was Archie Murphy who police identified as a New World member. "We have information that Murphy and others recruited youngsters, some as young as twelve, and trained them in firearms, hand to hand combat and other techniques. The New World is a paramilitary group. Their ultimate goal seems to be the overthrow of the Nation of Islam, an established religious group so they may use its power base to take over the city," Assistant Essex Prosecutor Anthony Mautone said. "They said we were a crime family with different crews of brothers in Newark, Florida, and New Brunswick." Hijr Najee says. But that was far from the truth.

"They were studying us. They said we were causing too much havoc in the street. We had a nice following. A lot of young guys were looking up to us. We had a nice close brotherhood." Hijr Najee says. Samud Ali goes deeper, "The New World Nation of Islam is what saved us. A movement toward our way of life. Before that we were dead." Rafi Ali agrees, "I needed to be a part of people who were teaching and working to help unite our people and establish a society owned and operated by us. The movement was deep. The brothers and sisters involved were thorough. A strange mix of religion and bank robbers, but Hijr Najee keeps it real. "Some brothers lost their lives because the New World was in a war, a war of ideals and a war for their way of life. In any war, casualties always play a part."

Police Director Hubert Williams was infuriated with the group and told a press conference that the religious sect had been using religion as a guise to carry out criminal activities. "Holdups, robbing banks and killing cops have no place in religion and is clearly contrary to the tenets of Islam. What we see rather is a distortion of the religious value system. They have crafted a sort of hybrid and grafted onto religion, criminal activities." Williams emphasized that the NWOI was, "A highly disciplined group with a code of secrecy, organized quasi-military. They use their religion as a guise to further their criminal designs. I have tried to make it emphatically clear as possible that what we're talking about is a radical element within a particular religious sect called the NWOI. Their activities in no way reflect the peace loving manner in which Muslims go about their life and worshipping their faith." Employing the age old tactic of divide and conquer, the police director attempted to differentiate between Muslims and the New World.

Police Detective Captain George Courtney compared their techniques to those of famous bank robber John Dillinger, "He'd stick up a bank after he staked it out and built a mock up of the bank. He'd study it and practice jumping over the counter before hitting a bank. He was well-prepared like the Muslims are today. We're not talking about religious law abiding Muslims. We're talking basically about a bunch of former convicts using the guise of religion to veil a serious criminal intent. The FBI has told us there is a new trend involving Muslims who are pulling bank holdups and are heavily armed. These Muslims are pulling bank holdups to get money to buy drugs and weapons. They're always looking for weapons." But the New World was looking for so much more. Hakim Ali explains, "We want to uphold the truth and be black, to do something for self as a Black man with a God, religion and a purpose in life to save our people." The Sister Hijrah Ali breaks it down further, "It is a movement towards establishing independence as a nation of people." But the movement wasn't without its pitfalls.

After all these years most of the members of the NWOI are out of prison and back in the world. They stayed together, stood firm and didn't blink in the face of adversity. Their belief was death before dishonor and even though they spent 25 years or more in prison for their beliefs they are still fighting for their people and are involved in programs for youths and more in Newark today. Plus NWOI member Wahida Clark started publishing her Thug novels from prison and emerged in 2007 as one of the top writers in the urban fiction genre. Through it all they have never wavered in their beliefs or their goals. Now that is gangster. That is what a street legend is all about.

"Looking back on all that we have gone through, I see the great wisdom taught by my teachers in the New World. Every exercise program, lesson, essay that was written helped to make the person I am today. It saved me. I have no regrets and I blame no one." Rafi Ali says. And Al Dickens, the General, breaks it all down. "We're about trying to save our own black people." He says. "It's a matter of first making our black people realize that they are an independent people. And that they have a right, just like everybody else to have a place in the sun and some of this Earth to call their own. We never turned around, we kept Elijah's teachings alive. We are proud to have kept our Nation's flag flying high while most fell away. That is the military training given to men in Islam. FOI means Fruit of Islam."

In its existence the group has boasted a light heavyweight world contender, a well-known street lit author and numerous soldiers in the movement who were down for the cause, no matter the consequences. They took theirs on the chin and kept it moving. Never giving in or wavering in their faith or chosen path. All of these brothers and sisters set out with noble intentions, and wrongly or rightly, their actions remain of pure intent. They fought a criminal justice system that was set up to hasten their demise. And through their defiance and refusal to bend even one inch, their exploits and misadventures in crime and life have become legendary. Their organization has gone down in infamy in street lore. They are the fallen soldiers that rose again like the Phoenix. They are the real, the unafraid, the unbended, resolute in their ideals and identity. They are the original gangsters, the ones who stayed true to the code of the streets and the tenets of the faith.

IV

THE
DRUG GAME

SEVENTEEN

My Brother's Keeper

W HEN THE CRACK era in New York was jumping off in the 1980's, a lot of street legends were born in a hail of gunfire. Business minded and ruthless dudes seized the opportunities afforded, and certain individuals out of the city's five boroughs became synonymous with the definition of the new era black gangsta. Characters and cliques that seemed to evolve straight out of the pages of a Donald Goines novel rose to prominence and became larger than life figures and ghetto stars in their respective hoods. Just like Hollywood catapulted the Mafia into the mainstream with "The Godfather" movies, "New Jack City" documented the devastating crack epidemic and the drug crews that terrorized and held sway in the city's projects.

Nino Brown was a fictional character, as was his crew, but you didn't have to look very far to find their real life counterparts who dominated the headlines of New York's papers. Drugs, murder, kidnappings, shootings, more drugs and more murder were the rule of the day. They called it the game but in reality it was a vicious attempt to come up by any means necessary. In the late 80's the mindset was get mine or be mine, and nobody embodied this attitude more then the Supreme Team, the most legendary street gang of its time.

Besides Hollywood paying court to the team, a number of homegrown rappers, who were shorties in the '80's, started namedropping the teams exploits in verse. First was 1994's Memory Lane where Nas spit, "Some fiends scream about Supreme Team a Jamaica Queens thing." But the more famous couplet came courtesy of Queens native son Curtis Jackson (aka 50 Cent) who rhymed on 2000's Ghetto Qu'ran, "When you hear talk of the southside/you hear talk of the team/see niggas feared Prince and they respected Preme/for all you slow mutha-fuckers I'm a break it down iller/see Preme was the businessman and Prince was the killer." Street tales, real life crimes, newspaper head-lines, Hollywood sensationalism and rappers rhymes have perpetrated, promoted and created a legend of mythical proportions that has grown exponentially over the last 20 years, keeping the Supreme Team name ringing bells from coast to coast. As one of the most notorious crews from a deadly era, the team towers above its contemporaries in stature, notoriety and infamy. But it's not all hype. Infamy has its price.

The Supreme Team was a street gang organized in the early 1980's in the vicinity of the Baisley Park Houses in Jamaica, Queens New York, by a group of teenagers who were members of a quasi-religious sect known as the "Five Percenters," court documents say. Under the leadership of Kenneth "Supreme" McGriff, with Gerald "Prince" Miller his nephew, as second in command, the gang concentrated its criminal efforts on widespread distribution of crack cocaine. At its 1987 peak, the Supreme Team's receipts exceeded $200,000 a day and the gang regularly committed acts of violence and murder to maintain its stronghold on the areas drug trade, court documents reveal. After McGriff went to jail in 1987, leadership of the Supreme Team was assumed by Miller. Miller solidified his control by increasing the se-curity force and employing it against rivals and against team members suspected of disloyalty.

The Supreme Team's narcotics operation used dozens of em-ployees, including layers of drug sellers to insulate the gang leaders from the street-level activity, court documents relate. Team members communicated in coded language and numerical systems. To thwart law enforcement efforts further, Miller used armed bodyguards and deployed sentinels with two-way radios on rooftops. The sophistication of the gang's operation enabled it to survive the periodic targeting of various members for prosecution by the NYPD and the Queens County District Attorney's Office. But like other hood stars of the age the team wasn't immune from the feds.

Back in the day Queens was a notorious breeding ground for brutal, progressive thinking gangstas. Fat Cat, Pappy Mason, Tommy Montana, The Corley Brothers, Pretty Tony and Hymee all hailed from the southside. But the two most infamous cats out of Jamaica were Supreme and Prince. They led a team that was said to be over 200 deep and rivaled the Mafia in structure. The notoriety of Supreme is well publicized and his transformation from gangsta to hip-hop icon and rap maestro has been well documented, as has the feds blatant vendetta against the man. Supreme and Murder Inc. are now in the first stages of overcoming the government's latest and boldest assault on the rap industry since they tried to unsuccessfully take down Death Row records in the mid 90's. The feds just can't stand it when a gangsta goes legit. Its okay for the Kennedys, but when a black man goes legit, it's a federal crime. But there is another story to be told, one that centers around Supreme's nephew Prince, who is doing seven life sentences in the feds. Newspaper accounts say Prince inherited the leadership of the Supreme Team in 1987, when his uncle Supreme was arrested, charged as a kingpin and ultimately sentenced to a twelve-year prison term in the feds.

At the time the papers called the heir apparent, Prince, Mr. Untouchable, because he was like the Teflon Don, nothing would stick. Everybody's heard the raps, read the newspaper headlines and the magazine articles but what was the Supreme Team really about? What was the real story? You know Gorilla Convict keeps it real and to that end we contacted a real gangsta, a man who stood tall in the face of adversity and went to trial at Prince's side, a man who's been buried in the guts of the belly of the beast for the last 15 years. Meet Supreme Team member and true soldier, Ronald Tucker (aka Tuck) who's going to take us back to Jamaica, Queens, circa 1986.

The working class neighborhoods of South Jamaica, St. Albans and Hollis that Tuck grew up in lie in the 103rd and 113th precinct, which are a 4.8 square mile perfect box, encompassing Van Wyck Expressway to the west, Hillside Avenue to the north, Francis Lewis Boulevard to the east and a jagged line that runs along the 110th Avenue to the south. Around 125,000 people live within its borders, 62 percent of them black. Tuck describes his days prior to getting down with the team, "I was in high school working at D'Agostinos. It's a famous supermarket. I was a delivery guy, seventeen-years-old and delivering groceries to fucking people." He says. "I lived next door to my man, Black Born. We were walking to the store one day and this guy Bishme told us about Prince coming home. He said he was trying to put the team back together. I had never heard of a Supreme Team before that and I lived in Jamaica all my life."

"I met Prince in June 1986, almost 19 years ago in front of Baisley Projects," Tuck says. "I went from making 100 dollars a week at the grocery store to a thousand dollars a day. I was selling hand to hand, a worker. I was seventeen and didn't have any goals. I thought I could sell drugs forever." But forever is a mighty long time, and looking back Tuck admits, "I chose to make the streets a part of my life. I lacked guidance in the form of a father figure, so I looked to the streets for that which I couldn't find at home. Prince became somewhat of a father figure to me. Someone I could look up to." And someone who could show Tuck what it meant to be gangsta.

"Baisley Park," Tuck says. "That's where I hustled at. Five Buildings. This was where I ate." Under the red-brick towers of Baisley Projects, an around-the-clock crack cocaine trade that operated more like a corporation then a drug outfit prospered selling 25,000 crack vials a week, according to newspaper accounts. "It seemed like the team controlled everything in Jamaica, from Liberty Ave and 171, 115th and Sutphin Blvd, to 121, which is several blocks," Tuck said. "It was crazy."

Street tales tell how the team kept the whole area in check. Whenever Supreme went to prison, Prince was the boss. And when the feds got Supreme, it was Prince's show. There was no free styling. Either you were down with the team or else. That was how it played out in the streets. And the team placed a premium on loyalty. Tuck was one of the most loyal, a gangsta to his core. About his relationship with Prince, he says, "I don't think Prince and I ever had a friendship. I believe it was all business. I do know that most people would rather have Prince on their team than have to oppose him. This was because Prince was about his business. As they say in the streets, he handled his."

Tuck breaks it down about the two legends he came up under: "Preme is a dude who will rationalize, talk it out. He's very diplomatic and charismatic. I remember the name Supreme as someone who always was spoken of highly. I don't know if it was out of fear or respect. But usually when people spoke that name, they were speaking of something greater then themselves." And this image reflected downwardly as neighborhood residents said the Supreme Team was generally courteous and respectful to residents of the projects.

"Prince is a real good dude also," Tuck says. "Very well respected and feared too. He was highly motivated, very organized and extremely intelligent, a real master at gamesmanship." Under Prince the team was run like a military operation, newspaper accounts say, with a chain of command and everything. Dudes who stood strong and held their mouth were given more responsibility. Those who didn't, the feds would have you believe, were murdered.

Tuck started off selling hand to hand to the crackheads. The team used a color coded system for the vials of crack. Each color signified whose cocaine it was. There was a color for every lieutenant of the organization—yellow, orange, red and blue. "I had yellow." Tuck says.

Crackheads from the era remember yellow as being Prince's color. This was the scene back in the day. Workers like Tuck were caged in by the handball court at Baisley Park. As soon as the crackheads got in the park, they would yell the colors out—for example, yellow to signify whose crack they wanted. And there were strict rules also. There was a line on the handball court and workers couldn't cross that line to make sales. They had to wait for the crackheads to come to them. And they couldn't knock somebody's customer out the box. If the crackhead wanted yellow, then yellow it was. Another rule was no singles, no shorts. Workers would be chanting to the crackheads: "No singles, no shorts," meaning no one dollar bills and don't come short with the paper trying to cop.

"I knew that if you were my customer, then on your payday you were gonna give me all your money," Tuck says. The crackheads were crazy, too. Tuck explains: "They'll take the joint and tap it. Try to switch it with an empty vial or one with soap in it. Or you'll take the vial out of your mouth with your spit on it and the crackhead would put it right in his mouth." Tuck relates an even more bizarre incident: "One time this bus driver came to cop. He parked his bus and copped. That's the illest shit I ever seen. People were still on the bus. The power of this drug."

Tuck adds: "Fifty of 500. That's what I made. But I was selling 10 grand worth of crack a day. So it was like a grand a day. If the drugs weren't in the community, Jamaica Queens could have been a beautiful place to live. But drugs were easy and fast money. As a seventeen-year old my thoughts were: why go to school when I'm making more money than the chairman of the Board of Education?"

Court documents say the gang under Miller included Wilfredo "C-Just" Arroyo as second in command, Harry "Big C" Hunt as Miller's bodyguard, Ernesto "Puerto Rican Righteous" Piniella as head of security and Roy "Pookie" Hale, Shannon Jimenez and Julio Hernandez as security workers. Tucker and Teddy Coleman managed retail spots and supervised crews of workers; long time gang-member David "Bing" Robinson helped to supervise the drug operations and kept records. Raymond "Ace" Robinson assisted in arranging cocaine purchases, provided security during drug transactions, supervised the processing of cocaine into crack and delivered crack to sales locations.

Prince was considered by law enforcement officials to be one of the most violent drug dealers in the city during the 1980s, but here's Tucks take on Prince: "I looked up to him. He was everything that a young kid from the ghetto aspired to be. He had money, tons of women, power and respect." In the streets they called Prince "The General." He was known to be cool, calm and collected and in control at all times. Legend has it he survived hit attempts and dealt with an iron fist. In the drug game there's no tolerance for bullshit, because the game breeds larceny, and anyone who can keep their cool in the face of all that deserves their stripes.

As for the other Supreme Team members, this is how the streets remember them. C-Just was known as a real quiet, soft-spoken dude who never raised his voice. Bonifide, you heard. Big C was known as Prince's right hand man, a real serious and intimidating cat who had dreads, wore dark glasses and tank tops that showed off his huge arms, which were like pythons. Pookie was a known gunman from back in the day, who did a rack of state time and came back out to hook up with the team. Ace was a dude fresh out of prison who just got down with the team before they went down. But he stood up like the old school cat he was. Shannon was, as the prosecutor dubbed him, "a lifelong member of the Supreme Team." He was known as a loyal dude who would do whatever for the team. These dudes according to court documents were Prince's security team.

The security team had a fearsome and well deserved reputation in the hood and they dressed accordingly. Tales from late 80's Queens claimed that the army fatigue-look was a Supreme Team signature. Their war gear was black fatigues and jackets, bulletproof vests, black

Timbs and hats, the drawstring joints or baseball caps. And their weaponry consisted of AR-15's, Mac-10's, Nines, 45's, 357's, Techs-you name it, they had it. And when they were on a mission shit got crazy. They would be jumping out of mini-vans like a taskforce. And when dudes on the block saw them they'd start running and scrambling praying that the team wasn't coming for them. Because don't get it fucked up. Real gangstas do gangsta shit. It was even said that Prince had a bulletproof baseball hat and newspaper accounts talk of a James Bond Mercedes 500 Prince had that was equipped with bulletproof windows, oil slick and everything. The Supreme Team wasn't playing.

About his life of drug dealing Tuck says, "I had no foresight to say I'm gonna make a certain amount of money and get out of this. Selling drugs is like an addiction. The dealer is just like the fiend. The dealer is addicted to the money. Just like the fiend is addicted to the drugs." And Tuck, Bing and Teddy were known as the money men. Bing, according to court documents was arrested with Supreme on a 1985 case and when he got released in '89, he got down with Prince. Teddy and Tuck were the youngsters of the team who rose up through the ranks from workers, according to court documents, to lieutenants who ran spots. Bing, Tuck and Teddy were the ones bringing in the paper. They all had their own crews and were making crazy money themselves and for the team.

And the team's structure was well organized. They had the security force, the retail spots and the stashhouses where chicks worked around the clock bagging up vials of crack on glass tables just like in "New Jack City."

A Queens native sums up the whole era and what it was all about. "Drug dealing, killing, more drug dealing, more killing, cops getting murdered, parole officers getting murdered for violating nig-gas, crooked police getting paid off, police issuing beatdowns, families getting murdered because other family members are testifying in court, you know, basic hood shit." Prompted by the February 26, 1988, murder of Officer Edward Byrne, the Tactical Narcotics Team or TNT was formed. The coordinated, city wide multiagency approach was the first to employ the concerted resources of many government agencies to combat crime and TNT covered the 103rd, 105th, 106th and 113th precincts- 22 miles of Southeastern Queens. Locals said that once you crossed the tracks into Baisley Projects it was a war zone or at least it was back then and the newly formed TNT task force agreed. After they took down Fat Cat and Pappy Mason the task force made Prince and the Supreme Team their new target.

The Supreme Team saw over more then 110 of its members arrested and convicted in the early 90's. By targeting the area bounded by 110th Ave on the north, Sutphin Blvd on the west, Merrick Blvd on the east and Baisley Blvd on the south, the TNT task force waged an all out war on the Supreme Team and brought them down. Newspaper accounts said the Supreme Team held the projects hostage, but according to people who lived in the projects things were done for the residents of the community that wouldn't have been done by the city, including turkey dinners, trips to Great Adventures for the kids and bills being paid for those who couldn't afford it. But was the good enough to outweigh the bad? Showing love to the community is all good, but like they say, what comes around goes around and when you deal in death sooner or later you'll have to meet your maker.

In court documents the state explained that it had been investigating the Supreme Team for some years and had nearly exhausted its battery of traditional investigative techniques with little success. Using normal techniques, the state had been unable to penetrate the Supreme Team or gain sufficient admissible evidence against any members other than those of the lowest echelons. The team's leaders had insulated themselves from police contact through extensive use of body guards and lookouts and when the state applied for wire tap authorization it had yet to identify all of the upper and middle level members of the Supreme Team or to determine where the narcotics and illegal proceeds were kept or to identify the teams suppliers. Tuck keeps it real, "For real as far as I'm concerned there was no Supreme Team. I pled not guilty and after 15 years I'm walking out the door still not guilty."

On March 21, 1990, 130 cops from the TNT task force fanned out to 15 area apartments for simultaneous 6 a.m. raids. The arrests were results of a year-long investigation of the group and came on the heels of Prince being found not guilty by a jury of a drug-related murder. The papers screamed their outrage about the vicious drug gang that turned a neighborhood in South Jamaica into a killing field.

"That was the last of the posses," said Lieutenant Michael Geraghty, commanding officer of the Queens Narcotics major case squad. "It is not an end to the drug problem in Southeast Queens by any means. But it puts an end to the Supreme Team. Prince was known as an untouchable. I think this dispels that myth." Investigators said Miller and his henchmen terrorized the area, murdered suppliers they double-crossed, confederates who fell out of favor and potential rivals. To law enforcement authorities battling the relentless drug trade in New York City Gerald Miller was one of the most savage and successful of the flashy young kingpins who dominated the lucrative crack business.

"They are an extremely volatile group," said Queens DA John J. Santucci at the time. But the much feared and tightly run organization had run its course. Miller, the heir, to the Southeast Queens crack trade, police said, was through. His gang that had used violence and intimidation to establish and maintain its crack selling operation were all in jail. But Prince's arrest only managed to increase his and the team's infamy as the murder cases started stacking up.

Prince was charged with the murder of a 19-year-old drug dealer who was shot once in the head at point-black range at 9 p.m. on August 21, 1987, at the corner of Foch Boulevard and 142nd place in Jamaica. But the jury found Prince not guilty. On July 13, 1990, while he was incarcerated fighting that murder he was indicted for the second set of murder charges in two years. A quadruple homicide of four Colombians, the papers reported. The Queens District Attorney's office said Miller ordered the killings from jail and that he operated his drug empire by using telephone code words to direct his underlings. "The fact is, these four people were slaughtered," said DA Santucci. "They were handcuffed, gagged, strangled and then they bashed their skulls."

In opening statements to the jury for Prince's 1990 quadruple homicide case, Queens Assistant DA Eugene Kelly called Prince the mastermind behind the so-called Supreme Team, which controlled the drug trade in the Jamaica section of the borough. Local detectives testified that since Miller was arrested in 1990, homicides had dropped by more then 30 percent. But for the second time in two years, at the State Supreme Court in Queens, Prince was acquitted. DA Santucci said he was startled and dismayed at the verdict.

"Prince beat four or five bodies in the state and beat eight or nine in the feds," Tuck says. "He was back and forth fighting murder cases. They called him Mr. Untouchable in the papers because every single case he beat at trial. That's what made the feds come and get us. It's called the Silver Platter Doctrine. The state said we can do nothing with 'em. You take 'em. They handed us over to the feds on a Silver Platter." Court documents describe Trent "Serious" Morris as the team's primary drug courier who negotiated deals by telephone with William "Willie G" Graham, a supplier linked with the team who had Colombian connections. Serious testified at the state murder trial that Prince confessed the entire crime to him and showed him where the bodies had been dropped. Ernesto "Puerto Rican Righteous" Piniella, who according to newspaper accounts, was head of security, didn't turn out to be very righteous. At the state trial, Piniella described how four men were tricked into coming to Baisley Projects with cocaine to sell and how they were each systematically beaten to death. Their bodies were put into plastic bags and dumped. Puerto Rican Righteous agreed to testify against Prince in exchange for a promise of a sentence of eight to sixteen years for trying to kill three police officers.

Court documents say after Morris testified against Prince in the second state murder trial, his sister-in-law and her father were killed and the first letter of Miller's nickname, "P", was carved into their torsos. The incident outraged the feds. The witnesses and their families had been put on notice—don't come forward. Tuck breaks it all down, "That is straight bullshit. None of that was ever proved and some dude admitted to the murders in 1997. They just put that all on the team to get the feds to take the case because the state was gonna have to let everyone go. Prince was acquitted of the murders and the wiretaps were all thrown out. All the feds had were the snitches who were saying anything to save their own asses."

Court documents say approximately 80 witnesses were at the federal trial, including Ernesto Piniella, Julio Hernandez, Trent Morris and Ina McGriff (no relation to Supreme), a corrupt former parole officer who traded info to the gang in exchange for sex and money. In 1987, the Supreme Team, according to court documents, was allied with another drug gang led by Lorenzo "Fat Cat" Nichols, who supplied the Supreme Team with powder cocaine. Nichols suspected two men, Henry and Issac Bolden, of robbing Nichols' organization. While Nichols was incarcerated, he sought Miller's assistance in locating the Boldens so that Nichols crew members could kill them. At the trial Ina McGriff testified that Fat Cat asked her through Miller to obtain info on the Bolden brothers to facilitate the murder, and from the Witness Protection Program which Fat Cat entered when he turned state, Fat Cat corroborated this.

The feds indicted Prince and his co-defendants on a 14-count racketeering indictment that included counts for drug-related murders, drug conspiracy and drug dealing. The drug ring that terrorized Southeastern Queens during the 1980s was indicted in a string of violent acts that included at least nine murders. Investigators described the Supreme Team as one of the busiest and bloodiest of the trafficking rings that plagued Queens at the height of the crack epidemic. Court documents say the substantive narcotic distribution charges against the defendants focused on the period from December 1989 to March 1990, during which the state was monitoring the gang's activity with wiretaps. During that period, the Supreme Team conducted its business in the Baisley Park House projects. Looking back Tuck says, "The feds can make anything look however they want. It's the United States of America versus you. That's the whole fucking United States! Their resources are unlimited. Why do you think the feds have a 99% conviction rate?"

Court documents say at the Miller trial the government presented voluminous evidence, including tapes and transcripts of more than 100 wire tapped conversation among Supreme Team members, telephone records, fingerprint evidence, photographs of assembled Supreme Team members, firearms and ammunition, narcotics paraphernalia and assorted documents. "At trial during the opening statements," Tuck says, "One of the jurors went back and told another juror, 'This trial seems just like New Jack City.' And the jurors told the judge. The judge didn't know what "New Jack City" was about, so he went out and watched the movie that night." As Tuck and them went to court, more treachery was uncovered. Julio Hernandez joined Puerto Rican Righteous and Serious as a snitch. "Julio was the only one indicted by the feds who flipped." Tuck says. "He was the only one who had access to all the floors at MCC New York. Seven South was notorious for rats and Julio was on 7 South. He swore to god he wasn't telling. He was coming to our co-defendant strategy meetings with all the lawyers. He's sitting there in the room, going back and telling the feds our trial strategy. What they call a spy in the camp."

And during the prelude to the trial the judge reported that Prince who served as his own lawyer in pretrial proceedings was making carefully orchestrated maneuvers to delay the trial as long as possible so that witnesses could be intimidated into not testifying against him. Jumping on this, authorities insisted that not only was Miller a remorseless killer, but he blended lethal wickedness with legal wiliness. It was a dangerous combination, according to the feds. In reflecting, Tuck sums it all up. "Coming up in the hood is rough. You see all types of shit and it's not pretty. Sometimes when you're young you make decisions that affect the rest of your life. You have to pay the consequences for your actions. You can't say I got to find a way out of this. Dudes want to play monopoly all day but nobody wants to go to jail. Everybody wants that 'Get out of Jail Free' card. If you're gonna play the so-called game, then play it right. When your number is called, and your number will inevitably be called, be willing to handle the jail shit just like you handle that street shit, gangsta."

The federal prosecutor was Leslie Caldwell. She had made a career of prosecuting Queens's drug dealers. She was the prosecutor who put away Fat Cat and Pappy Mason. She was ruthless in her pursuit to clean up the streets in Queens. She attributed the Supreme Teams longevity to its unhesitating use of violence. And the only place for members of the team that she said left a four-year trail of bodies and terror in South Jamaica was in the federal penitentiary.

"When I went for sentencing I was mentally prepared to do the rest of my life in prison," Tuck says. "Teddy was the first one sentenced. We were in MDC Brooklyn and he came back and told me he had thirteen. I thought he was telling me 13 life sentences. Imagine that." The gang that the feds said were responsible for 20 murders and countless shootings beat almost every single murder count. "Prince beat them all except one: facilitation of a homicide (the Bolden murder) and for the 848," Tuck says. "He damn near beat every murder except this humble shit. Big C beat seven murders, Shannon beat four and Prince beat eight and a half. They beat them shits but still got hit in the head."

"Prince was sentenced to seven life sentences. C-Just to three life's, Big C got two life's, Pookie got life, Shannon got 30 years, Bing got 19 years. Ace, 15 years, Teddy, 13 years and I got sentenced to 14 years." Tuck says. "When they gave me 14 years instead of a life sentence, I thought I was blessed." Tuck goes on. "I would never in a million years do what I've done all over again. I don't give a fuck how much money you have. No amount of money is worth 10, 15, 20 years of a life sentence. When I was younger, I didn't give a fuck. It was all about getting that paper. However, as one gets older, one's perspective on life changes. When I look back I see that all my friends are dead and none of them died of old age."

Judge Raymond Dearie, U.S. District Court Judge for the Eastern District of New York, told Tuck at sentencing, "You people have stuck together. I'll give you that. And you have proven your loyalty. I'll give you that. But there's a real high price to pay for that loyalty and you're going down in flames. I cannot understand it, but it's not for me to understand. And even if I could understand it, I could not excuse it." Are you your brother's keeper?

Convicts

Pappy Mason

Wahida Clark

Rick Ross

Fray and associates

Lorton   Supermax Florence

Seth Ferranti

Rayful Edmond   The World of Islam

WANTED
BY U.S. MARSHALS

NOTICE TO ARRESTING AGENCY: Before arrest, validate warrant through National Crime Information Center (NCIC).

United States Marshals Service NCIC entry number: (NIC/ W552151253).

NAME: FERRANTI, Seth Michael

ALIAS: JOHNSON, Michael; JOHNSON, Mike

DESCRIPTION:
Sex	MALE
Race	WHITE
Place of Birth	LEMOORE, CALIFORNIA
Date(s) of Birth	JANUARY 2, 1972
Height	6'1"
Weight	180
Eyes	HASEL
Hair	BLACK
Skintone	MEDIUM
Scars, Marks, Tattoos	TAT UL ARM BABY DEVIL
Social Security Number	....
NCIC Fingerprint Classification	19 TT 16 17 15 21 06 15 14 11

SHOULD BE CONSIDERED DANGEROUS

FERRANTI FAKED HIS SUICIDE PRIOR TO SENTENCING. HE HAS A PREVIOUS HISTORY OF DRUG ABUSE.

WANTED FOR: CONTINUING CRIMINAL ENTERPRISE
  Warrant Issued: EASTERN DISTRICT OF VIRGINIA
  Warrant Number: 9383-1019-8022-8

DATE WARRANT ISSUED: OCTOBER 8, 1992

MISCELLANEOUS INFORMATION: FERRANTI was a member of a drug distribution organization in Northern Virginia. The organization was involved in the distribution of LSD and marijuana to students at numerous high schools and universities.

If arrested or whereabouts known, notify the local United States Marshals Office. (Telephone: 703/235-2713).

If no answer, call United States Marshals Service Communications Center in Arlington, Virginia.
Telephone (800) 336-0102: (24 hour telephone contact or (800) 423-0719 (TDD). NLETS access code
is VAUSM0000.   PRIOR EDITIONS ARE OBSOLETE AND NOT TO BE USED

Form U294-151
(Rev. 4/90)

Seth Ferranti

Lamont Fridge Needum   Jose Platero, MS-13   Terrell C. Wright

Char "Shocker" Davis with daughter

Fat Cat and Pappy Mason

Shocker with homeboys from Queens

Kenneth "Supreme" McGriff

Terri Woods

Eyonne Williams   Mexican Mafia   Kwame Teague

Joe Black

Wahida Clark on left   Robert Booker, Jr.

Lorton

Michael Santos

Ron Chepesiuk

Nikki Turner

Scott Wilson

EIGHTEEN

Adventures of a
Meth Monster

"

BACK IN 1984, is when I first experienced crystal," says Big Coop, a self-proclaimed "professional tweaker" who "robbed banks on the side." This go-hard white boy and mountain of a man, is now locked up in the feds for those same telltale bank jobs. In prison, the hulking tattooed convict is usually a pretty mellow dude, except for when he is cracking heads, that is. But on the street, the dude was tripping. I'm talking certifiable meth monster.

The meth scene has traditionally been associated with white, male blue collar workers. But in this new millennium, the cheap, easy-to-make and instantly addictive crystal meth is burning a hole through America. A longtime biker staple and West Coast mainstay, meth is now surging across the nation. But this homegrown drug epidemic didn't sprout from any foreign shores like the Southeast Asian heroin Triads or the Colombian cocaine cartels. Meth was born and raised right here in the good U.S. of A. And it has long been reported as the dominant drug problem in the San Diego, California area, which happens to be the hometown and stomping grounds of Big Coop.

"San Diego, I would say, is the Meth capitol," says Cooper. "Where I am from, you can buy it almost anywhere. If you know the slang words people will know you're cool and you'll have it. If you walk up to somebody whom you think looks cool and say, 'Dude, where can I get some shit?' More likely, you'll have it within minutes."

Meth is also called crystal, go fast, crank, or dope, but Big Coop says, "The two main hip words are tweak and shit." If you go anywhere in sunny southern California crystal will be around. Coop elaborates, "In North County, Oceanside, Carlsbad, Vista, Encinitas, and Cardiff by the Sea, the tweakers rule."

Big Coop admits to snorting, slamming, and smoking meth. "Back in 1984, I snorted it up to about 1988, then I experienced slamming it, which is the ultimate. I've never been so out of it. The rush is so intense."

He says in 1993, he was introduced to smoking meth. "This is where they get calling it shit. Because that is exactly what it taste like," Big Coop reveals. The Coopster claims to be an equal opportunity meth head though, alternating between snorting, slamming, and smoking. "I've been going through the different ways of doing it. It depends on the type of people I am around at the time. I don't want to be slamming around people that don't. It just doesn't make good relations." And that is a perfect example of tweaker etiquette.

The history of meth is a storied one. It first appeared in medical literature as far back as 1887 and was propagated as a Victorian cure for narcolepsy. Years later it was being prescribed by doctors in the U.S. and abroad in an aspirin-like version as a bronchial aid. In World War II, it was widely used as a stimulant by Allied soldiers to stay awake while on duty. This led to the more modern use of meth by bikers and long-haul truckers, or by workers in any occupation that demanded long hours, mental alertness, and physical endurance.. It was either snorted or ingested in a pharmaceutical tablet-form.

For a long time, stretching from the '60s to the '80s, meth was largely underground and referred to as crank because it was hidden in the crank cases of motorcycle engines. It was largely a biker drug.

Brown colored, harsh on the sinuses, and crude. But finally in the 80s, a smokeable version appeared and thus was born the age of the tweakers. A once largely underground scene with limited cooks and chefs as they are called has exploded. The Internet boasts over 300 websites, which have detailed instructions on how to obtain all the ingredients necessary for making meth. Most of these fixings can be picked up at the local drugstore and home-supply shop. And recipes on how to cook it all up are all over the Internet.

Big Coop says, that meth "looks like a bunch of shattered glass. But then again it depends on where and whom you get it from. Different people make it different ways." The main ingredient is ephedrine, which is found in decongestants like Sudafed and Drixoral. This substance is easily whipped up in mom and pop shops, kitchens, and makeshift labs. Battery acid, liquid fertilizer, iodine, drain cleaner, lye, paint thinner, lantern fuel, and anti-freeze are the toxic solvents, which the nonprescription cold drugs are cooked up in. The cooking process is a volatile one, though, and explosions are known to occur. The compounds used can burn your skin off like acid. Many cooks have been burned, or worse, they have been killed when their labs have blown up.

And the police hate these labs also because they have to wear full-body hazmat protection suits when they raid those toxic-waste sites. The type of meth varies with the cook and solvents used. "I've had red, yellow, green, blue," Big Coop says. "It's all in how and what they rinse it with and the quality of the chemicals."

And prices vary and so, depending on the quality or who you know. "You can get a quarter gram for $20, but you try not to go that route because you get a better deal buying like an eight ball, which in some places you can get for $150," Big Coop says. "If you don't know anybody though, you can end up paying $100 for a gram." That's the break for being a tweaker.

So basically, the profit for a cook is 100 percent. No overhead, no Colombians or Triads to pay off, and the product can be made in the household's kitchen, that is, if you don't mind turning your kitchen into a potential disaster or toxic-waste dump. Coop says, "You get the best meth right after it is finished being made. You can't get no better." He concludes though, "You have to be careful on the amount you do, because some is more potent then others, depending on the qualities of chemicals being used. Everybody's recipe is different."

The effects of meth have been described as euphoric. It brings on a feeling of exhilaration and a sharpening of focus, with occasional episodes of sudden and violent behavior, intense paranoia, and visual and auditory sensations. That is why it is called tweaking, because people on meth are literally tweaking out of their minds. "It was such an exciting high," Big Coop says. "Everything was at a fast pace. The buzz was intense, full of energy, your mind constantly on go, go, go."

If you did a little line, you would be good for at least two of the three hours, and I've got to say it's the best weight loss program around," relates Coop. "You never have an appetite and don't even think about sleeping. When I was slamming, I once stayed up for 26 days."

Medical reports claim meth has a neurotoxin effect on users, damaging brain cells that contain dopamine and serotonin. It causes increased heart rates and blood pressure and can cause irreversible damage to blood vessels in the brain. Short term effects include irritability, insomnia, confusion, tremors, convulsions, anxiety, and aggressiveness. But for real- who's worried about some little chemicals in the bloodstream? Not Big Coop.

The Coopster says, "I became a tweaking bum. You talk about seeing shit, everything that wasn't supposed to be there was. Your mind would definitely play tricks on you after about a week of tweaking." And when you get a bunch of tweaking methheads together- it's not a matter of what they're going to do, it's a matter of what they're waiting to do. It's like Big Coop says, "Even if nothing is happening, as far as, activity, you still don't want to sleep for the simple reason that you might miss out on something that might happen. It's like the crowd of people I hung with. We were always together waiting for the same thing, something, anything, to happen."

According to published numbers, there are almost 10 million who've tried meth in this country. That is a hell of a lot of people tweaking out. Big Coop relates, "Everybody and their mothers are tweaking in San Diego. I honestly believe it's the way of life there." And apparently it's becoming the way of life in other parts of the country also. Meth is the new drug of choice for white, middle-class and rural America. It makes crack look like baby food. There is even a Top 40 song about meth that was in regular rotation on MTV a couple years back.

I wish I could get back there/some place back there
Smilin in the pictures you would take/doing crystal meth
It will lift you up until you break/it won't stop
I won't come down/I keep stock
With a tic tock rhythm and a bump for a drop
Then I bumped up/I took the hit I was given
Then I bumped again/I bumped again
-Semi-Charmed-Kinda-Life, 3rd Eye Blind

"All in all, my life has been pretty good, except for holding a job," Big Coop says. "After being on meth for as long as I've been you don't want to work. Once you become a tweaker, all your ambition is gone. Your mind is going 1,000 RPM's, but as soon as you decide to do something, you're over it just as fast." That is the price to pay if you want to be a tweaker and meth monster extraordinaire.

But it's not like it's all bad. Doing meth for weeks has its benefits. "By the end of the week you're basically starting your hallucinations. Some people are ready for bed. Well, those who can't hang with the big dawgs. Myself, I'm a 3 (weeker) tweaker," Coop says, with a smile.

His piercing blue eyes staring right through you, permanently frazzled from years of meth abuse. He continues, "Most people are mentally run down, tired of it. But if you are a true tweaker, you don't let the small shit bother you." Yeah, the small shit like motherfucking heart attack. But that is why Big Coop is the Meth Monster.

One of the big side effects of meth is the paranoia experienced by users. Crystal can over-excite the central nervous system to the point where a user feels paranoid, fearful, and anxious. Heavy users can experience psychotic episodes, medical jargon for losing touch with reality. Big Coop relates an episode, "I had just finished doing a blast, and I had to go pick someone up from the airport. Anyway I was a little late, so I decided to drive faster. I got pulled over by the police for doing 110 mph. Man, I was zooming out of my head, sweat pouring and my wife beater soaking wet."

He continues: "I know I had to look guilty as hell when the man came to my window, and asked for my license, which I didn't have. So he tells me to get out of the car, searches it and finds nothing. Luckily, I was carrying my stash inside the bottom cuff of my pants leg, but the police didn't know that, so he let me go with a speeding ticket. But I was paranoid as fuck. The whole time I was thinking of just running off the highway, leaving the car and all. Fuck it, you know."

Methheads are known to be super paranoid, and have a tendency to compulsively clean and groom, and repetitively sort and disassemble objects, such as cars, and other mechanical devices. Like this one tweaker Big Coop knew. "He was always taking apart his vacuum cleaner, swearing that there were bugs in it. He said he could hear the coded transmissions, and that big brother was onto him. So we would take apart the vacuum cleaner, literally hundreds of times, and spend all night putting it back together again."

It seems that meth permanently hijacks user's judgment. The meth fiend wallows in a binge-tweak cycle, which encompasses rage, delusions, and spontaneous violence. Meth, which some consider a mixture of laundry detergent, and lighter fluid, can lead to paranoia, or even worst, a wave of lurid crimes.

Big Coop is in federal prison for robbing banks. He was convicted on five counts. But he wasn't robbing the banks because of his meth addiction. He was robbing banks for the buzz. "When I started robbing banks the buzz was out of this world," he says. "It was like I was unstoppable. I had no worries, money to spend and tweak to do."

When asked if the bank robberies were meth induced, Big Coop replies, "Yes and no. Yes, because I've been using meth for almost 20 years. No, because I wasn't robbing banks for money to spend on tweak. I've always had all the shit I wanted." Big Coop says, he robbed banks, because "he found out how easy it was." He relates how he would "meet the newspaper guy when they filled the machines at like 4 a.m. just to see if my picture was in the paper," tweaking out of his mind, of course.

But tweaking wasn't the best way to rob banks, as Big Coop explains, "My first bank I robbed, that was pretty sketchy. Well, I didn't actually get to rob that one. I was all mind set to do the job, but when I walk in, there was like five tellers and no customers, and all the tellers turn their heads and look at me."

He continues, "I didn't know what to do, so I continued to the counter and asked for nickel, penny, and quarter rolls. I guess the way I looked (all tweaked out) caused panic, because the guard approached me and asked if everything was alright."

Big Coop sits there all casual like, smoking a cigarette in his too big hands, pausing for a moment and looking out the barred window of the prison cell. This huge, almost child-like, tattooed-convict seems to be reflecting, but then he turns with his two blue eyes beaming and the edge of a crazy smile on his face as he concludes, "Imagine being all tweaked out with the intentions of robbing the bank, and the guard pulls you to the side. I just about pissed my pants. But that didn't stop me, I went the next day and robbed another bank."

NINETEEN

Life and Times of a Suburban Drug Dealer

I DON'T KNOW why I became a drug dealer. Free drugs I suppose. It wasn't something I planned. It just happened. I used to buy quarter ounces of weed or hits of acid from my god brother and his friends. They had a party house by Springfield Mall. I was always cruising over to score. I was like seventeen and these dudes were all twenty-one or so. I idolized them. They didn't work or nothing. Just hung out, partied, got laid, and sold drugs.

I was bringing them crazy business. Finally I said fuck it. I can do this myself. But I needed some contacts. I asked my god brother to hook me up and he took me down to Kentucky. It was a long trip but worth it. My god brother introduced me to country boy Scott, who became my contact. He had a tobacco farm down in Monticello and grew a little weed on the side. He didn't fuck around though. He and his partners had it down to a science. These guys were straight-up country. I'm talking shotguns, moonshine, cockfights, muscle cars, and pit bulls. They planted and cultivated their weed to perfection. They showed me a patch once, way out in the deep forest. I thought they might try to kill and rob me and leave me buried out there. But they didn't. Their marijuana plants were like trees, easily fifteen-feet tall, with tree size trucks, and an IV-bag mainlined into the roots pumping in plant vitamins. It was some crazy fucking shit.

I still needed an LSD source though. My god brother said, "Go on tour dude."

The first Grateful Dead show I went to was in Deer Park, Indiana. I drove there from Fairfax with some Deadhead wanna-bes. I wasn't really into The Dead, music wise, but I needed an LSD connect. Dead shows were filled with LSD peddlers. The parking lot scene was a carnival, half circus, half flea market, with drugs, tie-dyes, hippies everywhere. I met this kid, Drummer Al, a hardcore Deadhead who was at all the Dead shows. They called him Drummer Al because he was always in the drum pit banging on the congas. This dude was skinny and really burnt out, with natty dreadlocks to his waist. He wore cut-off fatigues and Birkenstocks, but never wore a shirt. He sold me 2,000 hits of triple-set, blotter acid and gave me a number to call in Frisco to order more whenever I needed it. Mail-order LSD was only a phone call away. What an awesome connection, I thought. I figured that, with the Kentucky bud contact and the new mail order acid, my fortune was made.

Back home in Virginia things were jumping. I was becoming very popular. "You got the kind dude?" Someone asked. "Fuck yeah." Everyone welcomed me to the party. The scene was straight suburbia—Burke Centre, Fairfax County, 1988- hot chicks, cool dudes and imported brewskies and Stolis. REM blasted on the stereo. All was enjoyed in the confines of somebody's parents' house. I greeted the hostess, an exotic looking brunette with large brown eyes and creamy olive skin who was a freshman at Penn State. She was wearing a tight black dress that stuck to her curvy, lithe form and magnified the prominence of her breasts, which seemed to jut out at me. "Steph, where's the folks?" I inquired, trying not to stare at her tits.

"They're at the beach house, dude, all weekend." She beamed. "You can stay here if you want." She said with a hint of smile. Cool, I thought. I can set up shop and possibly hook up with Stephanie.

Everyone had money and everyone wanted drugs. Luckily, I was holding. I had the kind from Kentucky and the blue unicorn trips from Cali. Like the bluegrass state, I was open for business.

I made money but I spent it just as fast. It just seeped through my hands like water. More Becks for the party? Okay. I got it. Order Domino's pizza. No problem. A little trip to the Union Street Bar and Grill. Don't worry. I got the tab.

I would take my inner circle of friends out to eat at Red Lobster or wherever. It was always my treat. I was the king of my own court and I was always decked out. I bought Eddie Bauer, Polo shirts, Timberland boots, Doc Martins, Air Jordans, and whatever new CDs or Sega Genesis games came out. Shopping was an everyday thing. I would buy something, wear it once, and give it away.

And the drugs—I smoked weed constantly, like cigarettes. I loved going to parties and busting out a Cheech-and-Chong size joint. "Fucking hell, dude." They would say. "Is that all weed?" I would smile with satisfaction as I nodded my head and lit the stogie. I enjoyed being the man.

It wasn't long before drugs became my whole life. I bought them. I sold them. I lived them. In '89 I graduated from Robinson High School. It was a blast but it was time to move on. I was still living at home and I'm sure my parents knew what was going on, but not to the full extent. One time I gave my mom twelve grand to hold for me. She was like "Where'd you get this?" I told her I orchestrated a couple of drug deals. "Well you better not do it anymore," she said. I promised her I wouldn't. But I was lying because I was already planning on getting the next load, then cashing out and re-upping. I thought I was a businessman, a professional drug dealer. It was like I had a career or something.

As my clientele grew, so did my cash flow. I started looking for other sources and reached out to my Robinson High School buddy Zane who attended the University of Texas at Arlington. This guy was a first-class stoner. I'm talking weed connoisseur. He had his shit together though. He went to University of Texas full-time and managed a little bar-restaurant at night. He was a solid dude.

I would fly down to Dallas and cop thirty-pound loads of commercial-grade brick pot from Zane's source, Mexican Eddie. I would then wrap the bricks in hefty bags, pack them in my suitcase, and check it through baggage for my flight back to DC. I would pay someone $500 to pick up the load from the luggage carousel at DC National just in case there was any problem.

This proved to be a sweet connect as Mexican Eddie had a trucking company based in Matamoros, Mexico. He brought in five-hundred pound loads. He was always on. The weed wasn't as good as the Kentucky bud, but it was cheaper at $500 a pound. And it moved fast for $1,500 a pound. I also got it on the front so I didn't have to pay for it until I sold it.

This guy Mexican Eddie was a trip too. He had this apartment in Dallas where he entertained his customers and finalized deals. This place was jumping like twenty-four hours a day. Every time I went there, no matter what time it was, there was this fucking mariachi band playing their Mexican asses off in sombreros and Mexican bowtie suits. It was crazy. Mexican Eddie would be hooping and hollering like Speedy Gonzales, as some Latinas made burritos and served Coronas. A couple of big vatos stood in the background all silent like, acting as Mexican Eddie's personal bodyguards. I could never get over the sight of the mariachi band though at 2:00 a.m. in the morning playing loudly in the apartment's living room. It was like a Tijuana mescalin trip or something.

Most of my friends were at colleges now and they all wanted drugs. So I started hauling loads up to the universities. I had a set route. I used to drive south down Interstate 81 in Virginia from Fairfax to Radford and Virginia Tech where the Miller brothers took care of business for me. The older brother was an acid freak who moved crazy

LSD at Tech. The younger one attended Radford. His thing was pot and women. He hooked me up with a new cutie every time I rolled in. I would drop off Kentucky green. Brick pot. Acid. And I collected whatever money they had for me as I frolicked with whatever girl was at hand. I would then cut through the Cumberland Gap into Kentucky and meet up with country boy Scott, who always wanted trips to sell at Eastern Kentucky University.

Then I would drive north up Interstate 75 to Lexington and the University of Kentucky where this spacey, psych major Brandon bought acid and kind bud. Then I drove east to West Virginia University in Morgantown where my buddies in the Delta Fraternity sold drugs for me. This was definitely my biggest market and a major party place. I would stop and see the hot brunette Steph at Penn State, who knew a lot of dudes who could move a lot of drugs, before going back to Fairfax. At each stop it was like, "What do you got dude? Here's the money."

For a while I had this girl Kristi running drugs with me. She would do most of the driving and when I drove she would give me blowjobs. She was also a nymphomaniac and was up for sex whenever, a real dream girl. We did have some close calls on the road though, such as when a Virginia State Trooper pulled right up behind us on Interstate 81 when we were carrying. "You don't think he saw the joint, do you?" Kristi asked me.

"I don't know. Just drive normal," I told her. "And think of white light. Only white light. It will make us seem innocent." Kristi put the joint in the ashtray and turned down the car stereo.

"Are you thinking of white light?" I asked as the five-O flicked on his lights. Momentarily we were gripped with panic, but then the cruiser switched lanes and rocketed past us. Kristi laughed as she grabbed the joint, fired it up, and turned up the thumping bass lines of NWA's "Fuck the Police." I really loved Kristi, but eventually she dumped me for heroin.

Trip parties were also a big event in Fairfax, especially in the summer time when everyone was home from school. A house was always available as people's parents went on vacation. I would make sure to invite everyone and supply the acid. I convinced this girl Shawnthia to throw a trip party one weekend when her parentals cruised. She was a pretty blond chick from Robinson who just graduated. The party was crazy. The techno music was pumping LA Style's "James Brown is Dead" as we held our own mini rave. Everyone was dosed out, chilling, but this one dude started freaking.

"Fuck dude, I'm like totally tripping," he said. "It's like the colors are in my head, but they're floating and they're falling. I'm drowning in colors. They're everywhere. Don't you see them?" Shawnthia and I laughed as we tripped on the dude wigging out. I decided to make my play, so I grabbed Shawnthia's hand and pulled her into a bedroom. "What are you doing?" She asked.

"Trying to get some privacy," I answered as I guided her head down to my crotch. "Oh," she said, as she unbuttoned my jeans.

I loved my life. I was like a rock star. Drugs, girls, money, blowjobs. What more could I want? I was nineteen and on top of the world. Never in my wildest dreams did I think I would get busted. I mean, I was no criminal. I was from the suburbs. And I was white. They never busted people from the suburbs, especially not white kids. But I was wrong.

I was in Hawaii when I heard about the cop. The younger Miller brother was making moves via the mail-order LSD contact. Word was that a 16-year-old Reston boy tripping on LSD shot and wounded a Fairfax County police officer, Darryl McEachern. The pig chased the kid down while breaking up a field party in Clifton. Apparently the punk was running naked through the woods.

Somehow he snatched the cop's gun and shot him in the chest. Miller told me that our buddy Dave, a long haired metal dude, had sold the acid to the 16-year- old. We were fucked.

Soon thereafter, Dave the metal dude started working with the cops and upon my arrival in Fairfax, Miller and I were lured into a sting operation and arrested by undercover Fairfax County narc Mike Sullivan. This kid Scott, a small insecure kid who Miller was breaking in, was arrested with us. We were charged with LSD conspiracy by the state of Virginia.

The DEA was called into interrogate us. DEA task force agent Joe Woolf explained that the DEA was well aware of all my dealings and that if I gave up the shipment of LSD I had stashed they would make it worth my while. I told him, "I'm not saying anything until I see a lawyer." He yelled back, "Oh, yeah, well your lawyer's gonna want to suck my dick."

My parents bailed me out of Fairfax County jail, putting up their house to secure the bond. They were angry though. The DEA had ransacked our house, but no drugs turned up. Then disaster struck. Scott, the new kid, under pressure, cracked, confessing to police that he was holding 100 sheets of acid for me in his basement bedroom. It was time to see that lawyer.

My mother suggested this lawyer Michael Reiger. She had heard he was a hotshot criminal attorney. Not knowing any better, I agreed. In my first consultation with Reiger, he pressed me to tell him the whole story. So I did. I gave him six grand cash as a retainer. "This isn't drug money, is it," he asked.

"Like you fucking care?" I retorted. In my opinion there wasn't much to the case. I expected leniency because I was from the affluent suburb of Burke Centre and had no criminal record. I thought maybe I'd have to go into a drug rehab or something. My attorney, Mr. Reiger, seemed to take the whole affair lightly. But I hadn't taken into account the revenge factor of the Fairfax County Police Department.

At the urging of the Fairfax County Police, the case went federal. They portrayed me as an arrogant hothead who flaunted cash and sold LSD to unsuspecting high school students. The evidence against me consisted of fingerprints on the acid blotter paper and various written records of drug transactions. Mr. Reiger insisted we needed a federal lawyer to assist him. So I hired Tom Carter. The first time I met Tom Carter, he informed me that Christine Wright, the U.S. Attorney, was going to indict me on seven different ten-to-life counts consisting of LSD conspiracy and distribution charges. He counseled that I plead guilty to a Continuing Criminal Enterprise charge that carried a mandatory-minimum twenty-year sentence and that I cooperate with the government. The CCE charge was known as the drug-kingpin charge, something they would have slammed on Scarface. It didn't look good.

Following Mr. Carter's advice I pled guilty but I wasn't going to cooperate and I had no intention of serving any time. I always said I'd rather die than go to prison. I started making plans. One of the stipulations of my plea bargain was that I was to be released on bail. Judge Claude Hilton conducted my plea proceedings at the Alexandria Federal Courthouse in Old Town, Alexandria, on August 28, 1991. "How do you plead?" He demanded.

"Guilty." I answered.

"All right then," he concluded. "The court formally accepts your plea. You are released on bond until sentencing on December 13, 1991." I planned on being long gone by then.

My homecoming after the guilty plea was difficult. My parents were angry and disappointed in me. My mom, a religious woman, was particularly devastated. My dad, the military type, was standoffish, offended. I remember my mom crying, telling me I needed to pray to the Lord for guidance. Between her tears I decided all I needed was some luck to get the hell out of there. Luck and a solid bong hit.

I began to prepare for my flight. I had to be careful so as not to raise any suspicions. Christine Wright, the U.S. Attorney, was particularly fanatical about the case. Her nipples seemed to pop out of her shirt whenever she discussed the possibility of inflicting misery on others.

Her diabolical aura made her seem like a female Darth Vader. I felt like Luke Skywalker fighting the dark side of the force. The evil factions of the United States Government were arrayed against me, as I attempted to escape their clutches.

I contemplated suicide, but the prospect of death was terrifying so I decided to stage my suicide instead so the feds would think I was dead, throwing them off my trail and making my transition to a new life easier. If I never turned up, I would be declared legally dead in seven years. It was a good idea I thought.

Great Falls was the place where I would pretend to die. I had it all planned out. I would stage my suicide and then split. Great Falls was a National Park frequented by tourists and kayakers. Vast cliffs towered over the rushing Potomac and the jagged rocks below where class-IV rapids ran wild, representing the most accessible whitewater river in the world. I pictured my body being smashed and mangled against the rocks in the whitewater frenzy as it washed out to the Atlantic Ocean.

I left my wheels in the parking lot for the U.S. Park Police to find. On the banks of the Potomac, near where the Great Falls were crashing down, I left a half-empty bottle of Stoli's vodka, my jacket and wallet, everything necessary to establish my identity. I left a note in the Subaru—

Journey to the center of the star ain't that far
Boundaries are limitless in my head Now I'm dead
Such a tender young imagination Adds to my frustration
I crave death
Death is my maker
So ends the journey of a lost soul
Wrong person Wrong place
Wrong time

The note captured my feelings exactly. I'd rather have died than have gone to jail. The prospect of spending my youth in prison was too much for me to handle. My whole world had crumbled so quickly.

I just wanted to escape the situation. I felt so empty inside as all my hopes and dreams turned to dust. I was left with only one aspiration: To run.

As I walked away from the Potomac, I walked away from my shattered life. "Let's go." I told my god brother who drove me to DC National Airport to begin my life on the lam.

I flew to LA where an old girlfriend, Nancy, took me in. She was kind of slutty but sexy and pretty. Not too bright though. She lived at Point Magoo, a Navy Port, up the coast from LA. Her dad was the XO on the base. Her folks didn't know I was a fugitive.

This was the start of my fugitive lifestyle. I lived under a series of false identities, zigzagging from Hollywood to Dallas to St. Louis. At first I experienced extreme paranoia. I was always looking over my shoulder. I thought the feds were waiting around every corner to arrest me and take me to prison. It was all mental though. There were no feds, only me and my paranoid delusions.

For the first couple of weeks after my arrival in Cali, Nancy and I scoured the Washington papers for news of my disappearance. It was strange seeing the headline news in the Metro Section of the Washington Post, "Fairfax LSD Kingpin Missing: Suicide Note found in car." As I read the article I became distraught. Law enforcement officials had declared my suicide a hoax after the park police made an extensive search of the area and found no evidence of a body. It appeared my ruse was up.

When my cashflow ran out I ended up in Texas. My old buddy Zane put me up. He reacquainted me with Mexican Eddie and I started moving some brick weed. Zane's friends at UT were good customers but you can't make money selling weed in Texas. It's too cheap and plentiful. I was selling quarters to the Harrigans crowd when I met Jeff, a sleepy eyed, mellow guitar playing stoner who cooked at the restaurant. He started helping me make moves and I eventually found out he was from St. Louis. So I proposed a little trip.

We took twenty pounds of brick pot up to Missouri. The shit flew out the door. At a grand mark-up per pound, the market was good. Through Jeff I met Dan the Man, who had a glass blowing business and made some killer pipes and laid-back Dave who was a senior at the University of Missouri in Columbia. Both of those dudes moved some serious weight. It looked like my fortune was rising again. I went by Christopher Hoss. I had different fake ID's with the first name Christopher so when people asked my last name I said Hoss to avoid confusion. It sounded like a Texas name.

Dallas to St. Louis became my new smuggling route. I was running up twenty-pound loads every other week. The loot was rolling in as I started hanging with the TGI Friday party crowd. I was actually getting over all that paranoia shit. Then disaster struck again.

I got arrested in a Burger King parking lot with my partner, Jeff the Cook. The cops found a half-pound of weed in his truck. We were taken to St. Charles County Jail and got bailed out. Per procedure they ran my prints and all hell broke loose.

From watching episodes of "Cops" and "America's Most Wanted", I figured it would take two to three months for my prints to match up. What I didn't count on was my U.S. Marshal's top-fifteen status. My prints matched up in three days and the U.S. Marshal's Special Fugitive Task Force, led by Marshal Luke Adler, were hot on my trail.

Why was I top fifteen? Apparently this federali, Henry Hudson, was one of the U.S. Attorney's handling my original case in Virginia, and when I fled, I represented the black mark on his otherwise distinguished record. Coincidentally, Mr. Hudson left the U.S. Attorney's Office soon thereafter to head the U.S. Marshal's Service. Mr. Hudson moved my case to the Most Wanted list, making it among the marshal's top investigative priorities. This was another case of the revenge factor working against me

On October 1, 1993, at 6:45 a.m., U.S. Marshal Luke Adler and the Special Fugitive Task Force busted into my Econolodge motel room in Bridgeton, Missouri, and captured me. I was kind of half expecting it because in the preceding days I could feel them closing in on me. Jeff the Cook had turned himself into the marshals and became an informant. So due to his snitching ass, I was cut off from my clientele, friends, and money. I was stuck in the hotel room with eighteen pounds of pot that I couldn't sell. So I tried smoking it.

It was a relief to be caught. I could be myself again. No more fake ID's. No more running from state to state. No more making up phony stories to protect my identity. And at last, I could call mom.

I was taken to the North County Federal Detention Center. As soon as I was able, I phoned my mother. It was an emotional phone call. I hadn't talked to her for almost two years. She had been repeatedly harassed by the U.S. Marshal's during my absence. They threatened her, trying to get her to give information of my whereabouts, information she didn't have. She assured me everything would be okay. She would pray for me and call my lawyers. It was good just to hear her voice. "See you soon mom," I said. As I hung up the phone, I felt tears on my cheek.

I was extradited back to Virginia and brought before the judge. Amid the spectators attending my sentencing, I spotted my mother and gave her a smile. U.S. Attorney Timothy Shea told the judge I was a machine-gun- toting skinhead-LSD-marijuana freak who corrupted society and deserved to go to prison for life. My lawyer, Mr. Reiger, countered that I was a drug- addict mixed-up kid who fell in with the wrong crowd, but that I was really a good person at heart who wanted to change for the better. I felt more like a victim of circumstance, guilty only of being the wrong person in the wrong place at the wrong time. But I don't think any of that mattered to the judge.

Judge Hilton tried not to look bored as he contemplated my fate. His countenance grew grim as he shuffled some papers and pronounced my sentence. "You will be committed to the custody of the Attorney

General for a term of three-hundred-and-four months." After doing the math, I realized I had a twenty-five year sentence—more time than how old I was.

TWENTY

When Crack was King

"The city ain't been the same since then, especially with that bitchass Rayful telling. It almost seems as if he made it a fad. I definitely blame him for that."
-The DC Hustler

WASHINGTON DC WILL forever be known as the Murder Capital of the United States because of the drug violence during the crack era. The drug trade bred killers, and Dodge City in the late 80's was a virtual war zone with bodies dropping left and right on a daily basis. The shootouts, drivebys and execution-style killings were reminiscent of the brutal tactics used by Chicago gangsters in the 1920's. Thirteen people were even killed by gunfire in a 24-hour period on February 14, 1989, a clear reminder of the St. Valentine's Day Massacre in Chicago 70 years before when seven henchmen of gangster Bugs Moran were shot to death by Al Capone's gun thugs. And like the Capone-era thugs, many of the crack era gangsta's had huge egos and boasted of their exploits after seeing them depicted on TV shows like DC's "City under Siege."

Crack hit DC in 1986 and its effects were immediate. When crack became king, the streets of Chocolate City turned much deadlier. The police lost control of the neighborhoods and Washington became a mecca for crack cocaine, enabling dealers to become more feared than cops. Rival dealers spilt blood, dying everyday for drug turf and spraying DC's poor black neighborhoods with automatic gunfire, killing one another and painting the city with death. As crack tore through DC and people got hooked, crack babies, homelessness, carjackings, home robberies, kidnappings, lost homes, jobs and families became commonplace. Most of the drug dealers, drug users and victims of the drug-related murders were young black men, and the young black man who came to personify the city's drug wars was Rayful Edmond.

"Rayful was balling, but he wasn't like they made him out to be. A lot of that was for the media and public. He was just the wrong nigga in the wrong place at the wrong time." Mr. T, DC Blacks gang leader.

Rayful Edmond was a baller, as in world class baller. His flashy life style made him famous on District streets and his crack empire, which spanned four years, generated $2 million a week at its peak. The flourishing business afforded its young executives a style of life well beyond their working-class origins. And Rayful was president and CEO. His life consisted of flashy cars like Mercedes- Benz, BMW's, Porsches and a Jaguar convertible with gold-inlaid hubcaps and bling like a $45,000 Rolex watch on his wrist, $25,000 pendants, a 3-carat diamond stud in his ear and a $15,000 diamond covered cross around his neck. Does your chain hang low? Rayful's did. He took all expenses paid trips with his crew to the Super Bowl in San Diego, Mike Tyson fights in Atlantic City and Vegas title fights. $25,000 shopping sprees at Trump Plaza, Rodeo Drive in Beverly Hills and Gucci or Hugo Boss stores in chauffeured limousines were the norm too. Dom Perignon champagne flowed at trendy nightclubs and the flamboyant dresser made cash purchases totaling $457,000 over two years from Linea Pitti, a pricey Italian men's boutique in Georgetown. And this was just on suits, clothes and $600 shoes.

The king of cocaine was a folk hero to the city's youth and passed out $100 bills like candy to kids in his M Street neighborhood. They gawked at Edmond, his fabulous clothes, his glittery girls, his stylish cars and the famous basketball players like Alonzo Mourning who were his friends. Rayful was a charmer who was seen as a modern day Robin Hood. When his city-league basketball team played in area tournaments, the gym was filled with admiring young woman and adoring kids. The 6-foot, 190 lb. sweet shooting guard was an affable, courteous and intelligent young man who attributed his affluent life style to his winnings from gambling. He was a high roller who loved to gamble at craps tables and the numbers. Edmond liked the streets, he liked running around, people talking about him and women chasing him. He liked spending nights at high-stakes crap games and being the center of attention and adoration of the whole city. But he also had a darker side, rooted in the vicious crack cocaine trade that caused a drug crisis in the city like never before.

Open-air drug bazaars and the grotesque killings that plagued the city's spiraling drug trade, couriers going to LA by plane to buy kilos of coke carrying suitcases stuffed with, so much cash they could barely be lifted and seizures by law enforcement totaling nearly $4 million in cash were the lore of Rayful's reign. His exploits were legendary in the city where stories about his crew's drug dealing and penchant for violence that led to Rayful being linked to as many as 30 killings were rampant. As a big wheel of the drug trade he became a role model and employer of the area's youth, who, with the promise of fast money, became street dealers, lookouts or runners and made thousands a week. Edmond even had t-shirts made for his crew with his 'Top of the Line' slogan. Edmond spared no expenses and picked up legal fees, if necessary, or funeral expenses for soldiers gunned down in the line of duty. Network members were almost always represented by paid lawyers, an unusual sight in DC Superior Court for youths with no visible signs of employment and the deceased's families were taken care of and provided for.

"Rayful was very generous," a prosecutor said. "He provided his people with the avenue to get all their acquisitions. It was the lure of money that made them turn a blind eye to the immorality of the drugs and death around them and embrace the business wholeheartedly." And Edmond made mind-boggling sums of money. He had so much money coming in that he once recalled having $15 million in denominations ranging from 100s to 5's at one time in his house. Despite his millions he had no bank accounts, checkbooks, ledgers, money orders or cars, houses or apartments in his name. "That's the way the police catch you." He said.

"He's the Babe Ruth of crack dealing," U.S. Attorney Eric Holder said at the time. When a detective tried to serve him with a grand jury subpoena in connection with a shooting, Edmond arranged to meet the detective at a certain time on a street corner. "Exactly at that time, Rayful pulled up in a white stretch limo with a driver," the detective reported. And city educators knew about Rayful too. "The youth of this city know more about Rayful Edmond than great civil rights leaders," a District high school teacher complained. And she was right. The man, who was so fresh he got three haircuts a week and who 20/20 called the $300 million dollar man, has gone down in infamy. His story, one of brutality, power, money, murder and betrayal, deserves its place in the annals of the black American gangster. And here it is, straight from the penitentiary, The Rayful Edmond story, uncut and uncensored.

"I was real jazzy. I'm like, let's try to have a lot of class." Rayful Edmond

"They said he had fags up in the limo." Da Kid from SE

"I made between 35 to 40 million easy." Rayful Edmond

"They said slim had some rather homosexual tendencies." The DC Hustler

"Just having a lot of street knowledge and being honest and putting a lot of work into it." Rayful Edmond on building his crack empire.

"Rayful Edmond is no hero. He is simply a thug with a wasted past and a hopeless future." The City's Top Prosecutor said.

A 43-count indictment filed on June 20, 1989 charged Edmond along with 29 others, with a variety of narcotics related activities, weapons offenses, murder and other crimes of violence in regards to the operation of a large scale cocaine distribution conspiracy. At trial the government presented evidence that Edmond led a group of family members and friends who conspired to distribute large amounts of cocaine in the NE Washington neighborhood where many of them lived and where Edmond grew up. Court records indicate that those involved in the conspiracy were Edmond; his friends, Melvin Butler and Tony Lewis; Edmonds half-brother, Emmanual "Mangie" Sutton; his half-sister, Bernice "Niecey" McGraw and her husband David Mc-Graw; Edmonds cousin, Johnny Monford; Edmonds aunt, Armaretta Perry; and Edmonds sister's boyfriend Jerry Millington; along with Antonio "Tonio" Jones, Keith "Cheese" Cooper, Columbus "Little Nut" Daniels; Edmonds mother, Bootsie Perry and other relatives and associates.

"It was run just like a major corporation." a detective said. "You had the chairman of the board and it went down from there." Many of the family members supervised the retail side of the street operations, which included counting the money, packaging and distributing the cocaine destined for the open-air market at Orleans Place NE. Rayful's grandmothers house at 407 M St NE served as the networks headquarters, and law enforcement officials said his "organization was as slick and well run as McDonalds. Crack was available any time of day or night and dealers had customers form lines that stretched one hundred buyers long." Rayful was allegedly responsible for 60 percent of the District's cocaine market in the late 80's and he ran his organization with careful precision.

According to the government's evidence, the conspiracy involved a multi-layered operation. Its focus was on a two block area of Morton Place and Orleans Place NE, known as the Strip, which Edmond ran and maintained from 1986 through 1989. In operating the drug business, sellers, paid by the day or week, worked in 8-hour shifts. Demand for drugs along the Strip was so intense during that period that sellers sometimes sold out their supplies within minutes. Individuals dubbed lieutenants of the organization, including Cooper and Sutton, supplied dealers and even juveniles with bundles of cocaine, collected money from them and shouted warnings when police entered the area. These lieutenants, along with Millington, Jones and Monford, supervised the Strip, controlling the supply of cocaine and overseeing sellers. To supply the Strip several family members of Edmond, including David and Bernice McGraw and Armaretta Perry, packaged cocaine at various sites. Once packaged, the cocaine was stored at various houses and apartments of the conspirators, court records indicate.

The government also presented evidence that the Edmond organization-acted as a drug wholesaler. According to the government, the Edmond network received the cocaine that fueled its activities from Colombia through a series of transactions with Melvin Butler in California. The government presented evidence that Edmond associates Royal Brooks, Alta Rae Zanville, Tony Lewis and Edmond himself made trips to LA in the late 80's to arrange for and pay for shipments of cocaine to Washington. Tony Lewis and Edmond pooled their money to finance million dollar multi-kilogram cocaine purchases from LA groups, including the Crips, who served as brokers for the Cali Cartel. The two youthful drug lords also formed a loose syndicate in DC with other major dealers in an effort to quell the violence bloodying the drug markets, court records indicate. But the violence associated with Edmonds crew couldn't be averted and it would eventually come to a head.

But how did Rayful get his start?

"If Rayful had all that money, how come his pops got busted with a punkass couple of kilos in Virginia after he got popped." Said Mr. T.

"I am not the person the U.S. government is trying to make me out to be." Rayful Edmond said. "A lot of kids from my community, they look up to me and think I was right for selling drugs. I want them to know I was wrong."

"Rayful comes from a long line of hustlers," Mr. T says. And police concur, reporting that the Edmond family was linked to old-time drugs and numbers rings, which operated in the 1950s and 1960s. "He learned the business from his relatives at an early age. That includes counting money and holding drugs." Mr. T continues. Prosecutors alleged that Edmonds father gave his son his start in the drug business in 1986 with a kilogram of cocaine, which Edmond flipped, setting up the foundations of his operations at Orleans and Morton Place, which are short, narrow, parallel one-way streets connected by a series of alleys. Florida Ave, a major east-west thoroughfare, was a short block to the north for easy access and fast getaways. When the strip was running at full capacity, dozens of coke dealers sold little bags to customers who came on foot or slowly cruised through in cars with Virginia or Maryland plates. If a police car ventured into this maze lookouts would yell, "Olleray, Olleray, Olleray," pig Latin for roller. The narrow alleys were barricaded, so if the cops gave chase on foot, it was an obstacle course of old tires broken-down washing machines, trashcans and trip wires. Juveniles would lob foam footballs that had been hollowed out and stuffed with coke up and down the block as a kilo a day was moved in $50 bags.

"I don't know if he was running shit back then, but everyone associated with slim was getting some bank. Some more than others but no one was hurting." Said Christopher Johnson, a DC soldier who's forever tied to Rayful. And Edmonds operation grew so fast that by 1987 he was making $1 million a week. "If you introduce Pepsi-Cola into a new area, you're going to create a demand for something new," said Eddie McLaughlin, Narcotics supervisor for the Washington office of the FBI. "Edmond knew the potential for the market here. He was an early entrepreneur and he helped in its proliferation."

Edmond became a hometown hero. He made sure neighbors had turkeys on Thanksgiving. He bought meals for the homeless, cars for his top staff, clothes for his friends and sponsored area basketball teams. With his flair and street persona he drew workers and admirers by always traveling in an entourage and in cars like Porsches or Jaguars. He was a walking employment advertisement. "There goes Rayful and them. They getting it." They said in the city and the street smart, cunning young man from a large tight knit family was getting it. "Slim was having shit his way," says Da Kid from SE. "I remember Slim pulled up in my hood and gave all us lil' niggas $100 a piece and told us to take out lil' asses to school. I was like seven-years-old then and to me he was a star because he was getting out a limo."

"When people saw Ray they saw flash and personality." Christopher Johnson says. "I don't think he was feared himself or respected as an individual but the dudes that were around him were respected and feared by many. That's how it's supposed to be. Everyone played their position." Edmond avoided arrest because he dealt only with a small group of associates and he rarely had direct contact with drugs or money. But his business really took off when he got hooked up with some major suppliers in California. The cocaine road to Edmonds distribution area in NE Washington began in Cali, Colombia. It was in LA that he laid the groundwork for large shipments of Colombian cocaine to the streets of Washington. And it was in Las Vegas where he made the connection.

Edmond said: "People get killed, people lose their jobs, people get strung out. A lot of my friends from my neighborhood lost their lives because I brought drugs into the community. Some babies probably were born from crack because of me. I feel bad about it now but back then I was just thinking of power."

He noted: "All of us are loving and caring people who have kids. We're ordinary people, just like everyone else in Washington."

"Rayful Edmond and his family were a scourge to the streets of DC." DC resident

"Any drug dealer then and now would enjoy doing business with Edmond. It would be a claim to fame. I could see how each and every one of them would like having that on their resumes." DEA agent John Cornille

Among the thousands of high rollers who converged on Las Vegas in April 1987 for the Sugar Ray Leonard/Marvelous Marvin Hagler title fight was an unusual delegation from Washington DC led by a flashy 22-year-old Rayful Edmond. The flamboyant Edmond and his crew caught the eye of LA Crip gang member Melvin Butler who attended such events for the precise purpose of finding men like Rayful, out of state big city drug lords. Butler was a cocaine broker who hooked up with kingpins like Rayful and connected them to Los Angeles wholesalers. The complex system that evolved and started to supply Edmonds organization with drugs was built on an informal and mutually profitable set of relationships between him and three West Coast figures, the aforementioned Butler, his fellow Crip Brian "Waterhead Bo" Bennet and Mario Villabona, a Cali Cartel cocaine wholesaler who used his Crip connections to move thousands of kilo's of coke.

During the 18 months following the Leonard/Hagler fight, Edmond imported more cocaine into Washington than any drug dealers in the city's history, federal law enforcement officials said. The drug pipeline that fed Edmond was a graphic illustration of the reach of the global cocaine networks controlled by Colombian drug cartels, which supplied 80 percent of coke imported to U.S. markets in the 80's. Law enforcement officials note that the increase in cocaine abuse in the city closely tracked the period Edmond was tapping into that pipeline that, during '87 to '89, brought a seemingly unlimited supply of cocaine into Washington. "Slim made a grip." says the DC Hustler. "It wasn't a problem or a factor for slim to be known for money gettin. I can jive go for that."

The methods used to supply Edmonds' organization illustrate the meticulous and increasingly sophisticated way drug traffickers used the nation's highways and airports to transport massive quantities of cocaine. During the two years the LA to Washington pipeline was in operation, a highly organized transcontinental supply system operated with virtual impunity, thwarting the best efforts of federal and local law enforcement officials. Some shipments as large as 200 kilograms of cocaine were driven across country in rented trucks or recreational vehicles. Smaller shipments of about 20 kilograms were brought to the District in the luggage of couriers. An elaborate protocol extended to all business dealings. When Edmond met Bennet, they talked and they partied, but money and drugs did not change hands between them. Associates attended to those chores. Edmond took care to separate himself from them.

"You know that with money comes power and strength." The DC Hustler says. "Ray had a crew of almost 200 working for him. He was powerful and slim had folks that he fucked with that were very real men, so respect came with the territory. Dudes have respect for those who earn respect." And with the Colombian coke connection Rayful got that respect, and he got that money, too. "He was from Northeast but he was supplying a great portion of the whole city." Da Kid from Southeast says. And it's said that Rayful even acted as a cocaine liaison for other drug kingpins in New York, such as Alpo and AZ. But it didn't last. In May 1988, Edmond's elaborate, cash-rich corporate style drug operation started to cave in when four men were arrested in California for offering an undercover $1 million for a cache of coke. Eventually the men talked and the man they talked about was Rayful Edmond. Three other key members of Rayful's organization were arrested and agreed to participate in the case against him.

WHEN CRACK WAS KING

"I didn't know how bad my situation was or how it was going to turn out." Rayful Edmond

"Ray just got too big, too fast. You just knew the feds were gonna come get him." Mr. T

"When Rayful got busted it was big news. I mean big news. It seemed he was the biggest drug dealer the world had ever seen." Da Kid from Southeast

"All I know was at that time Rayful was the man. Before all the other shit." The DC Hustler

Edmond recalled: "Everybody had incentives to lie. Royal said a lot of things about me. Me and him was like brothers. I couldn't believe him coming to court saying things like that about me."

The U.S. District Court Building occupied an entire block on the North side of Constitution Avenue, where it intersected with Pennsylvania Avenue at Third Street. Constructed of buff-colored limestone. It wasn't an unappealing structure. The small park to the one side with the expansive courtyard in front gave it an open, unimposing feeling. The National Gallery's East Wing was directly across the street and the Capitol was just four blocks up the hill. It was a court for trying corrupt senators, judges, spies and federal officials. It was also a venue to try local drug dealers.

The Edmond case provided one of the first detailed glimpses of how the cartels fed the inner city drug markets. The trials were a culmination of three parallel investigations into Edmond and his District associates and their suppliers in LA conducted over two years by more then 200 federal, state and local law enforcement officials. The investigation, which began independently stretched over three continents, revealing an international drama of smuggling, money laundering and secret wiretaps, which traced a drug pipeline that began in the valleys of the Andes and ended on the narrow, tree-lined blocks of NE Washington known as the Strip, where Ziploc bags of cocaine sold for $50. Witnesses included drug and money couriers, buyers, street lieutenants, sellers, a member of the Crips, a security guard and a lifelong friend and associate of Edmond, court records indicate.

"I wasn't too surprised when his crew went down, because they were doing a lot of back and forth beefing prior to his arrest." Christopher Johnson says, referring to the June 23, 1988 murder of Brandon Terrell. Columbus "Little Nut" Daniels allegedly shot the rival dealer seven times on Edmond's signal to kill him. Edmond rewarded Little Nut with a $50K Mercedes-Benz for the Terrell shooting, court records say, and got a 16-year old to take the blame for the killing of Terrell outside the popular Chapter II nightclub. But the police didn't buy it. "Nice try," a detective said to Edmond, "but we still want Little Nut." The execution triggered the turf battles, which gave DC the reputation as the world's drug and murder capital. Little Nut was eventually gunned down at a barbershop and paralyzed from the neck down, but Rayful escaped unscathed.

"It did shock me when the people told on him though. His mom killed him by bragging to someone that was wearing a wire. I couldn't believe she was talking like that." Christopher says, referring to how Edmond's mom described his rise in the drug business in a body wire recording played at the trial. "When he started out it was just like hand to hand on the street corner and then he just got too big. He just up and went out on his own." Bootsie Perry said while secretly being recorded. "That's not something I said, ladies and gentlemen, but his mother." The prosecutor told the jury.

"They were actually executing slim without the death penalty," the DC Hustler says. "He had Mayor Barry at his trial along with others. That's when he had respect, when he was in the ring with Rome clutching."

And the trial was not without controversy. The cocaine conspiracy trial was the city's first criminal trial with an anonymous jury and the public was excluded from the proceedings, leaving the media to act as its surrogate. A daily series of outbursts and unexpected events overshadowed the courtroom testimony. The complex, multi-defendant drug trial had allegations of witness harassment, death threats, prosecutorial misconduct and judicial bias. One hundred and sixty witnesses and 800 pieces of evidence, including tapes filled with coded discussions about drugs in sometimes undecipherable pig Latin, were presented in the 56-day trial, which U.S. District Court Judge Charles R. Richy presided over.

"There was the general feeling that because of the bulletproof glass, the anonymous jury system, the number of Marshals ringing the courtroom, the way in which the jury was selected, the general hype about the case and the amount of pretrial publicity, it was going to make it difficult for Rayful to get a fair trial," Edmond's lawyer said. The most damaging evidence was the testimony of Alta Rae Zanville and Royal Brooks, a childhood friend of Rayful's who testified in excruciating detail how he stored hundreds of pounds of cocaine and millions of dollars in cash for Edmond. He described ferrying millions of dollars to LA at Edmond's instruction to pay for cocaine. Edmond bragged to him that he could package cocaine faster than anyone because he was "raised bagging stuff." A police officer testified that he saw 30 transactions a minute at the Strip and a former worker testified that she sold 500 $50 packs, $25,000 worth in two hours. The testimony painted a picture of an efficiently run business with regular paydays and work shifts and Sundays off.

"This is the most significant law enforcement operation here directed at a cocaine distribution network," said U.S. Attorney Jay B. Stephens, who was flanked by local and federal officers at a news conference in front of the courthouse. "This is the principal case, based on our intelligence, Edmond's group distributed 60 percent of the cocaine coming in. It was a closely knit family organization with enforcers, runners, lieutenants and money counters."

The three-month trial dominated headlines and newscasts and was the first to be carried out under extraordinary security measures, which included an anonymous jury, more than 15 U.S. Marshals in the courtroom, and the bulletproof shield separating the attorneys, judges and jury from the courtroom audience. None of the defendants took the stand to testify in their own defense and six witnesses linked Edmond directly to drug transactions. The jury of two men and 10 women announced their unanimous verdicts of guilty for all defendants shortly after 10 a.m. on December 6th, 1989. It took five days of deliberations in what was the longest and costliest drug trial ever held in the district.

"We've taken down a major distributor in the city," DC Police Chief Maurice T. Turner said at the conclusion of the trial. "That sends a message to the community that we are serious, that we are going to close this drug distribution market down." U.S. Attorney Stephens also hailed the convictions as a victory "for all the people of the District of Columbia" and a warning to other drug dealers that law enforcement officials "stand shoulder to shoulder with the people of this community to turn the tides of drugs that have so devastated this city." The convictions capped a massive two-year investigation by the DEA, FBI and DC Police, which pursued Edmond as his operation grew from its base in a quiet residential neighborhood in Northeast Washington. Edmond, who smiled through much of the trial, appeared shocked when the verdicts were read. "For those young people who have seen Mr. Edmond in his smiling ways over the years, they should have seen his crying ways in jail this morning." DEA agent John Wilder mocked. But Edmond would get the last laugh.

"I think that me, and my family, and my friends all should have been found not guilty." Rayful Edmond said. "I felt railroaded. I honestly think I was. Everybody in DC knew about the case. I said to myself the jurors were not going to have any choice but to find you guilty."

"We were on trial for three months and they came back in four days." Rayful Edmond

"People are sitting in prison, making drug deals." Rayful Edmond

Rayful kept on dealing even after he went to federal prison for life. He masterminded the shipment of more than two tons of cocaine from the coca fields of Colombia to the District of Columbia from his cell block. Edmond took advantage of every privilege while at the Lewisburg PA federal prison using the phones to arrange introductions of Washington dealers to Colombian suppliers. He often made 60 calls in less than five hours occasionally using two lines simultaneously to conduct his business. His contacts on the outside set up conference calls for him to Colombia, and he used the prison mail and visiting hours to work out details of the meetings of the various parties. He even mediated disputes, persuading the Colombians not to kill Washington drug dealers when they fell behind in their payments for cocaine. One afternoon he made 54 calls to five states and two foreign countries. He spoke pig Latin to his boys in DC using the contacts he made while serving two life sentences to expand his drug trafficking operation in prison.

"He was exceeding that which he did when he was running what had been the largest drug operation in DC history," U.S. Attorney Holder said. And Rayful said in interviews after the fact that it was "much easier (to sell drugs in prison) because you're right there where the people that have direct access to the narcotics that you need-Colombians, Cubans Mexicans." Sharing the same cell block with Edmond at USP Lewisburg were Dixon Dario and Osvaldo "Chicky" Trujillo-Blanco. The brothers connection went to the heart of the violent Medellin cartel and they became Rayful's new Colombian connection. Lewisburg was bustling with convicted dealers who were doing major business setting up deals for friends on the inside and outside. When Rayful met the brothers they were not a year away from being paroled.

Osvaldo "Chicky" Trujillo-Blanco was cocaine royalty, son of Griselda Trujillo Blanco, better known as the Godmother of the Colombian drug underworld, a founding member of the notorious Medellin drug cartel. By October 1991 an informant told the FBI Rayful was back in business arranging deals from prison. From April to October of 1992 the FBI listened in on four prison phones as Edmond brokered deals between the Colombian brothers and various DC drug traffickers in arcane codes to discuss and arrange large cocaine deals. As matchmaker, Rayful collected commissions based on the amount sold.

"His name was still ringing in the city." Christopher Johnson says. "After all he was one of the biggest dudes to come out of the city. His crews name was still ringing too. Still does for that matter on a respect tip." As Rayful's name stayed in the streets, he got visitors to smuggle small amounts of cocaine, heroin and marijuana to him. He said he quickly learned it was easier to deal drugs from behind bars to people on the outside. He had access to phones on the B cell block practically whenever he wanted. He estimated he hooked up 20 or so Washington dealers with Chicky who sold them close to a thousand kilos of cocaine. "I just enjoyed it," Rayful said of his continued drug activity. "It was something for me to do. I was in jail and I had nothing to do. I wanted to make more money. At the time my mindset was I had to still have people look up to me and prove that I was still capable of making things happen. It's just about everybody inside the jail in some way, shape, form or fashion is dealing drugs, either directly or indirectly." Not to justify it, but Rayful was definitely balling from inside the cell block. The authorities were not amused.

"It is intolerable that criminals who were incarcerated for the precise purpose of protecting our citizens have instead been able to use the prison facilities as their home offices for creating and commanding narcotics enterprises that have left nothing in their wake but death and destruction on the streets of our city," U.S. Attorney Holder said upon revelations of Edmonds activity. "Today's events demonstrate the shocking fact that inmates in federal correctional institutions have been able to participate in international cocaine conspiracies from behind prison walls." Lane Crocker, the agent in charge of the FBI's Washington field office, sharply criticized the federal Bureau of Prisons, blaming its lax management for allowing international drug deals to be orchestrated from prison. But this story still had an unexpected turn.

"Dude stayed up in the law library. He always said he was working on a way to get out, but I had no idea he would do what he did," recalled a USP Lewisburg convict.

"I could stay in here 100 years and it's not going to change anything," said Rayful Edmond

He also predicted: "I'll be out in two years. I'll be back on the street."

"Rayful is the ultimate stand up guy. That persona just sucks people in. Rayful Edmond would be the last person anyone would think was a snitch." Said James W. Rudasil, Attorney at Law.

"The feds sent a nigga named Donald "Worthy" Wortham to set Ray up in Lewisburg." Christopher Johnson relates. "After the Colombian dude Chicky got killed, it slowed things down in the city for a second. Through Ray the city was getting blessed by Chicky. The feds knew this but couldn't get to Ray until Donald caught a case and couldn't do the time. They knew that Donald knew Ray so they sent him to Lewisburg and Worthy hit him with the good story. 'I got a man that has the money but his connect is not steady.' Ray bit and plugged Worthy's man (the feds) in with the connect. The feds went to Ray and let him know that he was through. Told him he was going back to Marion and that his appeal on the first charge didn't mean shit. That's right that whole crew was coming back on appeal except for a few people. So all that shit about he did it for mom is propaganda by the government."

When authorities ensnared him in the above mentioned sting in July 1994, Edmond said he saw that as a chance to break his addiction: selling cocaine. He never used the stuff, let alone smoked a cigarette or drank a beer, and with his man Chicky having been gunned down in a Medellin nightclub, Rayful must have been tired of it all, the hassle, the hustle, the deals-living up to the name, Rayful Edmonds, and being the wheeler dealer everyone expected him to be. "I had been giving it a thought for a while that I wanted to stop selling drugs, and I figured this was the best way for me to stop," Rayful said. He started working for the feds shortly thereafter.

"We gained tremendous intelligence when Rayful Edmond said to the FBI he wished to cooperate with the government," Assistant U.S. Attorney John Dominguez said. The immediate results of Edmond's work were the arrests in DC of 11 people, five of whom authorities described as the biggest drug dealers in town at the time. Edmond set them up and arranged for them to meet an undercover agent, DC Police Detective Jesus C. Gonzalez, who posed as a representative of the Trujillo-Blanco family from Colombia. The men and their associates met with Gonzalez in Newark to work out the details of their purchase of 60 kilos of coke for $1 million with $375,000 to be paid upon delivery. Christopher Johnson, who was then 28, was one of the men set up by Rayful. Two other men, Michael Jackson and James Corbin, were set up and indicted in Pennsylvania.

This is how the setup went down. "It was easy." Christopher says. "Ray called and said that Chicky's brother was in town. Shit, niggas was happy as a motherfucker. All the time a nigga think he's meeting Chicky's brother he's talking numbers with the feds. Them bastards tricked everyone. Kept a nigga on hold for months. They would call once in a while and tell you to be ready. All that good shit." Christopher ended up getting 150 months for being caught in the sting operation and the knowledge that he was set up by the biggest drug dealer from the city ever, Rayful Edmond.

"I consider myself a loser," Christopher says, "Not only did I see the police that day. I just didn't want to believe it. And of course being greedy and loyal to the niggas I was with…. But I'm a loser cause I don't have a pot to piss in or a window to throw it out of. I've learned that if you heard a nigga was hot and he went and put work in and smashed the dude for saying it, it doesn't mean he ain't no rat. It just means he's a tough rat."

U.S. Attorney Eric H. Holder announced that Edmond delivered five up and coming drug traffickers to the FBI and the DC police. Edmond pleaded guilty to even more drug counts and agreed to forfeit $200,000 of the profits he had racked up during his prison cell dealing. As a reward for his cooperation, his mother's 14-year sentence was reduced. The feds put him in a little know Witness Protection Program for convicts. He lives under an alias in a different prison where it's hoped those he betrayed won't find him. His testimony for the prosecution against Rodney Moore and Kevin Gray of Murder Inc. in 2002 was the third time he set up or testified against his former friends or business associates. It was reported he did this to regain visiting privileges with his mother. The old Rayful who swaggered through DC streets in fancy threads and expensive jewelry and who always seemed to have beautiful women on his arm, was no more. He was a witness for the prosecution. A rat. A snitch.

"I was in Lewisburg with Rayful and when I got out the nigga was calling me trying to get me to do some things with him on the coke tip. But I had just got out and wasn't trying to hear that shit. I'm glad I didn't cause that was when he started setting niggas up." Revealed a USP Lewisburg Convict.

"Edmond was such a notorious figure it was unpalatable for the government to consider reducing his sentence." AUSA John Dominguez

"They said that Colombian Chicky got killed for fucking with Rayful. His people knew Ray was a snitch." Da Kid from SE

"He was setting dudes up and getting good men a lot of time." The DC Hustler

"When it got out that Rayful was snitching, all the love turned to hate, dudes started saying slim was a faggot and all types of shit." A USP Lewisburg Convict

The Edmond lore of fancy cars, gorgeous women and basketball stars still circulates in neighborhoods near his old base of operations in the 400 block of M Street NE. His rise and fall have become milestones in the city's drug trade, a market previously dominated by smalltime dealers in constant search of supplies. The man who was voted most popular at Dunbar High in his senior year of 1982 and who was most definitely the undisputed king of District drug dealers during the 1980's, still illicits controversy whenever his name is mentioned.

"Rayful's legacy to me is bitch," says the DC Hustler. "He put a black eye on the face of DC. His antics single handedly gave out of state bammas the green light and weak bitches the green light to get down first. What type of shit is that? They even got fake gangsters on TV making bitchass movies portraying bitchass dudes talking about telling, snitching, ratting on dudes in DC. Why not huh? One of our own set it off." Edmond means different things to different people even to this very day. But he was definitely an urban (DC) legend whose true-life story is far from imaginary hood myth. Rayful was king of the city, the drug tycoon/mob boss that a lot of rappers nowadays portray themselves to be. Edmond's sophisticated enterprise that moved thousands of kilos of coke received significant regional and national publicity, making Edmond one of the most infamous drug dealers of our times

"Yes," the DC Hustler says. "But he's infamous for being one of those with the ability and know how but not the heart to hold true to the code. History in DC will always know Rayful for being a bitch. We don't remember nothing that he did before the day he snitched. True DC niggas don't honor no rats." But still Edmond's exploits have been documented in film and in print. "The Life of Rayful Edmond" was released in 2005 by Kirk Fraser, a former Howard University student. "This is the first real movie about DC." Fraser said. "It's about Edmonds rise and fall in the game. How he made it and what brought him down." Instrumental in the making of the film was Curtis (Curtbone) Chambers. The film has received positive reviews, even though it's said to be sympathetic to Rayful. In the film Ray's attorney and Curtbone both describe how Ray didn't really understand how much evidence was piling up against him. Ray thought because he didn't actually touch the drugs he was safe. But that wasn't true. And the movie omitted the defining characteristic of Edmonds whole ordeal-that he became a rat. So much for a true story.

"History will remember Rayful Edmond as a snitch," the DC Hustler says. "As a coward, as a turncoat. He is part of the reason why Rome is so hip to us the true players and macks in the game. As one of those who broke down like a bitch and gave Rome the upper hand. Remember how Rayful Edmond and those like him got a lot of warriors fucked up. I know I will."

And to finish this piece, we'll conclude with one of the men Rayful set up: Christopher Johnson. "It's like this with me. If you're in the game period, not just drugs but anything illegal, and when your ass get caught, shut the fuck up and stand the fuck up. Go to trial or cop out but don't drag nobody else in your part. You crab ass nigga. That's for all the hot niggas reading this."

"He snitched because he was fucked up that dudes in the street owed him money and wouldn't pay. He didn't do that shit for his mom," Mr. T.

"A rat is a rat anyway you look at it and slim is a world class snitch." USP Lewisburg Convict

"Slim fucked up. He's a rat and a faggot." Da Kid from SE

"We don't recognize hot bammas." The DC Hustler

The Sentences

Rayful Edmond - two life sentences
Johnny Monford - 405 months
Columbus Daniels - life
Jerry Millington - life
Armartetta Perry - 405 months
Antonio Jones - life
David McGraw - 292 months
Emmanual Sutton - 320 months
Keith Cooper - 320 months
Bootsie Perry - 14 years (reduced)
Tony Lewis - life
Bernice McGraw - 235 months
Melvin Bulter - 405 months

Those Rayful set up

Christopher Johnson
Adolph Jackson
Darrell Coles
Jimmy Robinson
Anthony Smither
Marcus Haynes
Lecount Jackson
Rodney Murphy
Richard Deane
Johnny Cherry

TWENTY ONE

Holding Down the Neighborhood

I N THE CHRONICLES of gangsta lore, the big city drug barons get all the love. The New York City drug crews, Detroit kingpins, Washington DC coke dealers, LA gangbangers and Chicago gang organizations receive all the shine, newspaper headlines and publicity. Just like the big market sports teams, they remain in the public's eye. Rappers like 50 Cent, Snoop Dog, Common, Nas, Jadakiss, Ice Cube and Ja Rule have honored these street legends in verse, making their names ring from hood to hood, across the ghettos of America, by broadcasting their exploits and name dropping them and their crews in their rhymes.

But as the emergence of the street literature genre has shown us, there are hood tales from all over the United States just as vivid and intriguing as the big city tales. From the dirty south down to Texas and all the way back up to the Midwest, dudes on the bricks are getting theirs. Vickie Stringer from Triple Crown fame was the first to give the 411 on Columbus, Ohio's drug trade in her bestselling book, "Let that be the Reason." With that book she exploded onto the urban fiction scene making her Triple Crown publishing house a leader in the industry. She has gone on to much success but there is a back story to all this that leads right back to the ghettos of Columbus, Ohio, to a place called the Short North.

Back in the day there was a crew on Columbus' North Side that was holding it down. In the late 80's and early 90's they regulated their neighborhood and held gangsta status throughout the city due to their deeds. They called themselves the Short North Posse and they have gone down in infamy. It was said that any outsider who dared to sell drugs in the Short North Posse's territory was beaten and robbed or even killed. Wars for control of the neighborhoods streets raged as hustlers from Detroit and Indiana tried to move in on the area's to no avail. They were repulsed, violently if necessary.

U.S. Attorney Edmund Sargas characterized the Short North Posse as the Columbus areas "largest and most violent gang." It's said the heavily armed posse gang, which sold crack and regulated crack sales in their neighborhood for five years, was the terror of inner city Columbus. "This gang was a cancer on the city's North Side, it turned neighborhoods virtually into war zones," a federal judge said of the SNP. But neighborhood residents begged to differ. They remembered a clique that sought to protect them from outside exploitation. "The Short North Posse held it down for Short North, period." Says one longtime resident. "They didn't let no outsiders run our streets, let alone set up shop."

And Essence bestselling author and street lit queen Vickie Stringer played a part in bringing them down. But we'll get to that later. First let's go back to the 80's and take a look at the North side of Columbus, a place called the Short North and explore the reasons for the formation of the Short North Posse. Because keeping it real and bringing it to you gangsta is what we do.

"I knew that area since forever. We called it the Short." A Columbus native we'll call the local says, "In Columbus the area goes from 1st Avenue to 11th Avenue. The reason we call it the Short is because of the street numbers. It only goes from 1 to 11. As soon as you leave out of downtown that's where the Short North is, north of downtown. The Ohio State campus is right there. The campus is right in the hood." Columbus is a huge city, 210 square miles, in comparison all five boroughs of New York are only 230 square miles, so imagine all that space. Columbus is three times the size of Cleveland and within that 210 square miles are 800,000 people. That's just the city itself, not including the suburbs. Short North is a real small area within the city and even larger surrounding area. But it has a rich history. "The Short been off the hook since the 60's," the local says. "When we used to go to middle school in the 80's, 4th and 8th was in the Wall Street Journal as a top 10 percent toughest street corner in America and eventually reached number one before 1986. The O.G.'s was the Snap Dragons from the 50's, 60's and 70's. The Short been trippin' all that time." The roots of gangsterism grew deep in the Short and the Posse were just continuing a long standing tradition.

"It's a rough area. You got to be strapped." The local says. "If somebody got shot over there the police would take forever to respond. There was a lot of prostitution, a lot of crack whores. It's all rowhouses. The main drag was 4th Street. Fourth Street and 8th Avenue was like the main area in Short North. There was a bar called The Eighth Avenue Lounge, a hangout for cutthroats and killers, on the corner. On 4th and 11th Avenue there was a little Arab store where everyone congregated. They hung out at the payphones and parking lot. People would pull up and bullshit. That's the border of Short North."

The Columbus Dispatch reported that the Short North Posse allegedly formed in 1989 in the Short North area of Columbus, Ohio, to control local sales of cocaine base by excluding from the area drug dealers who were not residents of the Short North. They allegedly terrorized the 42 block neighborhood bordering the Ohio State University area for up to six years. The violent prone youngsters began selling crack cocaine and firearms in August 1989 in an area bounded by East 11th Avenue, Grant Avenue, 5th Avenue and North High Street. They used cellular phones and pagers to communicate. Much of the gang's drug dealing occurred along North 4th Street between 7th and 9th Avenues. Other sites were near a certified gasoline station at Summit Street and 11th Avenue and a Kroger store on North High Street.

The Posse's unofficial headquarters was Kelly's carryout at 1521 North 4th Street. Its social club was the Golden Eight Ball pool hall at 222 East 11th Avenue. An illegal after-hours bar called the Juke Joint on East 9th Avenue between Grant Avenue and North 6th served as the gang's distribution center where they could pick up cocaine and guns to sell in the neighborhood. "The name Short North Posse, it was a bunch of kids, but they went hard. They handled their business." The local says. "There's always been Crips there, then Folks came. The SNP was mainly Crips and Folks."

The Posse formed in 1989 after a friend was shot in a drug trafficking incident. Robert "June" Dotson and Marshon Mays decided to band together to form a group that would offer protection to its members in the area directly north of downtown Columbus. They began selling crack on the north side in the 42 block area south of East 11th Avenue. It was nothing new. Crack had hit southern Ohio in 1984. But the youngsters coming up wanted to do it their way. Dotson and Mays then came up with the name Short North Posse to describe their clique. Gang members bought hats and shirts with the letters SNP on them. After Therhan Jones was wounded in a shooting by a competing gang the SNP became even more determined to keep outsiders from their territory. It was a get mine or be mine mentality.

The group of street level dealers were tried and tested gangstas who ran a retail operation in their hood. Representing and holding it down for their area. Due to the government's and media's propaganda, several myths have been perpetrated as truth. As the dude from the era says, "That shit was printed to get them convicted. Myth #1- they didn't terrorize residents. Actually, when the feds came in, there was a lot of protest from the Short North natives, young and old, black and white. Myth #2- the Short North Posse did not rob people. They were gangstas. It was the crackheads robbing other crackheads. The reality of it is that the SNP are legends in the city for being real dudes, not bitch ass niggas." From their inception the SNP aspired to protect their hood and to prevent anyone outside the Short North from selling crack in the neighborhood.

"Most of those Short North dudes were gangbangers," the local says. "A lot of weed, everybody was smoking that weed. They were on the corners hanging. You couldn't go up in there. They lived up in the rowhouses with their baby mamas. They were young boys, but they held it down. They were like baby gangstas. The dudes that had the biggest names were Trouble, Ant and Fridge." They were the dudes in the Short North who were getting big props at that time. Theirs were the names that were ringing. And because of our reputation in the streets, those are the dudes we talked to.

What was the SNP about?

Lamont "Fridge" Needum: I love my hood 'til this day. Short North—just saying the noun makes me want to throw four fingers in the air. Anyone fortunate enough to be there in its glory will tell you ain't nothing like it, the air, the buzz. I honestly think the place is haunted because it's something about the Short that makes folks excel from Ohio State University football to street niggas getting it.

Anthony "Ant" Gibbs: The Short North Posse was a group of people who all grew up in the same neighborhood and went to the same school coming up.

What was your neighborhood like?

Fridge: Short North is just what it says it is: the shortest part of the north side coming off of downtown. Columbus is the largest city in Ohio. Columbus is full of all the things that make cities pop, but the mentality of Columbians is- come, kick it, then get the fuck out.

Anthony: It was like a well knitted family that didn't take no shit from anybody and always had each others back no matter what. We took care of our own, whether they were nine months old or 99-years-old. We were one big family.

What types of things were you exposed to growing up in that neighborhood?

Fridge: Regular hood shit, but if an old person wanted to walk the streets of the short at midnight for no apparent reason, they were free to do so, and not only were they not bothered, nobody else better not fuck with them, that's how it went down. It was beautiful to see black men standing for one love and one hood.

Anthony: Just like any other hood I was exposed to—everything from pimping, robbery, the dope game, beat down, murder but, most importantly, loyalty.

Fridge, Ant and their crew were from the old school of thought. They didn't disrespect old folks or mess with kids. They protected their own. The youngsters banded together and went to war with outsiders to keep their hood sucker free. It wasn't a matter of selling crack, making money or none of that, although that played a part, it was more about neighborhood pride, representing to the fullest and holding it down for everyone that lived there.

It was about holding down the neighborhood, but then again it was about so much more. "They was young and thuggin' like a muthafucka," the local says. "It was money, cash, hoes but more than anything they was violent niggas." And their violence was directed at any fools blatant enough to try to sell crack in their hood. The dudes from Detroit, Indiana and other places all tried to muscle in and set up shot, but they were all sent running. Short North didn't bow to anyone.

What was your all's mentality and attitude?

Fridge: If you brought your ass in the short to put your goon hand down, that ass was toast, no exceptions. Our turf was our domain. My old ass will always rep the short side of town for life. I'm not the same guy I was before. As you grow, your priorities shift, but surviving the bloody years of the short makes me a strong man. Short North for life.

Anthony: My mentality was shit first and eat later. I was just one of them laid back niggas that you didn't cross.

What kind of clothes, footwear, whips and the likes were you all rocking?

Fridge: I know folks read this book to hear about cars and jewels and bitches and shit, but I can't find it in my heart to come with that. Those are merely the residuals of the game. What I loved more than anything about the Short North I lived in was the unity amongst its people, young and old, black and white.

Anthony: Back then there wasn't really a dress code, but you could find niggas rocking Polo, Tommy, Coogi, Guess, Nautica, Gucci, Nike shoes, Bally's, Tims, Gators. Really, you could find a nigga in just about everything that was in style back then. New cars, Vets, Iroc's, old schools, Benz's, Lex's, Regals, Caddies, Monte Carlos. When we roll, you knew it was us.

Fridge: I was wearing platinum when niggas assumed it was silver. Styles haven't really changed in the last 15 years, 'cause young niggas just do what we did with more glitter. We had all the flash, but it's so lame now. That shit is outdated and overrated. The things that impress me are integrity, proper displays of valor, little black kids striving to be great, real love, not that canned shit.

"There was a lot of hype. They started making big noise in 1990," the local says. "All you would really hear was it's getting wild over there. Fourth and 8th was where shit was jumping off and shit could get violent real quick." Dudes were known to get robbed, too, even a federal agent. In the first month of the probe into the Short North Posse's activities, Rodney Russell, an undercover agent from the U.S. Bureau of Alcohol, Tobacco and Firearms, allegedly was robbed at gunpoint by Fridge who was 18 at the time. Fridge allegedly walked out of an apartment and pointed a Tec-9 semiautomatic pistol loaded with a 32 round clip at Russell's head and cocked it.

But locals dispute this. That's the government and media line they say. What they sold to the masses to create a media storm that assured the SNP would be assumed guilty until proven innocent. "The biggest myth created by the feds in the whole case is that the ATF agent got robbed," the dude from the era relates. "Rodney Russell was a crackhead who smoked up all the feds money and then started lying about being robbed to conceal his smoking activities. That dude was dirty. I was there. He was smoking." And in his crack induced haze, the agent invented a robbery scenario and pinned it on Fridge.

"At first I thought he was going to try and sell it to me. Then he pointed it at my head and put his hand on my shoulder. This guy weighs over 300 pounds." Russell said. For a few tense seconds Russell said he believed that Fridge was going to kill him. "I thought someone had tipped him off that I was an undercover agent and I was finished." Russell said creating the scenario for the papers. He said later that he kept his hand on his gun, which was hidden beneath his untucked flannel shirt throughout the incident, to portray himself as the cool ATF agent under pressure.

"You're too busy thinking about your options to be afraid," Russell said, playing the hero role. "I didn't want to take him down. I was thinking if I shoot this guy now it's all over. We'd have to shut down the investigation." To hear Russell tell it, he kept his cool and allowed Fridge to lift more than $400 from his shirt pocket. But the dude from the era tells a different story. "Fridge sold the agent crack at his spot but he didn't rob nobody. The nigga's like 350 pounds. Nobody looks like him. Why would he rob somebody at his own spot? All Fridge did was snatch dudes shirt pocket off because he saw a list with beeper numbers sticking out. He thought dude was five-o and wanted to see whose beeper numbers he had." Russell's boss, Don Mapley, Chief of

Columbus' ATF, laughed about the incident afterward. "The biggest mistake they made was robbing him. That made him more determined than ever to get these guys." But was it all done under a crack induced haze of an investigation?

The state and federal governments continued conducting their extensive undercover investigation, with Agent Rodney Russell of the ATF leading it. Russell prowled some of the meanest streets of the North Side, making almost 100 drug buys from Posse gang members. From April 1994 until March 1995, Russell bought $40,000 in cocaine from Posse dealers and smoked a lot of it. "These guys are very aggressive," Commander Nick Panzera of the Columbus Narcotics Bureau said. "We're supposed to target the most violent offenders. We key in on quality targets, the armed career criminals and narcotic traffickers. We're finding more and more drug dealers are involved in street robberies and sometimes we are the victims of these rip-offs." And the feds found it was hard to identify SNP members because they all went by street names.

"Street names allow them to remain anonymous. They cause a bit of a problem for us identifying people." ATF Chief Mapley said. The dealers rarely used their real names and matching nicknames with actual identities often took months of investigation. Still, the ATF persevered. With one of their own allegedly robbed at gunpoint, they weren't giving up at all. "It's a macho thing with some of them. We found out Antwan Woods was known as Trouble and he tried to live up to that name. Lamont Needum was known as Fridge because he was as large as a refrigerator." ATF Chief Maply said. But in truth, the ATF chief had it wrong. The local corrects him. "That name was given to Fridge out of respect by his niggas because of his athletic abilities. He got that name when he was nine."

Police and federal agents were intent on smashing the Short North Posse, though, despite the obstacles. Actually they went after them with a fever. And the youngsters made it easy for them by wearing openly in their hood SNP t-shirts and hats that included the language 'Death Row' and 'Caps get peeled' along with images of tombstones and references to shootings. Because being a member of the gang was an honor in the hood. The SNP thought they had everything on lock but the feds had other ideas.

"These guys are well aware of what they're involved in. If they're going to use guns and we find out about them, they're looking at a severe hit." ATF Chief Mapley said. "When it goes federal, they're in for a big shock. This isn't state court. If they don't like the sentences that are being handed out, they need to find another vocation." At the end of the investigation, an associate of the SNP identified Russell as a federal agent, but by that time, he had been buying drugs from the gang for 10 months. Everybody thought he was just another crackhead. "They didn't know whether to believe their own informant." Russell smirked. During one cocaine buy, Big Fridge became suspicious of Russell. He asked the undercover agent, "Are you a cop?" But Russell didn't answer. Fridge turned to the crack addict who had introduced Russell to Posse members, "If he's a cop, I know where you live." But by the time the SNP found out for certain, it was too late. The crackhead agent had enough info to get them indicted.

Authorities found a cache of handguns in a September 1994 raid at Woods' home at 690 East 4th Avenue, and they confiscated many semiautomatic handguns and assault rifles during their investigations, along with all the buys that Russell made. On March 23, 1995, a federal grand jury charged 46 people with a total of 210 federal charges relating to drug dealing, money laundering and the illegal use of guns. The newspapers were about to up the ante with a series of headlines portraying the Short North Posse as vicious thugs and hoodlums who terrorized their neighborhood. But in reality it was much different. "The Dispatch disrespected the shit out of those kids, especially Fridge. Those kids are stand up niggas. They held it down and stayed true. The whole indictment was some straight bullshit." The dude from the era says.

"46 Face Federal Drug Charges; Lawmen Round Up Reputed Short North Posse Members"--the Columbus Dispatch reported on March 21, 1995. They were arrested without incident in night and morning raids on North Side bars, houses, apartments and street corners. The raids were conducted by the Columbus police, U.S. Deputy Marshals and agents for the U.S. Bureau of Alcohol, Tobacco and Firearms. The arrested were held without bail in the Franklin County jail. The arrest capped a one-year investigation by local and federal undercover officers.

Tell us about the indictment and trial?

Fridge: It takes a conspiracy to create one, and no one is better at doing that than the feds. Our problem was that we were too close to O.S.U. In 1993 an ugly incident took place. An Ohio State student was raped and killed behind the campus by an unknown pervert. Last year through DNA evidence the punk bitch was nabbed. His name is Jonathan Gravely. The state allowed this whore to cop to 25 to life. Me and the homies are pissed. That bitch did something unthinkable and he brought major heat on us. With all the shit popping in the hood, it was the proverbial straw that broke the camel's back. O.S.U. is Columbus. Something had to be done. First my cousin Jason (RIP) was killed in an accident in the Short. He was a linebacker at O.S.U. Then this. The powers that be had to show they were in control. That coupled with the visions of the prosperous and the Department of Justice's mission to fill prisons under the Clinton Administration made us prime targets. Rather than find the sick motherfucker they decided to give 46 young black dudes over 300 years in prison. Everyone from the judge to the then mayor (Greg Lashtuka) were state alums.

Anthony: Our case is really about politics. It's a long story that Fridge touched on. The police needed a scapegoat, so they sacrificed

46 blacks to kill two birds with one stone. It was fucked up. I'm a drug dealer, so I knew I was guilty. The reason why I went to trial is to see if them hot ass niggas had the heart to look a nigga in the eyes while they testified and they had the heart. I couldn't do nothing but grit and nod my head.

Tell us how you felt at trial?

Fridge: A black person should stand up every time they get the opportunity. Our lack of stick-to-it-ness is why we have no rights in federal court. A two point reduction for a selected few is not justice. People are being indicted for five grams of crack and being sentenced to life for kilos.

Anthony: My hearing was fucked up. My PSI officer lied about the amount of drugs to boost my time, so they gave me 353 months. I was 19 at the time, so I didn't think it was too bad until I went back to my cell and did the math.

Authorities described the Posse as one of the most vicious gangs in Columbus history. "When this happened it was big news," the local says. "The news kept running stories about the SNP, hyping things up. The news was calling the SNP a violent drug dealing gang that could only be handled by the feds." And one of the stories circulating in Columbus concerned the feds take down of Vickie Stringer's drug ring, which precipitated the SNP's fall.

Testimony during Vickie Stringer's plea hearing revealed that her ring supplied cocaine for several Columbus area gangs, including the Short North Posse. Testimony during the plea hearing revealed that dealers bought large amounts of crack from Vickie Stringer's smuggling ring and then sold the drugs to Posse street dealers. Stringer had already pleaded guilty to smuggling drugs to Columbus from New York. Terms of her plea bargain required her to testify as a government witness against members of her own ring and defendants in the Posse case. Carlos Hill also pleaded guilty. His plea bargain also called for him to testify as government witness against his fellow Posse defendants.

"For six years, this gang was terrorizing the neighborhood, spewing drugs on our streets," U.S. Attorney Edmund Sargas said. "We were able to take action against them because of the high level of cooperation among law enforcement agencies. The deals were made often in broad daylight, in apartments and outside of commercial establishments. The Short North Posse literally took over the neighborhood with violence." The government alleged that the goal of the group was to prevent anyone not living in the Short North from selling cocaine base there without permission. The government contended the SNP achieved this goal through threats and intimidation. The bulk of the government's evidence would consist of testimony from cooperating witnesses, most of whom were alleged members of the SNP who had pleaded guilty and turned snitch.

The gang that stuck together to protect the neighborhood fell apart when the feds came after them and started talking football numbers. "The feds started picking all the kids up," the local says. "We thought it was hype. The feds do large neighborhood sweeps in Columbus about every other year. But this time they were serious." And armed with their snitches their game plan was tight. Forty-six suspects were indicted in the SNP drug dealing case but fewer than a dozen went on trial. A rash of guilty pleas kept most of the alleged members and associates of the North Side gang from appearing in the first floor courtroom of U.S. District Judge George C. Smith. Thirty-six Posse defendants pled guilty to a variety of drug and firearm related charges and a big majority of them turned snitch. Among those that stood up to face the charges were Antwan "Trouble" Woods, Lamont "Fridge" Needum, Chad "Boss Moss" Gibbs, Anthony "Ant" Gibbs, Robert Curtis, Donneto Berry, Richard "Manual" Hough and Jimmie Reed.

The most significant pleas came from Therhan Jones, a reputed leader of the gang, and Raynard Wallace, one of the gang's cocaine suppliers. Terms of their plea agreements required both men to appear as government witnesses in the trial. Jones oversaw much of the gang's day-to-day drug dealing, the authorities said, and Wallace brought large amounts of crack cocaine from Detroit and sold it to Posse members. Antwan Woods, another reputed leader of the gang, maintained his innocence and went to trial. He was charged with seven felonies, including drug trafficking and firearm charges. Lamont Needum was charged with eight felonies, including three gun charges, the most serious of which was his alleged robbery of the ATF agent who spurred on the case.

The government would argue that the SNP was a drug conspiracy. The defendants conceded that they were street level crack dealers, but contended that the SNP was merely a neighborhood identification of a loose-kit group of friends and acquaintances, most of whom grew up in the Short North area. The guilty pleas left eight Posse defendants charged with a total of 43 counts to stand trial. The trial, which would last six weeks, commenced on September 27, 1995. Sixteen Deputy Marshals and courtroom security officers were assigned to provide security in the federal courtroom in Columbus.

Federal prosecutors laid out their case. They contended that the Posse had a monopoly on crack cocaine sales for six years in the 42-block area of the North Side called the Short North. Several members of the gang were making up to $10,000 every three days, agents testified. "They provided services 24 hours a day, seven days a week," Asisstant U.S. Attorney Salvador Dominguez said.

He displayed scores of items of evidence, including bags of crack, wads of money, gang t-shirts, six handguns and an assault rifle. Most of the bags of crack that Dominguez held up for the jury to view were worth only $30 to $50. "Crumbs of crack, perhaps," AUSA Dominguez said. "But guns are a part of crack dealing." The guns and drugs had been confiscated in raids on homes of some Posse members when they were arrested after the indictments. Other relevant evidence came from undercover officers, SNP members turned snitch and non-SNP drug dealers or users.

"It was easy money, quick and fast," Robert "June" Dotson testified. As to the origins of the gang, he explained how his friend got robbed. "We decided we're not going to let that happen again. We were going to stay together and protect each other." Asked by AUSA Dominguez what would happen to outside drug dealers who invaded Posse territory, Dotson said, "They'd get beat up, robbed. If you didn't know nobody you weren't allowed out there." The gang had no leaders and did not hold regular meetings, Dotson said. However, members of the gang "did get together for informal discussions." Also hatreds within the gang were put aside if a Posse member was threatened or got into trouble. "If anything happened to somebody you'd pull together even if you didn't like him." Dotson testified. Dotson's most damaging testimony was that he saw seven of the defendants selling drugs in the North 4th Street area between 11th and 5th Avenues.

Quinton "Q Dog" Clausell testified but was vague about the times and locations of the defendants alleged narcotics dealing. Andrew Jackson, though, gave the most detailed description yet of cocaine selling by the defendants on trial in the case. Jackson named seven of the eight defendants standing trial as regular drug dealers in the area. Clausell told of beating people up. "I take it out on them. It all depends on how I feel. I beat them down." Q Dog testified.

Prosecutors stressed how guns played an important part in the Short North. George Miller, a 32-year-old crack addict, testified that Antwan Woods brandished guns regularly. While complaining about police harassing his drug customers, Woods once pulled a handgun from his pants and said he was sick of police hassling "my clientele," Miller told the seven women, five men jury. Woods not only supplied Posse members with crack cocaine but also offered to sell them guns, George "Gee" Gladden a Posse dealer testified. Gladden said Woods offered to sell him firearms as they talked on an apartment porch along North 4th Street. "He would come to me and tell me, 'I got the guns you need,'" Gee testified.

Posse members didn't have any compunction about selling drugs near elementary schools, Jeremiah "Boogy" Berger, an 18-year-old former Posse member testified. He saw Hough selling crack across the street from Weinland Park Elementary at 211 East 7th Avenue, Berger said. A prosecution witness also recanted his testimony and said that federal authorities pressured him into lying about drug dealing activities by three defendants in the Short North Posse case. Defense attorneys said the surprise remarks of Reginald "Froggie" Crenshaw in U.S. District Court threw doubt on the testimony of the other government witnesses.

"When you testified about Donneto Berry, did you lie?" asked attorney George Luther. "Yes, sir," Crenshaw replied. He gave similar answers to questions from attorneys for Reed and Hough. Luther also asked the witness, "You would have said anything they wanted you to say, wouldn't you?" Crenshaw answered, "Yes, I had to say something. I was pressured for the whole testimony. I had no choice."

Lawyers for the defendants argued that the SNP was not a gang, and they claimed, more importantly, it was not a drug conspiracy. There was no business like a distribution network, a hierarchy of leadership or organization of members. The different members of the SNP claimed to have sold their drugs independently of one another, choosing their own locations, price points and working hours. Dennis Belli, Woods' attorney said Woods grew up with many of the defendants and even considered some of them his friends, "but mere association doesn't make a conspiracy." While some of the defendants were friends others didn't like each other, Belli said. "They engaged in turf wars," he told the jury. "There was no particular leader. There was no chain of command." Judge George C. Smith dismissed a total of seven charges against five of the defendants, Woods Needum, Reed, Curtis and Chad Gibbs, but they still faced a total of 25 counts.

"We've all heard stories about dope being used by everyone from three and four-year-olds to grandmothers in the Short North side,"

Steven Brown, Reeds attorney said. "But don't lump all the evidence together." He slammed the prosecution for putting a witness on the stand who testified about Posse members being involved in drug dealing and who later, as a defense witness, recanted his testimony. "Who are you going to believe government witnesses or government witnesses?" Brown asked. Judge Smith ruled that the jury should determine which version of testimony given by Reginald "Froggie" Crenshaw to believe.

After deliberating for nearly five days, on November 8, 1995, the jury convicted seven members of the SNP on 34 drug dealing and gun charges. One defendant, Jimmie Reed, was acquitted. The defendants showed little emotion as the guilty verdicts were read. The judge characterized the Posse as one of the most dangerous gangs in Columbus history. U.S. Attorney Edmund Sargas praised the ATF and the Columbus Police Narcotics Bureau for their joint investigation. "The convictions say a lot about good solid police work. It shows by working together we can make the community safer."

In April 1996, a federal judge imposed the stiffest prison sentences possible on the members of the SNP. A jury in the U.S. District Court of the Southern District of Ohio, George C. Smith presiding, convicted the defendants of conspiracy, drug trafficking and firearms offenses. "This was a street gang that was a plague on the community," the judge said. "They made life in the area unliveable. It is astounding to me the young age that some of you started dealing drugs. The brutality of threatening the life of an agent who was putting his life on the line in the war on drugs is untolerable." The judge was livid and hell-bent for retribution on the SNP.

"The sentence, forty-six years and one month," Fridge says. "I got a year for myself and one for all my co-defendants in what was the biggest gang conspiracy in Columbus history." Anthony "Ant" Gibbs was sentenced to 29 years 5 months, Antwan "Trouble" Woods to 40 years, Richard "Manual" Hough to 22 years, 6 months, Chad "Boss Moss" Gibbs to 33 years, Robert Curtis to 17 years and Donneto Berry to 10 years, one month.

"This is an indictment on the whole criminal justice system," George Luther, Berry's attorney said. "My client was a low level participant. This is an example of how the guidelines have disproportionably required judges to impose lengthy sentences that don't fit the crime. All these sentences do is warehouse these young men. You can't warehouse people and expect it to make a difference in the country's drug problem." But the war on drugs was in full effect and exerted its full force on the SNP.

"The gig was up. None of us really cared. Growing up in the projects was like growing up in prison. All my dudes were in with me, so it was like my high school reunion on steroids. At six-foot-four and with a top-billing reputation in the streets and the joint, crying was not an option. My niggas expect better of me and I demand class of myself," Fridge says. "We went to trial with an Ohio all star defense team. We chopped their asses up, but nobody talks about that. Nobody talks about the good we done." The feds were only spinning it one way. They wanted the SNP to go down and go down hard. They didn't care about the community the SNP protected.

"Clearly people are getting fed up with violent crime. The judge sent a clear message, if you're going to pick up a gun and use it in a violent crime, its going to be the biggest mistake of your life." ATF Chief Mapley said. "The sentences were appropriate," U.S. Attorney Sargus said. "The defendants were convicted of having played substantial parts in the conspiracy with a high level of personal involvement." And ATF Chief Mapley added, "If you don't warehouse them, they'll be back out on the streets doing the same thing. The money is too fast and easy." But justice would prevail at least to a point for the SNP, the sentences wouldn't stand.

"Members of Drug Dealing Gang to Spend Less Time Behind Bars, "the Columbus Dispatch reported on March 16, 2000. The stiff sentences imposed on seven members of the SNP were reduced because of a ruling by a federal appeals panel. The judges reversed a total of 12 convictions while upholding 21. The three-judge panel of the U.S. 6th Circuit Court of Appeals in Cincinnati found, "with respect to the other defendants, the government's evidence proved simply that these defendants independently sold a lot of drugs. Nowhere do we see evidence that a specific defendant agreed to participate in the conspiracy." The judges wrote.

"The case was bogus, I always thought they'd get some relief from the court/appeals." The local says. "It was a trumped up drug conspiracy. You know how the feds do. They twist shit however it suits them."

Antwan Woods' attorney, Dennis Belli said of the rulings, "It appears to be a general repudiation of the government's theory that simply because individuals are selling drugs in a certain neighborhood they're engaged in an organized conspiracy." The appeals judges ordered Judge Smith to re-sentence the seven SNP members.

Tell us about the re-sentence?

Fridge: April 1999, two days before my birthday. I received a precious gift. The Dispatch announced that we had won our appeal. We all knew the conspiracy was pretty much a stunt. Shoot, three months grinding it out in trial proved that. I'm thinking new trial, but they didn't grant a new trial. They re-sentenced me to 27 years.

Ant: The re-sentencing was cool, because I got the chance to see the Posse again. We had beat the conspiracy along with a couple other charges, but we still got fucked. I was re-sentenced to 248 months.

His co-defendants got similar cuts. Hough to 19 years, Woods to 33, Curtis to 8, Boss Moss to 19 and Berry to 8. It was a victory but the defendants wanted more, and they appealed to the judge who rejected their motions for leniency. "You were part of one of the most odious groups of criminals ever to exist in Franklin County." The judge said. "The only thing the system can do is keep people like you off the streets as long as possible. You spread a slow death to many members of the community through your dreaded drugs."

Big Fridge benefited the most because his gun convictions were overturned. The appeal judges ruled that Needum's gun conviction be reversed because the weapon was not used in connection with drug dealing. The alleged armed robbery of the ATF undercover agent occurred after the drug sale. The feds were outraged. ATF Chief Mapley said, "This definitely undercuts the dangerous job Rodney Russell did. I'm shocked and dismayed." The feds couldn't leave it alone either. "Two weeks later the feds called in a favor from the state and had them drop an indictment on me." Fridge says.

Needum was charged with aggravated robbery, robbery kidnapping and unlawful possession of a dangerous ordnance by Franklin County Common Pleas Court. "We want to make sure that he is in prison for as long as possible because we consider him a dangerous man," Assistant County Prosecutor David DeVillers said. Talk about vindictive prosecution and what about double jeopardy? "If a prosecutor is going to press charges, he isn't suppose to wait to see if you're going to win the appeal five years later," Fridge says. Fridge was facing fifteen to twenty-five years in the state. That is American justice there, but it seems only to apply to people of color. Fridge ended up copping out to three years, so in reality the case was really weak. The state knew the testimony of the crackhead ATF agent wouldn't hold up.

And as the Short North Posse members rotted in federal prison, they watched as the unrighteous made money and fame off of their blood. With the release of Let That Be the Reason and the founding of Triple Crown Publications, Vickie Stringer turned her life around after five years of prison and became rich and famous. After snitching on everybody she knew or even heard of in Columbus, including her own brother, because she couldn't take the weight and do the time for her own crimes, Vickie Stringer was sentenced to five years in the feds. She wrote her book in prison, but conveniently left out the part that she was one of the biggest snitches in Columbus' history.

Vickie Stringer got busted in September 1994 and agreed to plead guilty and testify against others even her brother in exchange for reduced charges, the Columbus Dispatch reported. "Stringers information was found to be accurate and was corroborated by other confidential cooperating sources and independent investigation," authorities said. "Everyone at the crib our own age knows what the deal is with her," the dude from the era says. But people in other cities don't. They are steadily reading and supporting her and Triple Crown Publishing as if they are really the epitome of the gangsta lifestyle that their books portray. In reality the real gangsters she snitched on are sitting in the penitentiary while she profits off their stories. And imagine how the dudes from the Short North Posse case felt doing decades of their lives in the pen as the person who caused their case to come about rocketed to hood rich and street star status off of their blood.

Tell us about Vickie Stringer and what happened with your case?

Fridge: Our case started a domino effect. Lames far and wide jumped on our case in an attempt to reduce their sentences. People lied about being our connects or getting dope from us or something to get a time reduction. Many of them couldn't identify us in a lineup, but the first to tell can tell their own stories. I've stopped talking to homies because they mess with certain hot niggas and figure its cool, because they didn't tell on us. Rats are spineless and their supporters are just as spineless.

Ant: Cases are like sequels to a book series, because one case leads you to the next. Because Rob Brondon got caught and he told on Vickie Stringer, she tell on niggas in her case, my case along with niggas on other cases. The shit goes on and on. A rat is a rat. There's no justifying that. Now, most of the rats in our case were niggas who brought me to the game. I guess you could say they took me out too. To name a few- Andy Jackson, Thomas Terry, Raynard Wallace, Robert "June" Dotson. Man, fuck them hot ass, bitch ass niggas. I'm not going to waste your ink on them.

Fridge: I'll acknowledge the facts, but we're not rappers. Real niggas don't broadcast their business. Yeah, she bogus, yeah, he bogus, but that's all I got to say. It's a warning to all those who may come into contact with so and so, but that's it. That's how real niggas operate.

On January 17, 2002, the appeals court ruled that SNP members could not get their prison sentences reduced a second time. So that was it, the gig was up. Appeal Judges Guy Cole, Karen Nelson Moore and John O'Meara decided one sentence reduction was enough. And as the years have passed, the area the SNP once considered their territory has changed dramatically. "Some real estate and investors were interested in that area. About $100 million was invested in that area. They had to devalue the property, create a high crime area," the local says. "Since they got the SNP out of the way, property values went up. It's called gentrification. The legacy of the SNP is that of a group of young black men who were negatively exploited by the Department of Justice due to real estate and commercial interests."

And in Columbus there was a big buzz after the prosecutions. "They were saying shit like they saved the Short North area from urban terrorism." The local relates. "That's some bullshit. The Posse was about their business, but it wasn't any different then what went down in other hoods." In reality, was the neighborhood saved with the SNP convictions or was the SNP just a convenient group of young black males to take the fall so gentrification could occur? They were unconstitutionally locked down for a case that should have stayed on the state level. We will probably never find out for sure, but still we are here to salute the Short North Posse and the eight dudes that took the feds to trial and stood up.

What do you think your legacy is?

Fridge: It's well known that we were not a threat to the university or our hood. We're old school; we respected the turf. Yet, they still caved in our little community, but there are reasons behind this that blacks aren't looking at. It's as easy as killing three birds with one stone. In the Clinton years, Clinton was responsible for the cleanup of NAFTA. All the factory jobs were pouring out of the country, but many of those jobs were replaced with prison industries, especially in rural areas. Blacks fill up those prisons. So here you have it. You indict whole neighborhoods of black males who are getting a little money, make them face doing life or telling on everyone they know, which causes a split in the unity forever. My legacy is as of yet unfulfilled.

Anthony: Well, being that only eight of us took it to the box out of 46, I would say that we are respected and looked up to by few. The reason why I say a few is because, if you are from a city that is filled with about 80 to 90 percent of hot snitch ass niggas, what can we expect. Few stick to the street code, but a lot of them break like sticks.

How would you like to end this?

Fridge: Look around. Projects are being destroyed left and right. The trap I grew up in has trees and gates and shit, and at the bottom of the Short is $100,000 to $300,000 condos with more to come. Incarceration reduces the black populace, because incarceration is castration. HIV and AIDS will take care of the rest. The state of black America is scary. But still I'm gonna be who I am. I slay dragons, not talk them to death. Nobody cares about a grown ass man, which is what I am. They want to worship hot niggas and shit. I say let them have it. Niggas like us need to worry about one thing and that's gathering real niggas. Connecting game on a boss level and wiping clean what you can when you can. I got to mention my man Sherman "Sugar Shack" Giles. Sherm is one of those real niggas who got out the way and didn't roll his tongue. He was a big boy on the turf who chose to hold true.

Much respect to him and all my other comrades. Real soldiers who go hard these days are a rare breed. I'm honored to associate with niggas on this level.

Anthony: I've ran into a lot of good niggas who may never touch the streets again, so I would like to send respect to them- the posse, Big Fridge, Trouble, Richie Rich, Boss Hog, Sherman, Gangsta, Crusher, Dan Dan, Tom Cat, Style P, Too Short, Mike G, Sneeky Lord, Soup (Cuz), those Ohio Playas, Creed, Philly, Man, M and M, Bones, Cheeze and last but not least Larry B.H. and all the rest of the real niggas who took one on the chin and is still standing. Real eyes recognize real lies. Loyalty ain't everything, it's the only thing. Death before Dishonor.

V

HUSTLERS AND GANG BANGERS

TWENTY TWO

Public Enemy #1

THE CRAZIER A gang member is the more respect he gets from his gang. And this works for inter gang relationships too. The more brutal and terrorizing a gang is the less other gangs want to fuck with them on any type of level. MS-13 currently holds the crown as craziest gang in the country. The headlines scream - MS-13 America's most vicious gang is spreading violence to cities and suburbs across the country. But you can't always believe the headlines, or can you?

"I believe that today things are out of control and there is too much violence," says Jose Platero a 37-year-old MS-13 member who's been down with the click for 22 years. Jose, an El Salvadoran national, is currently in the feds serving a sentence for illegal reentry. "Back in the days, MS were a group of juveniles that would get together to talk about ladies and getting high on marijuana and alcohol. There were enemies back in the day, but we used to resolve our problems with our fists instead of guns. Back when I joined MS, there were only a few who resolved their problems with guns." But that was in the 80's and nowadays papers are reporting that MS-13's alleged violent activities and careless disregard for the law has made them the most feared gang in the U.S. The Washington Times reported that they have ties to terrorist group Al Qaeda and that they're a threat to homeland security. Is it all hype or reality?

"I feel it's not fair because the news only reports on what kind of criminals we are and what kind of crimes we commit and how violent we are," Jose says. "But they never write about how we were produced and they don't understand the kind of childhood that the majority of the members had." But nonetheless the mainstream media has characterized the group as a violent and powerful gang that's been responsible for murders, rapes, attacks on law enforcement, drug smuggling, gun running, people smuggling, hits for hire, theft, drug sales, arson, strong arming locals, leaving dismembered corpses, malicious wounding, assaults and batteries, and drug and weapon charges. Sounds like the mob in their heyday, but these aren't middle aged wiseguys. It's mostly kids and teenagers. It's the group's mindless brutality that keeps making headlines. Their penchant for violence is renowned.

"I think it is such a big deal now because of the crimes that MS-13 commits. I think the world doesn't think enough of MS-13 because the problem is still there and is still growing." Jose says. The FBI reports that MS-13 has cliques or factions located throughout the United States and that they are actively recruiting in the U.S. young Hispanic males and females, of which there is an abundance both legally and illegally. They have rapidly expanded from LA, their birthplace, into more than 30 states across the nation. With more than a reported 10,000 members their reach goes well beyond their inner city roots and into the suburbs. But is the media correct in their portrayal?

"Yes," Jose says. "The media is correct with their portrayal of MS-13 and how the group is widespread. The world has to think more intelligently about the MS-13 to correct the problem. We need wisdom to educate the children of the future." MS-13 is known as the most dangerous gang around. They started in California in the 80's when more than a million Salvadoran refugees fled their war torn homeland for the U.S. and settled in the barrios of Los Angeles. "MS-13 originated from Los Angeles and we are the children of the Salvadorans who were running from the war that the capitalists started for the power of the government," Jose says. "I am a product of the war and I began while living on the streets copying the actions of the older criminals."The young immigrants bonded together for protection. It was an El Salvadoran thing in East LA.

"At the beginning of the story, MS-13 was only for original Salvadorans," Jose says, but since then MS-13 has opened its ranks to Hispanics of all origins. "The M is for Mara, the S is for Salvatrucha and the 13 is for Sureno." Jose says. "In the beginning, we were M.S.S. which was MS stoners." And as the original members were deported back to their home countries of El Salvador and Honduras, they recruited religiously and entered the U.S. again in staggering numbers.

The Hispanic males, now mostly in their teens and early 20s, are seen as Public Enemy #1 in the U.S. "It wasn't supposed to be that way," Jose says. "I believe this has something to do with the two presidents who are in power now. El Gringo y el Guanaco, it's a political thing."

But it's also a poverty thing. "Life in my country is inhumane for the poor." Jose says. "My homies over there are being treated with a criminal hand." And the prisons in El Salvador are awful. They might be responsible for providing a breeding ground for the gang.

"Prison conditions are very bad in El Salvador," Jose says. "There is poor sanitation, over population, terrible food. Actually, one could refer to prison in El Salvador as criminal factories. A criminal is a human being that has a right to be treated as a human being and not as an animal. That's why we have courts and judges and prosecutors. But if they are corrupt, that's another story."

And like many MS-13 members Jose's childhood wasn't easy. "I don't remember having one," he says. "I am a victim of the war. I was educated in the streets. I learned how to read and write in juvenile hall. I learned how to speak English from growing up in the streets. My background is my experience in the world of crime and I'm from that world." And a lot of his homies are from that world, too, a world that eventually leads to prison.

"I am in prison because of my criminal history and because I am not supposed to be in the USA," Jose says. "The system calls it Illegal Alien found in the United States Following Deportation." Jose estimates there are about 1,000 of his homies in American prisons right now, but with all the anti-gang bills being passed by Congress, which are specifically targeted at MS-13, there will probably be a lot more coming in. And after doing their time they will be deported again back to their home countries where the governments are unable to bring them under control. The result has been to further entrench their smuggling operations. And for any members wishing to drop out, that's a no-no.

"I will be a MS-13 member until I die," says Jose, "because once a member is brought in they're in for life." Death is the only means of escaping MS-13. Another defining factor of the gang is their absolute intolerance for anyone who informs the police of their activities.

"That's against the rules," Jose says and the well publicized murders by the gang of several federal informants have shown they are deadly serious. They'll stop at nothing to get their mission accomplished, and with ruthless enforcement of loyalty few have the courage to turn on MS-13.

From Chicago to Raleigh to Des Moines to Dallas, you can see MS-13 members flashing their blue and white colors, flashing gang hand signs and spray painting gang graffiti at playgrounds and schoolyards in an attempt to intimidate and gain new recruits. And once accepted into MS-13 it can be deadly to try and break free again. That has law enforcement struggling to find ways to cope with the group. The FBI considers MS-13 its top priority among criminal gangs and Northern Virginia, home to a sprawling community of Salvadoran outside the nation's capital, is said to be the gang's East Coast stronghold with a reported 2,000 members. Flexible, organized and highly violent, MS-13 has incorporated itself into out society and refuses to leave. Jose even knows that talking for this story can get him killed.

"To be honest, yes, I am afraid but my opinion in this matter is not going to change the ending of the story of my life," he says. "I am living on overtime anyway."

TWENTY THREE

Gang Reporting

THE MEXICAN MAFIA or Eme is one of the most notorious and powerful gangs in Southern California. They are allegedly running things from the penitentiary to the streets of LA. Not much is known about them or their operations. What little has been revealed has been in trumped up RICO indictments against the gang by the feds or in movies like "American Me," which starred James Olmos. But the reality is that the fall out from that movie included the murder of some people involved who angered Eme shot callers with their portrayals in the film. So an aura of mystery surrounds the Mexican Mafia. Enter the In the Hat blog.

The well respected website gives the 411 on gangs, crime, cops and politics in Los Angeles. In the Hat tells the stories that the mainstream media won't. It's been in existence since February 16, 2003, and has reported exclusively on the Mexican Mafia and Hispanic street gangs in Los Angeles. The author of the blog, who goes by Wally Fay to protect his identity, is also near completion of a book, "Southern Soldiers," which chronicles the Eme and their story, from the shot callers in Pelican Bay to their gang structure to the street soldiers in the barrio. The blog has been profiled in Don Diva magazine and the Los Angeles Times, but we have a first here. We contacted the camera shy writer for an interview so that he could tell us what In the Hat is all about.

"It's about Hispanic street gangs and law enforcement in Southern California and the politics that affect both of those areas," Wally says. "I try to keep it out of the Netbanger realm. I don't encourage shout outs and gang bravedo. Instead, I try to get a dialogue going and raise the level of discourse above the "your neighborhood sucks, mine rules" level. The reason I focus on Hispanic gangs is because they outnumber all the other gangs by a huge margin and they're responsible for most of the violence, drug dealing and street crimes. None of the other groups can compare in terms of numbers or influence on the street." And that's saying a lot as LA is home to the infamous Crips and Bloods. Two very well publicized gangs that have cliques across the country.

"The Eme is clearly the most powerful organized force in the prisons and on the street. There is no other organization that can compare to its power projection beyond prison walls and the number of soldiers under its command." Wally says. "Their intelligence network is phenomenal. Something can happen in Whittier this morning and by the afternoon the brothers in Pelican Bay know all about it. And by the next morning they've already issued instructions to address the problem. The Crips, Bloods, AB, NLR- none of them have that level of command and control."

And there's no sign of the gang culture slowing down. "Keep in mind that we're now going into our fourth and fifth generation of street gangsters," Wally says. "Diamond Street, for instance, was one of the original players in the zoot suit riots in 1942. That neighborhood is still around 60 years later and still producing shot callers and brothers. The gang culture, and by extension the Eme culture, has permeated deep into the Latino community. Eme friendly or Eme sympathetic individuals can be found in every occupation you can imagine- Sheriff's deputy, LAPD, DA's office, LASD, County Clerks office, the FBI field office in downtown- you name it."

And with the Mexican Mafias long tentacles how has Wally maintained his anonymity? "Nobody knows who I am and I prefer it that way. Notoriety, fame or any kind of public image is an obstacle to getting at people and the truth."

It hasn't been easy for the self-proclaimed Sureno/Eme expert. "I've gotten a few death threats, but my sense is that as long as I tell the truth and don't spin it or try to put cases on people or maybe speculating that could hurt a guy's case, then they're okay with it. That's where Olmos got his tit in a wringer. He made stuff up about Cheyenne Cadena and the brothers disapproved with extreme prejudice. Three people were killed over Olmos' creative license."

Still the danger is there. Anger the wrong person and Wally Fay could be tracked down but just like the Italian Mafia some of the Emes like reading about themselves. "I've been told that as long as I don't make shit up or put cases on people, I'll be tolerated," Wally says. "They like reading about themselves. They just don't like lies. One guy released from county told me he overheard two shot callers talking about it. He said they seemed to like it."

But still it's a fine line to walk as Wally's been told several times by Eme members not to write the blog. "Somebody thought I was a cop stirring up the pot on the web and they took exception to a post. So now I finesse stories and try harder to put stuff between the lines," he says, "it's worked so far. No death threats in quite some time."

But what angle is Wally working, law enforcement or the street? "A little of both. I try to walk right down the middle," Wally says. "I don't make judgments and I'm not rooting for one side or the other. What I'm rooting for is a decline in the death toll. I'm trying in some small way to put a stop to the waste of lives."

An admirable goal but what do the cops think? "Some cops think I'm too sympathetic to the hoods. I interview and pester the cops and DA's the same way I interview the homies and gangsters. Sometimes I get answers and sometimes not," Wally says and on the flipside, "Some homies think I'm a shill for the cops. So I must be doing my balancing act just right."

But still what is the reason Wally puts himself in danger of being killed just to write a blog? "I write about this because I'm trying to understand it," he says. "I'm pro not having kids killed. The gang life is a dead end. Every time a kid gets killed on his bike or blasted at his front door the politicians look sternly into the cameras and say crap like: 'This has to stop', but then nothing happens. They're clueless."

And it goes deeper. "I realized from my own experience and research into street gangs, crime and law enforcement that the legitimate media was thoroughly full of crap when it came to covering gangs," Wally says. "The press doesn't dig very deeply and only gives the public a top line version of the story."

So Wally Fay started In the Hat to keep it real and give the true story, no matter the consequences to himself. "I don't get paid a nickel to do this," Wally says of his blog. "It's a labor of obsession for me."

And he knows a lot of cops, homies and reporters read his blog. "I know some cops read it because they email me with questions. I've also gotten emails from more than a few journalists about specific crimes or individuals, but when I ask them for a byline or money they run away fast. Its amazing how uninformed these people can be about something that's staring them in the face."

And a lot of readers think Wally Fay is a homie but he's not even from LA. "I grew up in New York where I was surrounded by the original Mafia," Wally says. "Almost everybody in my old hood was connected in some way to the Mob. I moved to Cali and found the street gang phenomenon both familiar and alien. They operate a lot differently here than in New York. As bad as the Italian Mob is it never put as many bodies on the street as the Eme have done in Southern California."

And let's just hope that Wally Fay doesn't become one of those bodies because for real his blog is like that. Check it out at www.inthehat.blogspot.com

TWENTY FOUR

Inside a Blood Set

IN CALIFORNIA WHERE gangs are a way of life, LA is gang-banger ground zero. The Crips, Surenos, Nortenos, Eighty-Eights and Bloods all hold court in the streets and they all perpetrate in some form or fashion. Gangs in the City of Angels are recklessly rampant. Yet, gang activity doesn't just happen in the big city. The blueprints for bangin' have infested smaller towns and spread across the nation. The ideology has transgressed ethnic, racial and geographical boundaries. Gangbanging exists in the hood, the suburbs and even rural areas all over America. Gangs have become a trend and the gang mentality is accepted in popular culture and society as a whole to a large degree.

But how did it all start and what's it really like inside a set? Gorilla Convict decided to get the 411 and take a closer look at the Bloods and in particular the Rolling 20 Neighborhood Bloods, one of the largest Blood clicks in LA today. Legend has it that the Bloods started in the summer of 1972 when a member of the LA Brims, a westside independent gang, was shot and killed by a Crip member after a confrontation. Being heavily outnumbered by the Compton Crips and thus no match for them in a gang fight, the LA Brims turned for assistance to three other non-Crip gangs: the Piru Street Boys, Lueders Park Hustlers and Denver Lanes. Before the ensuing rumble, a meeting was called on Piru Street in Compton where the four non-Crip gangs met and metamorphosed into the Bloods. To distinguish themselves from the Crips and their traditional blue bandanas, the newly formed Bloods decided to fly red rags. And so the war of colors was launched.

Throughout the 70's, 80's and into the 90's the Blood/Crips rivalry grew as did the numbers associated with the gang and their presence in cities and areas across the nation. The warfare has raged on unabated. Bloods aimed to be known as Crip Killers but recently the state of the war has changed as more and more Crips and Bloods have been fighting a more common enemy. The fight in LA has turned from Blood versus Crip and black versus black to Blood and Crip versus Surenos (Mexicans/Chicanos) and black versus brown. It's rumored that the Mexican Mafia or Eme shotcallers have green lighted all blacks in Los Angeles. From their cells at Pelican Bay the Eme have started a war in the streets of LA. And this racial war has turned vicious. Because we are Gorilla Convict, we go right to the source for our interviews. In this case we went to the California Department of Corrections to speak with Rolling 20's Neighborhood Blood soldier and O.G., Terrell C. Wright aka Loko, age 38, who is serving time for a Beverly Hills jewelry store robbery. We spoke to Loko about set life, what being a blood is all about and what the current climate in LA is concerning gang warfare.

When did you first get involved with your set?

For many, many years I sustained that wanna-be status, amongst that rank and file who mostly stood on the side lines, jocking the gangsters shadows and presence. Until finally, I crossed that threshold of no return in 1982, blindly committing myself into that cesspool of violence, death and destruction.

What neighborhood do you all represent?

Me and my homies represent a gang calling itself the Rolling 20's Neighborhood Bloods. A gang that's reputable on the west side of Los Angeles, and practically one of the largest blood gangs inside Los Angeles today.

Did you grow up there?

As shocking as this may sound too many who may have never known this, but I didn't grow up in my neighborhood; at least not in the traditional sense of growing up somewhere. But I've been a part of the fabric and interior for so long, many probably haven't even noticed.

Was it always like that?

I would have to say yes. As far back as I can recollect it's always been the way it is today: the gangs, the drama, the shootings, the murders and those that are legendary inside the gang scene. It's always been like that as far back as I can recall.

What kind of things did you all get up to?

As far as the neighborhood was concerned back in the early 80's we mostly hung-out on Vermont and 29st, drinking, smoking and flirting with the women who strolled by admiring our machismo. That was then, but as the drama intensified across the city with all the gangs vying to be dominate over the next, me and my homies committed ourselves neck deep into that which was taking the city by storm — (The era of the drive-by shooters).

When did things start progressing towards crime?

From the first inception into the Neighborhood Bloods as a member I soon learned that crime was an intricate part of the gang-bangers persona. Committing a criminal act for the gang-banger was no different than eating, sleeping and breathing. Plus back then crime paid. Our earliest form of hustling, prior to crack digging its claws into the many communities and jurisdictions, was that of snatching purses, jewelry snatching, home burglaries, stealing cars and selling its parts. As I mentioned to commit a crime was the gang-bangers hustle. So it's always been there; an intricate part of the gang-bangers life.

According to Blood legend, the red symbolizes the first inception into the Neighborhood Bloods. I soon learned that crime was an intricate part of the gang-bangers persona. Committing a criminal act for the gang-banger was no different than eating, sleeping and breathing.

Moreover, back then crime paid. Our earliest form of hustling, prior to crack digging its claws into the many communities and jurisdictions, was that of snatching purses, jewelry snatching, home burglaries, stealing cars and selling its parts. As I mentioned, to commit a crime was the gang-banger's hustle. So it's always been there; an intricate part of the gang-bangers life.

Q: Give me a history and breakdown of your set?

A: Prior to my click -the 29th click of the Neighborhood Blood - becoming a part of the NHB's, we were known as the Vermont Villain Boys. Basically, we were youths who thought they were cool. And we had such names as Lover D. - soon to become Zig Zag; Ranger, soon to become Stranger; Baby Black, soon to become Big De Bopp; and me as Baby Boy, soon to become Mr. Loko. That's how we started off as players, wanna-bes, until finally we became known as the 29th click of the NHB's. Today, we're one of the biggest clicks inside the Rollin 20s gang. We have a few hundred click members from our click alone.

Q: Where are all your homies now?

A: Wow, that's deep to me, because I always think about the generation of homeboys I grew up with, especially my click of members. Homeboys like Lace Dawg, T-Dawg, Sparky, Boodha, Joker, Hen Dawg, Te-Bopp, De-Rock, Be-Rock, Nutty-Boy, Gumboe, Dez, L-Bone, Lil Jerr, Big-Tee are either retired, dead or strung out on drugs... and I haven't even listed those who are in jail. There are a few success cases, but not many. I always reflect back on my homies and those I started off with. I often wish I could go back to those early time periods so I could hang-out with the homies that I miss.

Q: Looking back, how do you reflect on it all?

A: I have many regrets in one sense. I would be lying if I said otherwise. And in the same sense I don't have many regrets. I don't know how much sense that makes, but that's the way it is inside my heart. I am what I am: a soldier of the field who's totally equipped for any shit that hits the fan. I'm that gangster who stands his grounds when many suckasses break and run, not certain of themselves. I am an epitome of a gangster thug. So looking back, I have regrets but not many.

Q: Why did you all form in the first place?

A: If you're asking as to why the neighborhood was started, I'm not exactly certain, as the voyage was a generation before my time. But as far as my particular click, the 29th St is concerned, it gave us the opportunity to be apart of something grandeur, majestic, mystical and dominating in the hearts and minds of those who stood on the side line, admiring and awing over the gang-banger's life.

Q: What is the history of the color?

A: The choice of red as the symbolical representation for being a Blood is beyond my reach in knowledge. In fact, I don't have the slightest inclination as to why the color red was chosen for the Bloods. I'm totally lacking in that area of history.

Q: When did you first get involved?

A: Before I was an official made-man on the gang scene, I had my few tumultuous years from about 1979 to 1981 as a wanna-be gangster. So I started in the gang-bangers track some time ago, and it wasn't much time later that I was ready to make that commitment.

Q: What's it like for the young kids growing up there?

A: It's a continual struggle for the youngster growing up in Los Angeles. It's a city where the gang-bangers aura has a strong grip on the minds of youth from an early age onward. They have to always battle the choice between joining the rank and file of those who came before them into the gang scene, or to march down a separate path. But in my humble opinion, it's a struggle in every aspect.

Q: How do you see things in your neighborhood today?

A: Today is no different than the old: gang wars, funerals, lives destroyed and many more adversities to overcome. The only difference today, is instead of having the traditional Blood versus Crip wars, and Mexican (cholos) versus Mexican warfare, the two predominate groups in Southern California, have now turned their guns on each other. It's the new trend of black gangsters versus brown gangsters. But it's a no win situation, as the only for sure outcome is that there will be more chaos and destruction than there was the day before. All across the LA county lines, and its many highways and byways, the black and brown gangsters are drawing up new battle lines, re-drawing and re-establishing new Demilitarized Zones, inside communities they once happily shared together, and are killing each other at an alarming rate. The excrement blood baths have the two groups taking it to dimensions of warfare that's considered something new to the many LA gangsters: racial targeting and culture clashes. It's the new trend, and sadly enough, it'll be here for a while. But as it buries itself deeper into the fine woven material of the LA scene, more lives will be lost, and many more heart breaks of family, friends, homies, brothers, cousins, fathers, and uncles loss of lives will continue to rise out of control.

Q: What are all the dudes into?

A: Nowadays, most of my homies are into grinding (hustling) and trying to attain that almighty dead president (money). Although it's rare in a larger sense, some are attempting to use their illegal proceeds to take a shot at making a legit living by starting a legalize business of some sort. But for the most part most of my homies are grinding it out on one level or another.

Q: How do you feel about all this?

A: I have no qualms with any of my homies. They are trying to find their niche and I'm trying to find mine. My philosophy is, you make the bed, so you sleep in it. That's how I feel.

Q: What would you do to change how it is?

A: If you're referring to the gang scene inside the blocks I grew up on, I'd be more than willing to take a step forward to try and bring about some type of change for the betterment of the neighborhood as a whole and for those who make up the community. I would be willing to make an attempt at trying to form a peace treaty of some sort to rid my neighborhood of the violence that have plagued it for so long. I'm at that point in my life where I'm comfortable saying that and sincerely meaning it.

Q: What can society do?

A: What can society do, huh? In my mind, society can assist in many, many ways. I would love to be a part of a (think-tank) from the many echelons of society and try and to come up with some radical solutions, viable solutions to bring about an overdue change inside the hood. I wouldn't mind doing my part, as long as society does its part. In the end, it's a group effort.

Q: Will it ever stop or just stay the same?

A: In my philosophical mind frame, nothing stays the same — absolutely nothing. To me the one thing that remains constant is change. So in my humble opinion, I have a philosophical inclination to say that it will change one day. But the mystery behind that fact of life is what type of change will come. Will it be for the worse or for the better? But as a collective it would be most wise to have a hand in the dynamic that will be so the change that is inevitable will hopefully bear something positive, not negative.

Q: Who were your biggest rivals?

A: Undoubtedly, the Rolling 30's Harlem Crips, are our biggest rivals, and always have been. We battle on sight, and the only time that we've had a tentative peace treaty with each other was during the 1992 LA riots. But keep in mind, it was a tentative agreement. We had rules in place. We would stop our drive-by against them, and they would stop theirs against us. And unlike most rivals during that period, who openly visited each other's turfs as a sign that the warfare was over, the Neighborhood 20's (my turf) and the Harlem 30's had an understanding, we were not to visit each others stomping grounds.

For months the tentative agreement held until one late night on Brighton Avenue and Adams Blvd my roll dawg, Lil Moe, was shot eight or nine times at close blank range. And despite the early rumors that the Hoover Criminal (Crips at the time) had done the shooting, the Republic of the Neighborhood Bloods took our boiling wrath out on the entire Republic of the Rolling 30's. We struck at them from every angle, sending out messages that the LA peace treaty was officially over with, on the West Side of the city.

Q: What did you all beef for?

A: In the early days we beefed simply because we were Bloods and they were Crips. That was the unique dynamic all across the city. We were from opposite ends of the spectrum.

Q: Does the animosity still exist today?

A: Yes! It still exists but not as it once did. The wars are fewer than it once was, but when they do commence, they're bloody and violent. It's unlike the old days when the wars were more rampant, as many LA gangs vied to be the biggest fish in the ocean. We did what damage we could with our simple revolvers. But in today's time when wars jump-off, the automatics are brought out and most times multiple body count of dead are the results. So most wars today are brief, but are very, very traumatic. But don't get me wrong either. It's always a state of warfare between the warring tribes.

Q: What do you have to say to all the young kids coming up?

A: To not follow in the gangster's footsteps, to stay focused on something positive, and to remain steadfast in some constructive belief that will yield positive results. And never ever join a gang.

Q: As an O.G. (Original Gangster) who are your contemporaries?

A: In my line of work, many of my contemporaries are either dead, doped out, or have fallen off the face of the earth. But there are some, and since I'm asked to acknowledge them, specifically from my particular tribe. I would have to say my homeboy Big Tray-Kay from the 27th St., Big Krazy-Kay from the Avenue's, and Big Spook from the 29th St. There are plenty, plenty more I could tilt my hat to, but those I mentioned, are active generals in the field, directing, showing and leading divisions of cadres on the field of battle.

Q: Who are the fallen soldiers that need to be recognized?

A: I have a laundry list of soldiers that I'd like to mention,. First, I would like to tilt my gangsta hat to my O.G. homeboy, Original Gangster Santa-Klaus. For years I ran underneath his tutelage, absorbing all the street knowledge he had. And he taught me well. Also my big homey, O.G. Thunder. And of course, I have a list of names that I'd like to tilt my hat to and whom I would want many to remember: Billy Rob (1978), Fish-Bone (1984), Stoney (1986), Dopey (1987), L-Bone (1987), Don Don (1987), Lil No-Good (1988), Sweaty-Teddy (1989), Tee-Lok (1990), Dez (1990), Lace Dawg (1990), Dipps (1991), Wicked (1992), Santa Klaus (1993), Lil Squidd (1993), Baby Reese (1993) Cee-Kay (1993), Lil Krazy-Kay (1993), Insane Wayne (1993), Killa Kal (1993), Wino (1994), Loko-Moe (1995), Lil Dee-Kapone (1995), Tiny-Spook (1996), Tee-Spoon (1996), Kay-Dee (1997), Belizean Jerry (1999), Fat-Man (1999), Gee-Kev (2000), M-Dawg (2000), Big Bee-Rock (2000), Nipples (2001), Dre-Dawg (2001), Ant-Dawg (2001), Tiny Evil (2002), Roscoe (2003), Ise-Man (2003), Jay-Bee (2003), Kool Boy (2003), Baby Tippy (2003), Evil (2003) Lil-Kay Kay (2004), Rick Dawg (2004), Jay-Dee (2004), Black (2006).

Q: What sets are around your neighborhood?

A: My neighborhood borders with friends and foes. To the south of our neighborhood, we have our allies the Fruit Town Brim Bloods. Next to them, on our south-west border, we have our arch nemesis, the Harlem Crips. To our immediate west end, we have our allies the Black P. Stone Bloods (City Stones) and to our northwest border, we have our enemies, the School Yard Crips. North of us, we have our rivals the Mid City Stoners-13, and the Playboys-13. But we have enough girth to feel comfortable inside our established borders. In fact, it's estimated that we have the biggest territory of any black gang inside LA We have five large clicks that make up our neighborhood, and we have a sixth click, that doesn't get much air play. They are called the BZP (Belizean Posses). They're small but ruthless. They hold their own, as the Neighborhood Bloods have been known to carry their weight inside the gang arena. Before I west side roll out, I would like to give a shout out to my homies the Homicide Neighborhoods Bloods in New York, the 8-Mile Neighborhoods Bloods in Detroit and Bakersfield Neighborhood Bloods in California. And a salute to all the Bloods across the country.

Besides being a Blood soldier and convict, Terrell C. Wright aka Loko is also an author. Check out his books, Home of the Body Bags and the upcoming To Live and Die in LA, which chronicle his journey as a Blood soldier from the streets to the penitentiary. For more info on his books visit www.senegalpress.com or streetgangs.com. To learn more about the brown on black violence in LA check out the In the Hat blog at www.inthehat/blogspot.com.

TWENTY FIVE

Twenty-One Years Later, Injustice Prevails

T HE ARTICLE BELOW appeared in the New York Daily News 20 years after Char "Shocker" Davis was sentenced to 405 months for his role in Lorenzo "Fat Cat" Nichols and Howard "Pappy" Mason's drug distribution networks. On July 27, 1989, following a jury trial, Shocker was found guilty of count 12 of a 15 count superseding indictment. Count 12 charged that between February 1988 and August 11, 1988, Shocker, along with others, conspired to possess with intent to distribute in excess of fifty grams of cocaine base. This was a violation of 21 USC, Section 846 and 841 (b)91)9A).

By association, the feds implicated Shocker in murders he did not commit, including those of Fat Cat's parole officer Brian Rooney, police officer Edward Byrne and Charlene Baskerville, who is mentioned in the New York Daily News article. Instead of being innocent until proven guilty, the feds found Shocker guilty by association. And now after 21 years in the belly of the beast, when relief from his draconian, unwarranted and disproportionate 405 month sentence is finally in sight due to changes in the federal sentencing guidelines for crack cocaine offenses, the feds are again bringing up unindicted, unproven, unconvicted and unsubstantiated allegations, while using the media to great effect in their war against black males.

Since the New York Daily News is giving the Brooklyn U.S. Attorneys office a forum to air false and unproven allegations, Gorilla Convict has decided to give Shocker a chance to speak. After 21 years of silence Shocker has decided to set the record straight on his crack reduction motion, the article in the New York Daily News, his case, Fat Cat, Pappy Mason and the Bebos. Here it is the Gorilla Convict exclusive with Char "Shocker Davis," the go hard soldier who earned his stripes under street legend Pappy Mason.

What did you do when the changes in the federal sentencing guidelines for crack offenses jumped off?

I submitted a motion to get a crack reduction in April 2008 when I was in Raybrook. I didn't hear nothing about it until I got to Loretto a year later. The case manager called me in the office and told me to sign a progress report. My probation officer from the Eastern District of New York wanted to see it because I might be getting a time cut. The probation officer called my sister and asked her where does she work at, live and her salary, and if I was released, could I stay with her and my sister said yes.

Have you heard back from the courts about your motion yet?

No, but seven, eight months later the article in the New York Daily News came out and made it seem like I'm not eligible. But I am eligible for it. However, my case reduction motion is still not decided.

When you read the article, how did you feel? What did you think?

I was floored. I couldn't understand it after all this time. I wasn't discouraged though cause I know it's just a propaganda machine. I know I'm supposed to get some justice. I called my sister on the Sunday before I even saw the article and she was crying, talking about how they don't want to let you come home. She told me about the article that was portraying me like a monster. A month after that I got in the mail, the prosecutors response trying to shut me down.

How do you feel about the feds bringing up uncharged, unproven allegations in the article?

I feel it's not right. My thing is I never got arrested or convicted for this. I can't fathom how they enhanced my sentence for something I was never charged with, and now they are still trying to deny me for a crime I didn't commit. What I really feel is that they got a hard on for us because of what happened to Byrne. They knew I was a Bebo, so I am guilty by association. They know I was part of that crew.

Switching gears, how did you get down with Fat Cat and Pappy Mason?

I was born and raised in Forty Projects. I met Pap first but Cat knew my family. He knew my aunts, my grandma worked at the diner on 150th Street. So I always saw him because he knew my family. Fat Cat was like a legend. But I met Pap first through Ruff, his brother, who I got cool with.

How did that happen?

I'm on 160th Street. I see this dude with dreadlocks on a pedal bike. The way he talked, his whole swag, he was like a gangster god. I already decided I wanted to be a gangster, but after I saw Pap I wanted to be like him. This was like 1983.

How did you get down with the crew?

I saw him again, and he told me he was opening a spot on the 4th floor of my building. He knew that I was already hanging out with his brother Ruff. I go up there with Ruff and I'm down. I'm working security, I got a walkie-talkie. One time the police run up. I get arrested but I don't say nothing. So I'm locked in for life. Basically I met Pap on the strength of Ruff.

What was up with the Bebos?

I'm an original Bebo. Bebos came like '84 or '85. That's when we started calling each other Bebo. Most of us had dreads. They thought we were a Jamaican gang but we weren't. There wasn't that many of us. We were around Cat, an extension of him.

What was Pappy Mason like?

There won't never be nobody like him. He was a gangster god. He did a lot of good for people. That's just the type of person he was. He didn't like seeing people get taken advantage of. Pap taught us to have honor. It was different then, not like today.

THE NEW YORK DAILY NEWS ARTICLE

Deadly drug trafficker Char (Shocker) Davis asks to be released from jail early By John Marzulli.

Daily News Staff Writer Sunday, December 6th 2009, 4:00 AM

He was a feared lieutenant in drug lord Howard (Pappy) Mason's "Bebos" crack organization that ravaged South Queens in the 1980s and assassinated NYPD cop Edward Byrne. Now, Char (Shocker) Davis, who bashed a woman to death with a cast-iron pan, says he should go free.

Davis has nine years left on a 33-year drug trafficking conviction in 1989, but he wants to be sprung early based on last year's changes in federal sentencing guidelines for crack cocaine offenses. The change, which makes sentences more lenient, is retroactive.

The Brooklyn U.S. attorney's office filed papers last week arguing that Davis doesn't qualify for a reduction in his sentence under the amended guidelines.

Brooklyn Federal Judge Edward Korman slammed Davis with the maximum term because he also found that Davis savagely murdered Charlene Baskerville with a frying pan in her Queens apartment.

Baskerville, whose head was stuffed into a garbage bag, was bludgeoned repeatedly for nearly 30 minutes. The blows were so hard the heavy pan shattered.

"Finally , Davis said to Baskerville, 'I told you about running your mouth,'" court papers say. "Davis enthusiastically participated in the violence that was a Bebos' trademark."

Then Assistant U.S. Attorney Leslie Caldwell urged the judge to throw the book at the drug thug.

"There is no reason to think that anything other than keeping him in prison will deter him from committing violent, vicious crimes like the ones he's already committed," Caldwell said, according to a transcript.

"This is the only kind of sentence that will protect society from the defendant," she said.

Davis, now 39, made the request for early release from his cell in Loretto, Pennsylvania.

Mason, his former drug boss, is serving a life term at the super-maximum prison in Florence, Colo., where the country's most dangerous inmates are locked up.

Mason ordered the murder of rookie cop Byrne from his jail cell in 1988 in retaliation for the NYPD dissing him on the street and busting him on a gun charge. Byrne was guarding the home of a witness against the gang when he was killed.

Davis' sister, Cherise Davis, wrote to Korman on her brother's behalf. She lamented that her sibling has missed many family milestones while incarcerated and said he "deserves a second chance to live his life as a responsible and productive member of society."

TWENTY SIX

The Mexican Mafia

L A EME IS one of the big four California prison gangs. They originated in the California prison system in the 1960s and have grown since then to rule a vast empire of criminal activities, stretching from Southern California to Arizona to Colorado. Virtually all the southwestern gangs of Mexican heritage (Surenos) are under their control. In prison and on the streets they are one of the most feared gangs in America. Recently there have been a bunch of books published about their activities- Tony Rapheal's The Mexican Mafia, Boxer Enriquez's The Black Hand, Mundo Mendoza's From Hitman to Alter Boy and Robert Morrill's The Mexican Mafia: The Story. To get you the 411 on this treacherous group we reached out to author Robert Morrill. Here is the Gorilla Convict interview.

Describe the Eme's growth since you first started investigating them?

La Eme was a well-established prison gang by 1970, and by 1971 they hit the streets to take over many criminal operations. That is when the Gang Task Force (established in April, 1972) first started. They soon spread to other states via the Bureau of Prisons system or by some Eme (Carnales) or Associates (Camaradas) who moved back to their home states upon release from California prisons. Often these gangs took on their own homegrown flavor, but also remained in communications with California Eme. They are now considered organized crime, and often Eme members have ties to the Mexican drug cartels.

What is the state of the Mexican Mafia today?

The Mexican Mafia today has been targeted by numerous RICO cases, however as with other prison gangs, this often spreads them out as more and more Eme members were moved to Federal BOP Prisons all across the United States. They have been impacted by Law Enforcement and Corrections suppression efforts and lockdowns, but prison gangs are very good at adapting to these efforts and circumventing us through abusing the system, by using dirty lawyers, and having other people such as Camaradas, wives, and girlfriends handle their business on outside of prison or out on General Population Prison Yards.

Have the federal indictments put a dent in their empire?

All of the federal indictments have put a dent in personal Eme empires, such as when their personal bank accounts and assets are frozen. But I have explained, they often adapt.

What do you think of the recent books on the Eme like Tony Rapheal's "Mexican Mafia" and Boxer Enriquez's "The Black Hand?"

No disrespect, but Tony Rapheal's "The Mexican Mafia" is a good recent case study of the Avenues street gang based on court transcripts. But his book does not paint a complete picture of La Eme and their ties to hundreds of other street gangs over the years. It also misses, in my opinion, many of the very early crime elements and important Eme figures that were investigated by the Gang Task Force. Boxer Enriquez's book, "The Black Hand," written with renowned television investigative reporter Chris Blatchford does a better job of showing the various ties between La Eme, street gangs, and how they operate on a daily basis inside and outside of the system, but Boxer was not around when many of the early Eme members were investigated. He does cover "Topo" Peters fairly well. Topo was a mentor to Boxer but later despised by him as he learned about all the treachery done by fellow Eme.

Have you ever read Tony Raphael's blog In the Hat? What do you think the Eme think of him reporting on him and his book?

Tony Raphael's blog, In the Hat, started off as a pretty good discussion board, but appears to have stopped posting. I do not believe the Eme were very concerned because most of the correct info posted on his blog and in his book are already pubic info and in court record.

Do you see more "American Me" type stuff happening in this day and age, what with the Internet and all the info on the Eme available?

American Me, which several Eme and Gang Task Force members were advisors to, was a good thing and a bad thing. It was more accurate than say "Blood In, Blood Out," but it also has some discrepancies, such as when they show La eMe killing the real Santana "Chy" Cadena on the tier at Chino's Palm Hall. That did not happen! He was killed by Nuestra Familia. Gang Task Force members advised against the film's producer and actor Edward James Olmos putting that in as well as the sodomy scenes. But it appears he thought it would have more Hollywood box office appeal and left it in. As a result some eMe and a former associate were killed. Olmos also had threats on his life. So future directors may not want to touch the subject, or at least not use real gang names, for fear of retaliation.

There is a lot of info on the Eme available, but a lot of is flat out wrong. People mix apples and oranges, California Eme with Texas EME, etc. Good websites with good info are available, such as Gabe Morales' site Gang Prevention Services, or articles written in Police Magazine by Eme expert Richard Valdemar, or DOJ Official Press Releases.

Some of the info out there is really bad, people should check the background of the authors. Most of these people never met or personally dealt with Eme. They just heard about them.

Has your life ever been threatened because of your book?

If an author or gang investigator sticks to the truth and only puts out info that can be proven in court, has actual pictures, and relies on good informants and validated criminal justice info, then they should not be worried about being threatened. Eme knows the real facts!

Who are the most powerful Eme members today and where are they located?

Many of the Original Eme members are dead. There are a few early members still around like "Champ" Reynoso, "Rube" Soto, "Blackie" Segura, etc. There are also newer ones like Francisco "Puppet" Martinez from 18th Street and La Eme, "Huero Sherm" Leon and "Bat" Marquez from San Diego. Many are locked down in the BOP-ADX or at Pelican Bay.

What was Joe Morgan like?

Joe Morgan (deceased) was one of a kind. He was named the "Honorary Godfather" by Chy Cadena. Morgan's time in California Prison predated La Eme. He had ties to the Aryan Brotherhood and Italian Mafia. He was always respectful to staff who actually dealt with him. He did not like the name "Pegleg." Very few said that to his face and lived. He was pretty close to the character shown as "J.D." in the movie "American Me." Even though he was white he grew up in Maravilla and knew the culture. He was deadly, but already made his bones early in life. Other people would kill for him or even take the rap for him. No other Mexican Mafia member has ever had the power that Papa Joe did. While the Mexican Mafia is supposed to have no overall leader, and in theory every Carnales' vote is supposed to be the same, some like Joe had "la palabra pesada." Their word and opinions carry more weight. People who disagree often end up being on bad terms with La Eme or end up dead.

What were the original Eme like compared to the Eme today?

The original Eme like Chy Cadena and "Huero Buff" Flores or relatively early Eme like Joe Morgan were a different breed.

It has been said they were like the "Coke Generation". Later members who joined like "Boxer" Enriquez have been called the "Pepsi Generation". Many of the ones around today are more like the "Sprite Generation" but there are still some Old School left in La Eme. There are still some killers, but as they have grown, many of the old rules about honor and respect have gone away. Many former Eme stated that is why they left after feeling disillusioned. Of course, many also left Eme for their own selfish reasons.

TWENTY SEVEN

Death Before Dishonor

T0 LIVE BY a code, to embody that ideal, to be the real deal that is death before dishonor. A lot of dudes talk about keeping it real and staying true to the game, but when they get busted and snitch, they say, "Charge it to the game." The drug game is fucked up; that's a fact. With mandatory minimums, the federal sentencing guidelines and our government's War on Drugs, snitching has become the norm. A man who sticks to his ideals is a rarity, a throwback to the past when principles, omerta and honor among thieves stood for something other than a rap video. This new "Stop Snitching" fad embraced by the hip-hop culture is all well and good but will it harken back to the times of old when men where men, gangsters kept their mouths shut and crossing your brother was obsolete?

With black gangsters newfound relevance in pop culture due to rappers putting them on pedestals and mythologizing their crime exploits in verse, a new kind of anti-hero from the inner city is taking their place, standing next to the Mafia and Billy the Kid in American folklore. With magazines like Don Diva and F.E.D.S., Ethan Brown's "Queens Reigns Supreme" and BET's "American Gangster" series wetting the public's appetite for the street legends long idolized by rappers, a movement is afoot. But for real, don't get it twisted. Let's not get it fucked up. A lot of snitches, rats and informants are getting their shine on and being held up as an example of the American black gangster. I'm talking about cats like Alpo, who was featured in F.E.D.S., and Freeway Ricky Ross, Fat Cat, and Leroy "Nicky" Barnes, who were profiled on BET"s "American Gangster." Just like the Mafia turncoats before them, they are getting all the hype. About the only publication that keeps it real is Don Diva, which refuses to pay tribute to snitches or to those who turn their back on and betrayed the criminal code and the drug game.

Don Diva goes hard like the Gorilla Convict blog and only honors true gangsters like Kenneth "Supreme" McGriff, who is going to trial in January and facing the death penalty. He is a man who embodies what death before dishonor means. To both law enforcement and a generation of rappers and hustlers, Supreme is a black John Gotti, a larger than life figure whose underworld reach seems limitless.

"The streets will always respect Preme for who he is," says David "Bing" Robinson, a former Supreme Team member who was with Supreme since the jump off in the 80's. Bing, who grew up in South Jamaica, first met Preme as a teen and was arrested with him on a 1985 drug case in New York City. Bing came home in 1989, hooked up with Preme's nephew, Prince while Preme was in prison and subsequently got a 19-year sentence on the infamous Supreme Team racketeering case from 1993.

"We always been good." Bing says, looking back on his association with the notorious gangster. "Everybody has their good ways and their bad ways, but Preme is a brother to me. I have no complaints. He was always good to me. We lived the life. I'll love that nigga forever." And for real when black American gangsters are mentioned, Supreme's name is at the top of the list along with Frank Mathews aka Black Caesar, who is still a fugitive from justice 30 years after he was indicted. All these other dudes got it fucked up.

"The biggest names come out of Queens," Curtis Scoon said in an Allhiphop.com interview in which he trashed fellow gangsta writer

Ethan Brown as a fraud. But who is Curtis Scoon? A Queens native and aspiring screenwriter who was a suspect in the Jam Master Jay homicide and who is now capitalizing on his notoriety and the gangsta craze. Along with Ethan Brown he appeared in BET's "American Gangster" segment on Lorenzo "Fat Cat" Nichols, and according to Scoon, he played a big part in Ethan Brown's book, "Queens Reign Supreme."

"I came up with the idea to put all the guys in Queens in one book and then connect it to hip-hop." He said. And with his Fat Cat piece in the new King, Scoon is really pushing Cat, who he said, "Is the biggest name in his time in the 80's." But it's been circulating that Fat Cat snitched on Howard "Pappy" Mason, his cohort in crime for years. Even 50 Cent rapped about that. But to a lot of Queens dudes from the era, Cat is still the man. But they don't know who Curtis Scoon is. With so many dudes jumping on the bandwagon, it's hard to see who's legit and who's not. But one things certain and two for sure- Kenneth "Supreme" McGriff is that dude, always has been and anyone associated with him is certified.

"They always gonna remember him as a top legend from the hood," Bing says. "He was one of the main generals who represented Southside Jamaica Queens to the fullest. He's a person the streets will always re-member as a legend. He repped the hood and made Southside Jamaica shine." But his legend has also been his downfall. Hence, his 2005 federal indictment and the allegations he provided seed money and muscle to record label Murder Inc., which has largely been disproven with Irv Gotti and his brother's acquittal last year. But still Preme has to face the music.

The feds contend that Supreme has been responsible for Mafia style murders while moving kilos of cocaine in multiple states following his release from prison in the mid 90's after 12-years in prison on a drug kingpin charge. The feds are trying to give Supreme the death penalty, alleging he directed co-conspirators to kill associates in Baltimore and that he arranged other murders in New York City. He was originally indicted with the people accused of committing the murders and the

Murder Inc. honchos, but his trial was severed several times until he stood alone and after numerous delays and no co-defendants he will finally go to trial in January.

"All I know is that they ain't letting no black man win no federal trial, no murder case." Bing says. "Especially a dude like him with his history. He got more shit against him then we did in the RICO act case. I don't think he can beat that. I hope he does for his sake." But with all his former co-defendants and those accused of the murders in the government fold ready to testify against him, it doesn't look good for Supreme. He even admitted as much in a Vibe magazine interview last summer.

"You can put the death penalty on me," Supreme said. "I've lived my life already. I've done everything I wanted to do. I'm gonna stick to my values and face certain death. Every shooting they point the finger at me, the bad guy." It seems in a way as if Preme has already conceded the government the victory. But how did it all evolve and come to this point?

"They painted this picture themselves," Antoine Clark the publisher of F.E.D.S. magazine, who recently appeared in the BET's "American Gangster" segment on Leroy "Nicky" Barnes and who regularly pays tribute to rats in his publication, said in a NY Times interview, about the whole Murder Inc./Supreme situation. "There's something that comes behind bringing in a kingpin to ride with you. There's a certain ghetto pride and ghetto respect, but there's also a police investigation into the ties." But to dudes like Bing, real dudes who know what's really up, the whole thing is a travesty.

"Shit was good. He was going legit." Bing says of Preme's hook up with Murder Inc. and production of the DVD "Crime Partners" in early Y2K. "I was glad for that. He was with a legitimate organization that was making millions of dollars. That was like hitting the lotto. Especially, how they looked up to him like they did." But with the subsequent investigation into Murder Inc., because of Supreme's past, it all fell apart, the dream of legitimacy that is.

"At first, I didn't think nothing of it, because they were always putting his name out there because of who he was," Bing says. "They linked him to everything because of his name." And Supreme's name stayed ringing bells, because of all the rappers like Biggie, Nas, The Game, and 50 Cent who big upped him and the Supreme Team in their songs mythologizing them for their 80's crime exploits.

"It was good they paid homage to us for who we were and what we did," Bing says of the verses. "But I felt different about it when I first heard that shit. It is what it is." And in Vibe, Supreme had even more to say about it. "When we was coming up, there was a code of conduct. You didn't speak about dudes who may still be in the streets." But in Y2K with everything gangsta going popular culture, the rules are all getting twisted. And this leads to the biggest allegation and one that is uncharged in his indictment: the allegation that he ordered the shooting of 50 Cent in 2000.

As everyone knows, 50 Cent was shot nine times in front of his grandmother's house in Jamaica Queens. He went on to rap about surviving the attack and even raised the question in verse of whether Preme had anything to do with it. "This dude sensationalizes everything. All his statements are incendiary." Preme said in Vibe. "The government believes every lyric and then he (tells the police), 'read my lyrics.' Where I come from, that's dry snitching." And in the Murder Inc. trial, super snitch Jon "Love" Ragin, who worked on the "Crime Partners" DVD with Supreme, testified that Supreme told him he put the hit on 50. The whole scenario will most likely be replayed in the upcoming trial. Could 50 Cent make an appearance? On the whole 50 Cent deal, Preme broke it down in Vibe, "Kid, you've never been through nothing. I was around wolves, man. I walked among giants."

Recently in XXL 50 fired back. "He fuckin on trial. He shouldn't be talking. He should be keeping his fuckin mouth shut. I'm sure if he had a lawyer his lawyer would tell him not to have done that fuckin article." 50 said, alluding to the fact that Preme has a public defender representing him and in the same interview 50 even questioned Preme's motives.

"Are you an organized crime mob boss or were you a nigga from Baisley Projects who sold crack?" 50 asked and went on. "Preme loves to be out in the eye. He wants to be a fucking celebrity. He was a nigga you would look at and say, he the real deal. But the nigga at this point is broken. You mean to tell me none of the crew is making enough money in the streets to handle your lawyer fees, I don't recall John Gotti ever having a problem getting his lawyers' fees paid." But maybe that solidifies the defense's point. Supreme was trying to go legit. There is no crew. This whole indictment is just some gangsta rap fantasy the government has concocted by lifting the evidence straight from 50 Cent's lyrics. Talk about reality TV.

"I feel for him," Bing says of his man Supreme. "But if you choose to live that life, you got to suck it up. Dudes getting life everyday. Everybody got to fight their battle. We fought ours back in the day. A life sentence is not a good thing but when you choose that lifestyle, it's one of the consequences."

Consequences for one's actions is what magazines like Don Diva stress in their pages. It's why they don't glorify or promote rats, because snitches don't pay the consequences of their actions. They put someone else in the line of fire. That is not honorable. And a true gangsta like Supreme represents what death before dishonor means. He prefers death, is willing to face death, rather then dishonor his name, his hood, and his reputation. And concerning the indictment, Supreme said in his Vibe interview, "It's like a desperation grab. I've never been known as a murderer, and all of a sudden I'm this psychotic killer." Even 50 Cent rhymed as much in Ghetto Qu'ran- "Preme was the businessman and Prince was the killer." So if the feds are really reading 50's lyrics, it seems they got it all fucked up.

VI

STREET LIT

TWENTY EIGHT

Gangsta Lit

FROM THE GHOSTS of gangsta past, notably Donald Goines and Iceberg Slim, a new generation of writers are taking up the mantle and resurrecting a long since dead and underground genre- street novels, and making it into a multi-million dollar industry. From the ashes of blaxploitation films like "Jackie Brown" and "Shaft," these new gangsta novelists are creating their own brand of blood-drenched tales of criminal life in American ghettos, reminiscent of "Whoreson" by Goines, and "Pimp" by Iceberg. And just like the rap game these authors are on one million and taking the game by any means necessary, with their intoxicating world of hip-hop fiction.

If Donald Goines and Iceberg Slim are the godfathers of street novels then Teri Woods is definitely the Queen Bee. Her novel, "True to the Game," which fictionalized the rise and fall of the notorious Philadelphia Jr. Black Mafia crew from the late 80's, has sold more than 500,000 copies independently since its mid 90's release. Woods has become the major player in the hip-hop fiction genre as an independent with her publishing company, Teri Woods Publishing. "True to the Game was really meant to represent a lifestyle," Teri said in Don Diva Magazine. "You write what you know. A lot of these books, and especially the ones that are real good with stories behind them, are leaving a piece of documented history. I don't really call what I do street fiction. I refer to it as true-to-life crime, and that's what I think my books represent. The crack era existed for black gangsters just like Prohibition did for the Italians and Irish." And Teri's company was the one that opened the flood gates. What began as a trickle is now an all out waterfall, as streets novelists are coming up out of the gutter and flooding the market with their independently released gangsta books. But authors are also literally coming out of prison, as novelist Shannon Holmes did.

Holmes wrote his first book, "B-More Careful," in prison, and after several rejections from the publishing world he contacted Woods in the late 90's who then proceeded to put out his gritty street novel. The book has sold over 100,000 copies, and made Holmes a star in the hip-hop fiction genre. Flush with success Holmes found a partner, another ex-con by the name of Vickie Stringer, and they formed Triple Crown Publications, which put out Stringers first novel, "Let that be the Reason," and a host of others by first-time authors such as Nikki Turner (A Hustlers Wife) and K'Wan (Gangsta). Triple Crown now has a roster of 25 authors, and has gone on to sell several hundred thousand copies of the various books they've published to become a leader in the genre. "Triple Crown is like Motown when they were hot back in the day," Vickie Stringer said in Inc. Magazine. "The name guarantees it will be a bestseller. Hip-hop is universal. But don't worry you don't have to go to the hood, we'll bring the hood to you." And Vickie remembers her humble beginnings. "I was a 29-year-old felon with no degree, no resume, almost no legal work experience, no money, and no prospects. My manuscript was rejected by 26 publishers, so I decided to self-publish. I will never forget the small African American mom and pop distributors, because they were there for me from day one when all I had was word of mouth." And distribution has been a big factor in the genre's success, or lack there of.

"Distribution and lack of structure in this book game is a problem." Says author Kwame Teague who penned the Dutch series for Teri

Woods. "It's just a scramble now as far as the book game goes. So many good writers aren't heard because of it. Still the industry is wide open to be organized and streamlined, feel me?" With all the success of the genre the majors have come calling. Holmes was signed by Simon and Schuster to a $400,000 two book deal, and Stringer signed on too. Both are on Atria Books, the African American imprint of S&S, and they are working with senior editor Malaika Adero for more mainstream success because the big companies see dollar signs in the genre. Holmes put out "Bad Girlz" and two other books on Atria, and Stringer did "Imagine This," the follow up to her first novel. But they haven't made the impact that their first novels did. More Triple Crown authors have been picked up by St. Martin's Press, another large New York house, as Vickie Stringer has turned agent. "I have now represented nine writers with contracts valued at over a million dollars." And another ex-con has capitalized too. Relentless Aaron who put out books on his own Relentless Content label signed to a major, too, in a reported six figure deal.

And with Nikki Turner, formerly crowned the princess of hip-hop fiction, making a claim for the Queenship, the genre is being shaken up. Her success at Triple Crown and Urban books enabled her to sign with Random House for a very large deal that included setting up her own imprint, Nikki Turner Presents. "I'm really excited about my new imprint," she says. "In addition to Street Chronicles, my short story collection, I just received a deal to do full length books." So just like the rap game, the world of hip-hop fiction is blowing up, going hard like Don Diva magazine with their violent tales of drugs, betrayal and money. The grimy and gritty world of the ghetto is coming in print to mainstream America. Even 50 Cent is getting in on the action with G-unit books who signed the aforementioned Nikki Turner to pen their premiere release. But back to Teri Woods who now boasts 10 titles out on her independent house.

Teri Woods has continued to publish herself, changing the game one book at a time, refusing to sign with a major, and steadily putting out books on the strength of her name alone. She has been described as a good marketer, and savvy businesswoman who knows what's hot and what will sell. Her fans have eagerly awaited the release of her second novel, "The Method to the Madness," but it has been long in coming, and Teri is still putting out novels by prison writers like Kwame Teague, and Kurt Pacino, and doing all the marketing, and book signings herself. Of the signings to majors, Teri said, "I keep telling writers stop taking these deals with these companies. You're already selling your own units, why would you let these companies eat off of you? Those little bullshit advancement checks don't mean anything. Don't break your bread with these people. Stay independent." But independent or not, the world of hip-hop fiction is exploding.

And Kwame Teague sees this as only the beginning. "I think the street book game is like hip-hop in '74. At first we told simple stories, simple cadences, simple vocabulary, then it evolved. Right now, we're telling the simple bang, bang sex, and money story." Nikki Turner takes it further, "I feel that the market is over saturated with a bunch of books that can't meet their full potential," she says of the crowded genre. "But the good thing is that hip-hop fiction is not fading. It's just like the rap game. You have those artists who fall by the wayside. Then you have the ones who hold their own. And when the dust settles the ones who are true to their craft will be the ones still standing."

Time will tell if gangsta lit is just a fad, but with sales of over $50 million annually, the genre seems to be entrenching itself in the market place. And with the majors throwing money around and several independents like Hampstead, Fastlane, Gorilla Convict, Ebante and Amiaya emerging to produce books, that readers are demanding the genre can only skyrocket like the music before it.

TWENTY NINE

Incarcerated Authors

JUST LIKE THE rap game before it, the world of hip-hop fiction is blowing up. Street lit as its called is now grossing over $50 million annually and a genre that started with self-published authors selling books out the back of their cars has quickly become a legitimate market that has harnessed the talents of writers either fresh out of prison or still in the pen. The books often published under pen names, following the lead of rappers, are in high demand, especially among young people indoctrinated in the hip-hop culture.

You know the publishers- Teri Woods, Triple Crown, Nikki Turner Presents, Relentless Content, Urban Books, Amaiya, Hampstead Publishing and Gorilla Convict- but do you know the authors, the best of who are still incarcerated. Real convicts with real time who write real books. These authors were living the life your favorite rapper is rhyming about. Ain't no studio or cardboard gangstas in this group. And Gorilla Convict would like to introduce them to you.

"I'm incarcerated in North Carolina for two counts of murder and kidnapping and an armed robbery charge for which I'm fighting to prove my innocence," says Kwame Teague the 33-year-old native of Newark, New Jersey (aka Brick City), who penned the Teri Woods produced "Dutch," "Dutch II" and "Adventures of Ghetto Sam." The author, who's been locked up since 1994, is serving two life sentences.

"My parole date would be after 40 years." He says. And the thing about it is Kwame's name doesn't even appear on his books, "Dutch" or "Dutch II," two of the best street novels ever. Teri Woods is listed as the author.

"Dutch is a fictional novel about crime and murder, and I'm trying to fight an unjust murder charge," Kwame says, explaining why his name isn't on the books he authored. "I don't want the book to become a factor against me."

That's understandable, but how did Kwame first get with Teri Woods? "Back in like 2000 she had an article in the Vibe," he says. "She had just put out True to the Game. I had just self-published Ghetto Sam through Iuniverse.com when I saw that. So I had my people contact her and sent her my book. She dug it. And it started from there." And now six figure book sales later, Kwame is still in jail, writing and fighting to overturn his conviction. But it hasn't all gone smoothly.

"When they truly understood how successful the books were," Kwame says referring to the prison administrators. "They put me in segregation for 60 days on trumped up charges and shipped me seven hours away from my family. They fear the influence I have over other inmates, their exact words. They also banned the books in every state prison." Harsh measures, but measures any incarcerated author might have to deal with. Kwame Teague is currently incarcerated at Taylorsville Prison in North Carolina working on future projects and fighting for his freedom.

Another noteworthy incarcerated author is Trenton, New Jersey native Wahida Clark who is doing a 125-month sentence at FPC Alderson in West Virginia. "My charges are conspiracy/money laundering, mail and wire fraud," she says. Wahida has three books out- "Thugs and the Women who love them," "Every Thug needs a Lady" and "Payback is a Mutha," which is her current release on

Kensington Publishing. Wahida, whose release date is next year, is an Essence Bestselling author whose books have sold over 50,000 copies. She writes what she calls reality fiction.

"Ghetto/street life from the hood," she relates. "Welfare, food stamps, government cheese, weed, boosting and partying." She started writing books after seeing black authors in magazines and reading their interviews. She told herself she could do that, took a creative writing class at the prison and boom--three books later, she is among the leaders of the genre with an imprint at Kensington and a new series, Ghetto Stories, coming out.

"A sista had to do what a sista had to do," Wahida says. "And writing a hotty novel on lock makes it feel that much better." She relates that there are advantages and disadvantages to being an incarcerated writer. Pros- "You have time to write. You have three hots and a cot, no worrying about lights, gas, car note, food." Cons- "On the business side, you can't really spread your wings and soar. You're forced to crawl. So like my friend Relentless Aaron said, 'While you're locked up, pump out as many novels as you can.'" Wahida, who was recently profiled in King Magazine, is currently getting her Ghetto Stories series ready for release.

Joe Black's name has been ringing bells in the feds for the last decade due to his various photocopied legal writing paper manuscripts, which have been sweeping the underground prison nation and causing a stir. They are like the mixtapes of the prison system. The 38-year-old Bronx native, who's been down since 1994, is doing 19 1/2 years for a drug conspiracy. After finally self-publishing his first novel, "Street Team," on illstreetz.com, he inked a deal from the pen with Hampstead Publishing who took "Street Team" national and plans to put out Joe's second novel "Squeeze" next. The author, who's been profiled in Don Diva and King, gets out in 2008.

"It's an autobiography of everyone who ever played the game," Joe says of his novel. And he admits to admiring Donald Goines and

Iceberg Slim, because "they didn't have to interview gangstas to bring me their stories. They were gangstas and when I read their books it was like they were in the cell kicking it with me." And readers of "Street Team" have come to the same conclusion. Real recognizes real.

"It's the closest you gonna come to being in the game without being indicted," Joe says of his book, and concerning life in the streets, he has this jewel to offer. "There's no pot of gold at the end of the rainbow. There's only a pot of cream of wheat in the morning at the mess hall or your casket in a plot with your name over it." Incarcerated authors like Joe have spent decades of their lives inside, but with his novel he tries to show the consequences of the drug game. And it isn't pretty. Check out hampsteadpub.com.

Robert Booker, Sr. out of Detroit, Michigan, is another incarcerated author whose work has the streets talking. The 40-year-old who's been in since 1994 is doing a natural life sentence in the feds for a cocaine conspiracy. His novel, "Push," available on Sims and Sims Productions, is a story of crime, sex, loyalty and murder on the streets of Detroit.

"I started writing in 2000 after I read Teri Woods' True to the Game," said Booker, who's incarcerated at FCI Gilmer in West Virginia. "I knew my stories were way better then hers because I was living in the streets. I write what I know. You change the name to get the fame." And the streets, prisons, plus the industry have recognized. Off the strength of "Push," Booker has signed on to do Deep in the Game with Hampstead Publishing.

And about having a book out while in prison, Booker says, "Everybody acts like you a star but it ain't nothing. I'm just another prisoner." But with acclaim coming from the streets and the prisons and with more books coming out, Booker is a writer on the come up.

"My writing skills are raw, straight from my mind onto paper like a rapper doing freestyle on BET'S Freestyle Friday," says the author who was profiled in The Ave magazine. In his novels Booker keeps it all the way real. "I understand street life. I understand the struggles in the streets." he says. "I'm a real nigga, I got served life. I know what gangstas do and what they don't do." And Booker, who's at FCI Gilmer in the feds right now, is cranking out more books and stories for his audience.

From the West Coast out in the California prison system is Blood gang member and convict writer, Terrell C. Wright (aka Loko), author of "Home of the Body Bags," a tome that tells the tale of a Blood soldier, which is out on Senegal Press now.

"I've always wanted to tell my story as a Blood soldier, the Neighborhood Bloods in particular," Loko says. And the 38-year old Loko, who is at Corcoran State prison in California, is serving time for a jewelry store robbery.

"I was born and raised in South Central Los Angeles," Loko says.

"By 1982 I was a full fledged LA gangsta and the rest is history as my book expresses in vivid details." And Loko has always wanted to write a book, but prison finally gave him the time to do it.

"I've always had an innate desire of wanting to share the Blood experience with the world at large," he says. "I've always felt I had an author dwelling inside me, but it was the addictive high of being in the streets which kept me from taking out some quality time for myself to sit and write." And with the success of "Home of the Body Bags," Loko has penned another book, "Thugs," which will be out on streetgangs.com shortly. Check it out.

Another convict author straight out of the Chocolate City is 29-year-old Eyone Williams who is serving 15 years to life on a second degree murder charge. His novel Fastlane, "Is a tale of the streets mixed with events of my youth and what I saw around me." The Northwest DC native says. And the book has sold several thousand copies to date without any distribution or major promotion.

"My wife and I were inspired to start our own publishing company when we saw how many big companies reject manuscripts from unknown authors." Eyone says. So they started Fast Lane Publications and put out "Fastlane," which takes a look at the lives of DC street hustlers. "My wife, Aisha Bailey, keeps everything together while I'm in prison by keeping up with the business side of running the company." Eyone says and they have plans to put out books by other prisoners.

"I've been pleased to see that the streets and the prisons have been feeling Fastlane," Eyone says. "All of my support has come from those places." And Eyone, who's been locked up for 13 years, is only beginning. He's been penning "Lorton Legends," which takes a look at the notorious DC prison. Look for it soon at fastlanepub.com.

Cuban-American author Michael Santos has been in the feds since 1987 serving a 45-year sentence for a continuing criminal enterprise conviction. And although his work isn't considered hip-hop fiction he has still made tracks in the genre. His current book, "Inside: Life behind Bars in America," is out on St. Martin's Press and has been compared to prison classics, "Hot House," Soledad Brother and "In the Belly of the Beast."

"As a long term prisoner, I recognize that writing provides the only opportunity to reach beyond these boundaries that hold us physically," says the 42-year-old Santos who is eligible for parole in 2013. "I want to connect with the world." And he has. With three other books- "About Prison," "Profiles from Prison," and "What if I go to Prison" - and his website, Michaelsantos.net. Santos has made himself an authority on life in prison.

"I am not a fan of the prison system," he says. "I am convinced that, if one was charged with the responsibility of designing a system that conditions men to fail in society, that person could not do better than the concept of imprisonment. In learning how to live in prison, the individual simultaneously learns how to fail in society. But I've always believed that the pen is mightier than the sword. So I write." And the world has taken notice of the author who is currently confined in the camp at FCI Lompoc.

As Y2k moves on, jailhouse writers are becoming more prolific. The flood of prison writing is a result of the alarming numbers of incarcerated African-Americans and Latinos, many of them casualties of the War on Drugs and the draconian sentencing guidelines now in place in most states and the feds. Like street fiction fathers, Iceberg Slim and Goines, who both served time, the new writers are capturing the life they know. The authors profiled here are only a few of the most prominent and successful, but still there are many more. In many prisons, men and women on lockdown are spending their hours putting pens to paper and finding words to describe their prior or current lives. Like they say, the streets are watching and the next big hip-hop fiction author might be composing his novel right now in some prison somewhere, dreaming of success, notoriety and freedom.

THIRTY

The Gangster Writer

RON CHEPESIUK IS well versed in the arts of street knowledge. This Canadian born and internationally educated scholar has jumped into the true crime genre and pumped out books about drug lords and gangsters like Lil' Wayne pumps out hits. Ron Chepesiuk is certified platinum, tackling and taking on black gangster street legends like Bumpy Johnson, Frank Matthews and Nicky Barnes while at the same time debunking the myths of bullshitters like Frank Lucas. With his well researched and investigated stories Ron Chepesiuk is to true crime books what Nas is to the hip-hop world- a lyrical poet who traverses in words that have meaning and scope, examining issues which are at once relevant and concise, demanding and precise- in both a popular culture, historical and scholastic context. Forget all those tired ass Mafia books you've been reading and check out Ron Chepesiuk's work on the black gangsters of America, especially his latest offering- Sergeant Smack. You know we keep it 100 percent official here at gorillaconvict.com so here is the Ron Chepesiuk interview. We sat down with the gangster writer of the moment to see where he's been, where he's going and what's good right now.

When and why did you first start writing about black gangsters?

My book, "Drug Lords: The Rise and Fall of the Cali Cartel," which I published in 2002, was my first true crime book and I really enjoyed the writing experience. I wanted to do another true crime book and was looking for a subject. I am a big fan of the so called Blaxploitation movies of the 1970s—you know the genre with titles like "Shaft," "Su-perfly" and "Black Caesar." Many of them were set in Harlem. I wanted to read a good but true book about the gangster era in Harlem of the 1960s and early 1970s but couldn't find one. I did some research and learned about such big-time gangsters of Harlem as Caspar Holstein, the numbers king, Bumpy Johnson, Frank Matthews, Robert Stepeney, Nicky Barnes, Goldfinger, the Black Dutch Schultz, Zack Robinson and I knew there was a book to be written. That resulted in my first book on Black crime—"Gangsters of Harlem."

What is your background and where are you from?

I have a background that's given me the type of experience I need to research and write about true crime. I am a Canadian by birth from Thunder Bay up in the frozen tundra where wearing three pair of socks in the winter is considered normal. I grew up poor in a tough multi-ethnic neighborhood that maybe included more than 50 nationalities. So I'm use to taking care of myself and dealing with people of all types of backgrounds. I was the first kid in my family to go to college. I earned a Master's degree in library science from the predominantly Black school, Clark-Atlanta University and a post graduate diploma in archival science from the National University of Ireland in Dublin, Ireland. I worked as a University professor at a southern university for several years before becoming a freelance writer. I already had published 15 or 16 books, mainly academic in nature, and at least 3500 freelance magazine and newspaper articles, before I decided to pursue my dream of being a fulltime freelance writer (see www.ronchepesiuk. com.) I've reported from close to 40 countries and met my Colombian wife on one those trips when I missed a plane. On another trip to Cuba I was detained by Cuban security and given 48 hours to get out of the country. I got out in 24. I live in small, sleepy southern town, but write true crime books about drug lords and gangsters in far off places like Colombia and Thailand and in the gangland of the inner city. Go figure but I love it. I'd say life has been a continuous adrenalin rush.

What documentaries have you appeared on and who have you talked about?

I serve as a consultant to the History Channel´s "Gangland" series and have been interviewed by NBC´s "Dateline," the Biography Channel's "Mobsters", The Discovery Channel's "Undercover" and Black Entertainment Television´s "American Gangster." I've talked mostly about black organized crime. I imagine that as I continue my research there will be other gigs, given the huge interest in true crime.

What did you think about the Frank Lucas "American Gangster" movie and all the hoopla?

I didn't think much of the movie. If you know nothing about the real Frank Lucas then the movie can be entertaining. But the movie is supposed to be based on a true story. So it was really quite amazing to see how the hoopla unfolded and know Lucas was able to pimp his bogus story. Talk to former gangsters from the era in which Lucas operated in and they will tell you Lucas is full of shit. I have done extensive research on Lucas' life and his relationship to Ike Atkinson, who appears as the character Nate in "American Gangster," and I would say about 80 percent of the life story Lucas has presented is a lie. Now his autobiography has come out and he has three versions of his life: the New York magazine article that got him the movie deal, the movie itself and now his autobiography. Each of them contradicts the others and is full of holes.

Here in a nutshell is the truth garnered from my research. Lucas was not Bumpy Johnson's right hand man. Ike Atkinson, not Frank Lucas, pioneered the Asian heroin pipeline to the U.S. Lucas worked with the Italian American Mafia contrary to what the movie and he claims. There was no smuggling of heroin in coffins and/or the cadavers of American servicemen who died in Vietnam. Lucas was big snitch who turned in his fellow gangsters and not cops. When Hollywood, the media and Denzel Washington are all pimping a movie, it's pretty hard to combat the myths they create. But my new book, Sergeant Smack (www.ikeatkinsonkingpin.com) I think, does that.

How did you get involved with the Sergeant Smack story?

Ironically, Frank Lucas led me to Ike Atkinson. I had interviewed him twice for my book "Gangsters of Harlem." The book has a chapter on him. In the interview he kept referring to his "cousin" Ike and how he helped him to set up the Asian drug connection. I had heard of Ike but did not know too much about him. I did a search and found he has been prison for nearly 31 continuous years. He had not given an interview during that period. Not a good sign for a journalist. Maybe he doesn't want to talk to anybody. But I wrote the prison where he was incarcerated, requesting an interview with Ike. They passed the message on to him. Fortunately, I mentioned in my letter some of the things Lucas was saying about him. Ike was curious and agreed to the interview. We did another prison interview. I learned that Lucas was not Ike's cousin as Lucas claimed and that most of what Lucas said about his relationship with Ike was bullshit. Ike and I developed a close relationship and continued to work together on his biography when he got out of jail in 2007.

How do you do your research?

After I decide on a topic for a book, I gather all the background material I can on the subject—books, articles transcripts, etc. by going to the Internet and library and talking to sources. I like to include a lot of historical background in my books to give the reader perspective. For instance, I have a lot of info in my Sergeant Smack book about what was going on in Southeast Asia when Ike arrived in Bangkok in 1966. I hope there are a lot of court records available. They are a rich source of information. I absorb that material and develop a list of the questions I will want to ask sources. I also develop a working outline for the book. I develop a list of sources to interview. Then I go out and find them. It's very important to find good sources to interview. I think quotes enliven the text. When I'm about 30 percent into researching a book, I start writing and revising. I write very quickly. It usually takes six or seven months to finish a book

Would you say your writing is your passion or your job?

It has to be a passion, given the economics of book publishing today. It's very tough to make living solely by writing books, especially true crime books, unless they make the big screen. Your visitors may be surprised to learn that I can make more money writing articles. A 3,000 or 4,000 word articles can pay $5,000 or more. Today, that's more than the average advance given an author who is writing a 100,000 word book. So I love what I do and will continue doing it as long as I feel that way. Life is too short.

What are you working on now?

Where should I start? My plate is quite full. We are starting to get nibbles about film rights for Sergeant Smack (www.ikeatkinsa-onkingpin) and we are sorting them out. I'm halfway through a book "Queenpins," about famous woman gangsters, which should come out early next year. I've just been commissioned to write a bio of Robert Stepeney, the so called "Godfather of Harlem", which I hope to have done by next April. I plan to restart my Frank Matthews project soon. I'm co-starting my own publishing company, Strategic Media Books, and we will be soliciting for manuscripts for a series of books we are publishing, titled Gangster Chronicles. I'm only really happy when I see a life full of possibilities. To stand the French philosopher Rene Descarte's famous saying on its head—I work therefore I am.

What other writers do you admire in the black gangster genre?

There are some real good writers out there. I recently read Mara Shalhoup's "BMF: The Rise and fall of Big Meech." It's a real good book and I can't wait for the movie. Ethan Brown's "Queen Reigns Supreme" is also good read, as is Tom Folsom's "Mr. Untouchable." As far as the Black gangster genre goes, there are a lot of one shot wonders. I hope these authors come out with more books in the genre. I also like Seth Ferranti's books. I think it's amazing what he does from where he's located. I've learned from these writers and will continue to learn. But I don't limit my reading to true crime. I read both great and popular writers to learn and enrich my life as much as I can. For instance, right now I'm re-reading Ernest Hemingway's collected short stories because I love his style. I also read a lot of John Grisham to learn how to writer cinematically.

Do you think this genre can be as successful as the Mafia and Colombian cartel books that came before it?

Oh, yes, the genre is just getting started. There are still so many good stories about Black gangsters out here begging to be written. Look at Robert Stepeney. He was one of the most powerful gangsters of the late 1960s and 1970s when the black gangster was asserting himself but Stepeney was low key and is little known. These stories need to be written. They are a part of African American history and the country's history. So they should be written with the historical perspective in mind and not just about the sensational aspects of the criminal scene. Publishing needs to move on from the Mafia and Colombian cartels. After all, how many more books need to be written about Al Capone, John Gotti and Pablo Escobar?

THIRTY ONE

The Life of Nikki Turner, Queen of Hip-Hop Fiction

"

A HUSTLERS WIFE," "Project Chick," "The Glamorous Life," "Riding Dirty on I-95," "Death Before Dishonor," "Forever a Hustlers Wife"- these are the titles of Nikki Turner's books, but could easily be superlatives to describe the Queen of Hip-Hop fiction and her life. The Richmond, Virginia author is on top of the game now, but it wasn't always like that. Still a come up is a come up and in the parlance of the streets, Nikki is what they call a big baller. But every big baller started somewhere and most came from humble beginnings.

"I started writing in 7th grade when my English teacher gave me a journal because I passed notes in her class," Nikki says. "From that point I knew I could write. I've always been a very outspoken person, but if I put my thoughts on paper or in a letter then I would truly get my point across. That's with anything, if I went to a restaurant or to a store and was mistreated, if I complained it was ok, but if I wrote a letter, I always got a surprising response. So it goes back to there." And from there it went to her first novel, "A Hustler's Wife," which was a look into the world Donald Goines and Iceberg Slim left behind, but from a female's perspective.

"When I first penned "A Hustler's Wife," there were not many street books on the market. So I thought, 'hmmm, I think I'll write a book.' And I did. Once I had it in my mind that I was going to do it,

thirty-seven days later I had the rough draft of 'A Hustler's Wife.'"
And now that rough draft, which found its way to Triple Crown
founders Shannon Holmes and Vickie Stringer and sold in the six
figures within the first year of publication, is being made into a movie.

"It's in production now and scheduled to hit the big screen," Nikki
says. But the Essence and Don Diva Magazine best-selling author
hasn't rested on her laurels. Besides "Project Chicks," "The Glamorous
Life," "Riding Dirty on I-95" and "Forever A Hustler's Wife," which
came out on Random House/Ballentine, Nikki put out the first two
books in her Street Chronicle series. "Street Chronicles is my baby."
She says. "Initially, I created it as a vehicle for new and upcoming
authors to be put on. In the process, I somehow ended up getting some
already published and established authors under the Nikki Turner
book line through Random House." She also co-wrote "Girls in the
Hood" with Cruchi for Urban Books. Part two is ready to come out.
Nikki launched gangsta rapper 50 Cent's imprint G-Unit books too
with "Death Before Dishonor." So Nikki stays grinding and getting
that dollar, but she has other responsibilities also.

"Some days I'm a soccer mom," she says. "I have two children, although, I have a live in nanny. I am still a very instrumental part of my
children's lives. Even successful as I am I still go through the struggles
and prejudices of being a single mother." Still writing is her focus.

"Other days I am consumed with my writing." She says. "Those days
I am strictly hugging the block, only the block, and it becomes my
computer and my project. I go hard. After I get three chapters into it, I
completely submit to it. I don't answer the phone, cook and most of the
time I don't leave the house. Outside of those doors are too many perils
and traps to get me side tracked and snatch away my focus. During my
writing time, I don't do anything but sit at the computer with my cute
pj's or some sweats and a wife beater and write."

Nikki draws a lot of material directly from her life. "Most of my
days are merely drama filled and can fit in between the chapters of any

Nikki Turner original book," she says. "Funny incidents, arguments, things that could only happen to me. Never a dull experience. You have no idea... you think my books are intriguing? Try a day in my actual life." And since signing a reported six-figure deal with Random House, Nikki Turner is definitely that big baller,

"My first book deal with Random House was for two books (The Glamorous Life and Riding Dirty on I-95)," she says. "That came about through my agent. He held an auction for the highest bidder, who ironically I didn't sign with. Random House was just the best place and deal for me." With her own imprint to put out, Street Chronicles, and to put new authors on under "Nikki Turner Presents," she is ready to take over the street lit game. But still it's all about the down time.

"During the small breaks, usually a couple of weeks or one month I take between writing, I'm usually a wreck," she says. "I have too much time on my hands, but I usually take this time to read through the submissions and other books." Nikki also enjoys traveling in her down time.

"Every time I finish a book, I take a trip." She says. "I do travel the world extensively. This is when I let go of a project and move onto the next." But even on vacation Nikki handles her business. "It's always about promoting my books. It has become a habit that no matter the handbag I carry or which one of my cars I'm driving, I always have my promo postcards/bookmarks. In my travels I never know whom I may meet." She says. "Of course, my favorite past time is shopping, shopping and more shopping."

And to Nikki it's more than just writing books. She explains, "I feel I represent every woman- the single mother, the sister, the mother, the cousin, the sister-friend, the wife, the ambitious, the heart broken, the confused and especially those who have a story to tell. I also feel I symbolize a woman who is the epitome of a real chic on mission. I am the true definition of real life drama in all its splendor, and as I pen every story, I want all my sisters out there to know that through me that their mission is considered accomplished."

That about sums up the life of Nikki Turner. She just inked another three book deal with Random House. About the book deal she says, "Inquiring minds want to know for how much? Let's just say that I'm eating and I don't miss a meal." The first book in the new deal is the sequel to "A Hustler's Wife," "Forever A Hustler's Wife." So it's back to the beginning for Nikki. What comes around goes around.

In closing she says, "I'm just thankful for all the blessing that have come my way. I'm just going to continue to do whatever God places on my heart and mind. There are too many people to name who contributed to me being where I am today but I can honestly say that I'm truly blessed." As we are being able to read this wonderful and talented authors' works, book after book after book.

THIRTY TWO

The New Jack Gangster Writer

T HE WORLD OF gangster writers is a small one. You got the originals like Tiffany Chiles, Antoine Clark, Cavario H., Kevin Chiles, Shabazz, Ethan Brown, Seth Ferranti and Ron Chepesiuk. But now you have the newer ones who are breaking on the scene as we combine our journalistic and literary might to push this urban outlaw genre into the limelight. Magazines like Don Diva and F.E.D.S. have been doing it since day one. The documentaries like Street Stars, BET's "American Gangster" and The History Channel's "Gangland" series jumped on the bandwagon. And Hollywood blockbusters like "American Gangster" with Denzel Washington have shown this genre can generate serious paper. Still, no one has gotten a book deal from being in Don Diva, AS IS or F.E.D.S. New Jack Gangster writers like Scott Wilson are here to change that. With his blog at www.scottsmindfield.com, his writing gigs at www.planetill.com and Don Diva Magazine and his new book "Straight from the Hood: Amazing but True Gangster Tales," Scott Wilson is on a mission. We got the exclusive interview with this new and talented writer. Here it goes.

What is the title of your new book and what is it about?

The title of the book is "Straight from the Hood: Amazing but True Gangster Tales." I co-authored it with Ron Chepesiuk. The title is pretty self-explanatory. The book contains many different stories that emanate from the world of urban gangsters. Some of them are fairly well known, others not so much. All of them are interesting and will keep readers engaged. I'm sure lots of people will be shocked and amazed. Some will even be amused. Ron and I tried to keep the stories varied and interesting. Some deal with the world of Hip-Hop and Hollywood. Others deal with the criminal underworld exclusively. I think that readers will have a lot of fun with it.

For example, we have a story about how Denzel Washington got his start on Broadway in a play called "Checkmates." The play was produced by former drug kingpin Michael "Harry-O" Harris, who also famously provided the startup money for Death Row Records and later won a $1.5 million lawsuit against the label. We also have a story about how Al Capone forced the legendary Fats Waller to play at his birthday party. Al actually had an interesting relationship with the Black Chicago that many people don't know about. Readers will find those stories and more in Straight from the Hood.

What got you interested in writing about urban gangsters?

It was a convergence of different factors and influences. First and foremost, I'm pretty much a product of American popular culture. When I was 11-years-old, I saw the movie "The Untouchables" by Brian DePalma. Remember the scene where Elliot Ness and Al Capone had the Mexican stand-off in the lobby of that fancy hotel after Frank Nitti merc'ed that accountant in the elevator? All of Capone's bodyguards pulled out semi-automatic pistols. He didn't even have to move. His men were prepared to gun down a cop to protect him. The idea of a "bad guy" having that much power fascinated me. The entire city of Chicago knew exactly who he was and how he accumulated such wealth. It was no secret. Yet he operated as if he was above the law. I found it interesting that guys like that actually existed. Years later I discovered the films of Martin Scorcese, and my fascination increased. You also have to remember that at the same time "The Untouchables" hit theaters, you had Boogie Down Productions doing songs like "9mm Goes Bang" and Just-Ice calling himself the "Hip-Hop Gangster" and using that kind of imagery in his music. You also had Kool G. Rap laying the groundwork for what would later become "Mafioso" rap. Over on the West Coast you had Too $hort, N.W.A., and other guys exposing the LA gang scene to the world.

Later I met various people throughout my teenage and young adult years that grew up in the streets. Some of them were friends and family members, others were just associates. I knew a guy who got murdered selling drugs back in 1992. I also lost a very good friend to senseless gun violence later that same year. I'd known people that'd been in and out of prison. I worked in law enforcement for a few years and got to see certain aspects of that life up close.

So really it was a combination of things. It wasn't any one particular thing. I think it's fairly common for people to have a fascination with such things these days. The success of shows like "The Sopranos," "The Shield," "The Wire," and "Gangland" can attest to that. Not to mention the fact that Rick Ross is still able to sell gold in today's marketplace. I'd also like to add that I think classifying anything as "urban" puts a certain stigma on it. "Urban" is basically used as code for Black. It's also sometimes a thinly veiled way of denoting a lack of quality. You've got a lot of very talented writers out there like yourself, Cavario H. and Frank C. Matthews. I think it's unfair to classify you guys as "urban" authors or to classify your work as "urban" literature. That's just a way to marginalize it and make it seem less legit. Black gangsters are gangsters, period. They don't need any special classification to denote their blackness.

How did you hook up with Ron Chepesiuk and SMB?

I read Ron's book "Gangsters of Harlem" in 1997 and enjoyed it quite a bit. I purchased some of his other books like "Black Gangsters of Chicago" and "The Cali Cartel". In September of 2009 I interviewed Ron for a website called Planet Ill where I write under the name Malice Intended. We kept in touch. I would show Ron movie reviews and other articles I had written from time to time. He thought I had real talent and he presented me with an opportunity to work with him. That relationship blossomed into our current projects.

What are your writing credits in this genre so far?

My career is really just getting off the ground. It's a work in progress. I interviewed former army master sergeant Leslie "Ike" Atkinson for a Don Diva cover story which I wrote. I also worked on subsequent stories and interviews for Don Diva. I recently completed work for the forthcoming issue. It should be on newsstands shortly.

Where do you see your writing efforts in this genre taking you?

As far as I'm concerned the sky is the limit. I will continue to work with Ron Chepesiuk and Don Diva magazine. I will also be seeking out other opportunities. I'd like to get into crime fiction, mysteries, science fiction, screenwriting, and comic books. I recently discovered the work of the great Walter Mosley and I have found it very inspirational. I also hope one day to uncover some strange yet true crime tale that hasn't been told yet, something that doesn't follow the usual pattern that we've become accustomed to. Ron was able to do that with Sergeant Smack. A great gangster or crime story is about more than dudes getting rich, flossing and killing tons of people. Just look at any of the classic gangster/crime films and novels. They aren't just exploitation. They are works of art.

What stories are you working on or what do you have coming up?

Ron and I are working on another book that should be out this fall. I worked on a story about Kwame Kilpatrick for Don Diva. I have my own Blog called Scott's Introspection Section (www.scottsmindfield. com). I cover a variety of topics: movies, hip-hop, true crime, comics. It's really just an extension of my interests and enthusiasms. I try to bring an intelligent and thoughtful perspective to whatever I write about. I have interviews with Michael Jai White, Kool G Rap, and many others. It's growing by leaps and bounds. I refine it as I go. I also continue to write for Planet Ill (www.planetill.com). I'm their resident movie critic and pop culture expert. That site also covers a variety of topics from a mature Hip-Hoppers perspective.

This summer I am going to try my hand at screenwriting. It's something I've always wanted to do. I've got tons of ideas running around in my head, and now I have a platform to express them. You'll be hearing a lot more from me in the coming years.

How do you do your research and get your interviews?

Let's just say that both Facebook and e-mail are invaluable tools in my line of work. Facebook has made it so much easier to make contacts and develop professional relationships with people. I was able to get in touch with Cavario H. that way. Sometimes it's as simple as sending out an e-mail. If I request an interview or some other kind of information from someone, the worst they can do is say no or just ignore my request altogether. It's not going to stop me from grinding and reaching out to others. Eventually someone will say yes and tell me their story.

The importance of reading cannot be stressed enough. Around 2005 I discovered the story of Frank Matthews while reading "Black Brothers, Inc.: The Violent Rise and Fall of Philadelphia's Black Mafia." I read about how he escaped with millions of dollars. I was so fascinated that I began looking for whatever information I could find on him. I did tons of Internet searches and what have you. I was able to get little pieces of information but nothing substantial. Then I found out about Donald Goddard's book "Easy Money," and I ordered a used copy of it from Amazon. I read it from cover to cover. I also devoured tons of street documentaries and magazines like Don Diva and F.E.D.S. Basically, I find the information however I can get it. We live in an age where so much is available to us. With a tool like the Internet at your disposal, there's no excuse to remain ignorant on any subject, if you truly have an interest in it.

THE NEW JACK GANGSTER WRITER

Who do you think the most notorious or infamous urban gangsters are?

As I said before, I think Frank Matthews trumps them all. This guy lorded over a drug empire that stretched out over 21 states. He openly defied La Cosa Nostra, and managed to escape with 15-20 million dollars. He's like a real life Keyser Söze. That's got to be one of the most outlandish true crime stories I have ever heard. I don't think anything can top it, at least not any of the other stories I've heard in recent years. Think about how amazing a movie about Frank Matthews could be. With the right director, screenwriter, and cast, a Frank Matthews movie could be incredible.

Then there's Leslie "Ike" Atkinson. He dispelled the myth of the "cadaver connection" as well as the mystique of Frank "Superfly" Lucas. He smuggled hundreds of millions of dollars in "China White" to the United States. He was never directly involved in any murders or gunplay, nor did he order anyone killed. He was a pure hustler. When you talk to him, he doesn't seem anything at all like the stereotypical gangster that has been popularized in movies, television and books. There are others. Rayful Edmond supposedly amassed hundreds of millions of dollars selling cocaine in the late eighties. For him to be that successful in that particular time period is unprecedented. He must have one hell of a network to be able to sell that much product.

Do you see these guys as modern day outlaw heroes and why? Are they comparable to Billy the Kid and Al Capone? Why?

Though I find these guys stories fascinating and interesting, I do not consider them heroes. Not in any sense of the word. I can see why others might. People tend to see gangsters as self-made men and super capitalists. They play by their own rules and defy the system. That characterization has some truth to it. However, very few people benefit from violent criminality. How many people have been killed and imprisoned as a result of the War on Drugs? How many innocent civilians have suffered at the hands of gang wars and the like? People have to actually live and work in the neighborhoods where gang bangers and drug dealers set up shop. Nobody wants to live around that shit. At the end of the day it only benefits drug dealers, law enforcement, the prison industrial complex and funeral homes.

I would definitely say they are comparable to legendary outlaws like Al Capone and Billy the Kid. The similarities definitely outweigh the differences. Nicky Barnes and Felix Mitchell have a whole mythology surrounding them especially in their hometowns. It's very similar to the mythologies surrounding the outlaws of the old west and the prohibition era gangsters. Al Capone may have been more rich and famous than Nicky Barnes, but at the end of the day, they were both notorious organized criminals who became rich by dealing in vice. The only differences are race, time period, and the vice in question. Every single ethnic group in the history of the United States has its own underworld culture. Crime crosses all boundaries. As long as capitalism exists, you will have crime.

How does the Hip-Hop angle come into play with these guys?

Well, Hip-Hop's golden era was taking place in the middle of the crack cocaine epidemic. This was also when the Bloods and Crips were beginning to migrate outside of LA to other parts of the country. Rappers came from the cities and neighborhoods that were most affected by those factors. So in a sense they couldn't help but be influenced by it to some degree, whether it be the glorification of drug culture or the warning of kids away from it. Their slang, style of dress and worldviews were affected by it.

I want to stress that the glorification of criminality is in no way unique or exclusive to Hip-Hop. Hip-Hop encompasses many different messages and worldviews. Gangsta Rap is only a single facet of it. You have backpackers, hipsters, horrorcore, politically conscious rappers, and some cats that are beyond classification. Rap music is as varied as any other form of entertainment. It's just that those other subgenres don't always get the spotlight. That may change in the coming years since Gangsta Rap is considered passé now. The kids have moved on to other things.

Also, rappers are not the first popular entertainers to have associations with known criminals. Gangsters and criminal organizations have always been involved with the entertainment industry, whether it was to launder money or transition over to the straight world. In many cases, stars and celebrities are a high class clientele for pimps, drug dealers and the like.

The only thing I think rappers have done differently is that they are more willing to openly flaunt their criminal pasts and associations. Perhaps more than any other popular entertainers in history, rappers are keenly aware of the general public's fascination with certain things. Eazy-E was a genius at marketing. He created a template that many other rappers followed. I think the downside of that is that too many rappers try to live their art, which is the dumbest and most dangerous thing an artist can do.